Adolescent Sexuality

Adolescent Sexuality

A Historical Handbook and Guide

EDITED BY CAROLYN COCCA

Children and Youth: History and Culture
Miriam Forman-Brunell, Series Editor

Westport, Connecticut
London

Library of Congress Cataloging-in-Publication Data

Adolescent sexuality : a historical handbook and guide / edited by Carolyn Cocca.
 p. cm. —(Children and youth: history and culture, ISSN 1546–6752)
 Includes bibliographical references and index.
 ISBN 0–313–33399–8
 1. Teenagers—Sexual behavior. 2. Teenagers—Sexual behavior—United States.
I. Cocca, Carolyn, 1971–
HQ27.A3617 2006
306.70835–dc22   2006021767

British Library Cataloguing in Publication Data is available.

Library of Congress Catalog Card Number: 2006021767
ISBN: 0–313–33399–8
ISSN: 1546–6752

First published in 2006

Praeger Publishers, 88 Post Road West, Westport, CT 06881
An imprint of Greenwood Publishing Group, Inc.
www.praeger.com

Printed in the United States of America

The paper used in this book complies with the
Permanent Paper Standard issued by the National
Information Standards Organization (Z39.48–1984).

10 9 8 7 6 5 4 3 2 1

Contents

Part II   Documents

Part III   Bibliography

Series Foreword

Pocahontas, a legendary figure in American history, was just a pre-adolescent when she challenged two cultures at odds to cooperate instead of to compete. While Pocahontas forged peace, many more now forgotten Native American, Anglo-American, African American, and other children contributed to their families' survival, their communities' development, and America's history in just as legitimate, though perhaps less legendary, ways. Contracts and correspondence from colonial Chesapeake reveal that even seventeenth-century toddlers labored. But the historical agency of the vast majority of children and adolescents has been undervalued and overlooked in dominant historical narratives. Instead, generations of Americans have credited fathers and other hoary leaders for their actions and achievements, all the while disregarding pivotal boyhood experiences that shaped skills and ideals. Reflecting these androcentric, Eurocentric, and age-based biases that have framed the nation's history, American history texts have reinforced the historical invisibility of girls and boys for centuries. For students searching libraries for scholarly sources and primary documents about children and adolescents in various historical contexts, this near-absence of information in master narratives has vexed their research.

The absence of children in standard history books has not only obscured children's history, but also the work of scholars who have been investigating youths' histories and interrogating their cultures since the turn of the last century. A new curiosity about children in times past was generated by the progressive era agenda, which sought to educate, acculturate, and elevate American children through child study and child welfare. In *Child*

Life in Colonial Days (1899), "amateur historian" Alice Morse Earl drew upon archival sources and material culture in order to examine the social history of Puritan girls and boys. Children were also included in Arthur W. Calhoun's *A Social History of the American Family* (1917) and in Edmund S. Morgan's *The Puritan Family: Religion and Domestic Relations in Seventeenth-Century New England* (1944), but few other professional historians within the male-dominated profession considered children worthy of study. Those children who made appearances in historical accounts were typically the privileged daughters and sons of white men of means and might.

In the 1960s, larger social, cultural, and political transformations refocused scholarly attention. The influence of 1960s youth culture and second-wave feminism and renewed interest in the agency of "ordinary people," youth in particular, laid the foundation for a so-called new social history. The confluence of a renewed interest in youth and the development of new methodological approaches led French demographer and social historian Philippe Ariès to study a nation's youngest population. Challenging a dominant assumption that childhood was transhistorical in *Centuries of Childhood: A Social History of Family Life* (1962), Ariès argued that over time, changing cultures and societies redefined notions of childhood and transformed children's experiences. Ariès's work on European children was soon followed by Bernard Wishy's *The Child and the Republic: The Dawn of American Child Nurture* (1968), which explored the changing nature of child-rearing advice in the United States.

Despite important inroads made by these and other scholars (e.g., Robert Bremner), the history of childhood became embedded within historical subfields during the 1970s. The history of childhood was briefly associated with psychohistory due to the controversial work of Lloyd deMause, who founded *The History of Childhood Quarterly*. It was largely historians of the family (e.g., John Demos, Philip Greven Jr.) and those in the history of education (who refocused attention away from the school and onto the student) who broke new ground. Essays appeared in scholarly journals in the 1970s but were not reprinted until the following decade, when *Growing Up in America: Children in Historical Perspective* (1985) brought new visibility to the "vitality and scope of this emerging field" (preface). That important collection, edited by historians Joseph M. Hawes and N. Ray Hiner, along with their *American Childhood: A Research Guide and Historical Handbook* (1985), served to promote research among an up-and-coming generation of historians, whose work would be included in another pathbreaking anthology. By placing children at the center of historical inquiry, privileging gender as a critical factor in childhood socialization, and expanding social history to include cultural history, historians in *Small Worlds: Children and Adolescents in America, 1850–1950* (1992) demonstrated that the relationships between childhood and adulthood and kids and culture were historically significant. By privileging previously overlooked and disregarded historical sources, reading material culture artifacts as historical texts, and applying gender, race, and class analyses to an age-based one, these historians continued the mapping of childhood's terrain. Creatively and methodically, they traced childhood ideals and children's experiences within cultures and over centuries.

In the early to mid-1990s those in the fields of psychology and education initiated a scholarly debate about the dangers that popular culture posed to the healthy development of female adolescents in contemporary America. Those scholars, influenced by a different scholarly trajectory— cultural studies and feminist theory—saw agency instead, illuminating the many ways in which girls and female adolescents (as other youth) resist, contest, subvert, and reappropriate dominant cultural forms. Moreover, scholars such as Kimberly Roberts brought to light the discursive nature of the contemporary "girl crisis" debate, just as others have uncovered numerous other discourses that create, reflect, and reinforce the cultural norms of girlhood, boyhood, and female and male adolescence. Trained in fields other than history (e.g., American studies, communications studies, English, rhetoric and composition), the latest generation of scholars has blurred the boundaries and forged new fields. Informed by the work of cultural studies scholar Angela McRobbie, "girls' culture" aimed to balance the boy-centered biases of the older "youth studies." Nevertheless, such late twentieth-century anthologies as *The Children's Culture Reader* (1998), *Delinquents and Debutantes: Twentieth-Century American Girls' Cultures* (1998), and *Generations of Youth: Youth Cultures and History in Twentieth-Century America* (1998) reflect a new multi- and interdisciplinarity in the study of children and youth that utilizes textual and representational analyses (as opposed to social history) to study the subcultures that children and youth have constructed within larger historical contexts. By developing new methods of inquiry and widening subjects of study, scholars have been able to examine "lived experiences" and "subjectivities," though most of the recent work focuses on teenagers in the twentieth century.

Today, there is an abundance of scholarly works (e.g., monographs, anthologies, and encyclopedias); book series on children (e.g., The Girls' History and Culture Series); national, regional, and local conferences; major academic journals; and in 2000, the Society for the History of Children and Youth was finally founded by two of the field's pioneers, Joseph M. Hawes and N. Ray Hiner. That professional organization draws together the many college and university professors who teach courses on the history of children and youth, girlhood, and female adolescence regularly offered in schools of education, in departments of history, psychology, political science, and sociology, and in programs on women's studies, media/communications studies, and American studies. But the history of children and adolescents has an even broader audience as media attention on bad boys and mean girls (e.g., "queenbees") generates new questions and a search for answers in historical antecedents.

To meet the research needs of students of all ages, this accessibly written work—as the others in the series—surveys and synthesizes centuries of scholarship on children and adolescents of different classes, races, genders, regions, religions, sexualities, and abilities. Some topics in the series have a gendered, racial, or regional focus, while others (e.g., sickness and health, work and play, etc.) utilize a larger multicultural perspective. Whichever its focus, each and every book is organized into three equal parts to provide researchers with immediate access to historical overviews, primary source documents, and scholarly sources. Part I consists of synthetic essays written by experts in the field whose surveys are chronological and contextual. Part II provides access to hard-to-find primary source documents, in part or whole. Explanatory headnotes illuminate themes, generate further understanding, and expedite inquiry. Part III is an extensive up-to-date bibliography of cited sources as well as those critical for further research.

The goal of the Children and Youth: History and Culture reference book series is not simply a utilitarian one, but is also to ultimately situate girls and boys of all ages more centrally in dominant historical narratives.

Miriam Forman-Brunell, Series Editor
University of Missouri
Kansas City

Acknowledgments

This volume would not have been possible without the great ideas, hard work, and good humor of the contributors: Vern Bullough, David Considine, Susan Freeman, James Reed, and John Spurlock. For their strong support of this project I am grateful to series editor Miriam Forman-Brunell and Greenwood acquisitions editor Marie-Ellen Larcada.

I am indebted to Stephen Swinton Jr. and Amanda Frisken for their advice on the primary documents. Also, David Klaassen from the Social Welfare History Archives of the University of Minnesota and Jordan Foley and Amy Rocen from Miramax were particularly helpful in acquiring images for the primary source section.

Special thanks to my friends from Latham Ridge, Shaker, Fordham, and Old Westbury as well as to my multiple families: Wilkes and McCallen, Botticelli and Cocca, Swinton and Goodman.

As always, extra special thanks to my mother, Anne McCallen Swinton.

This book is dedicated to my partner, Steven Goodman, and to my stepfather, Stephen Swinton Sr.

Introduction

As part of Praeger's series Children and Youth: History and Culture, this volume covers major issues in adolescent sexuality in the United States, from colonial times to the present. It provides an account of how adults—from policy makers to police to parents—have attempted to intervene in the sexual lives of adolescents and how adolescent sexuality has been and continues to be a subject of social concern and an object of social control. It also shows how adolescents themselves have reacted to these interventions and how they themselves negotiate sexual agency on sometimes dangerous terrain.

But what exactly is adolescent sexuality? The time period referred to as adolescence, encompassing, in general, one's teen years and looked on as a transitional phase from childhood to adulthood, has been discussed by some scholars as a socially constructed category as its borders and meaning have differed from era to era and from culture to culture. Others have argued that such academic discussions do not do enough to engage with the reality of the way the term is used in our culture, particularly the ways in which "adolescents" and "children" are often spoken of as the same—particularly when it comes to sex. Collapsing "adolescents" and "children" together tends to rouse fear and anger among the populace and gives the word real political and social power that can lead to public policies and cultural norms that may be serving other agendas and may or may not be helpful to adolescents themselves. Indeed, even those who research and write about the subject—while praised by many—have been regularly criticized as subverting religious beliefs and moral values, endangering the welfare of children, and even endorsing sexual abuse.

With all this in mind this volume discusses adolescent sexuality as encompassing a range of sexual activities by teenagers as well as sexualized representations of teenagers. In so doing, it examines the ways in which adolescent sexuality has more often than not been constructed as dangerous and deviant and the ways in which it has been repeatedly linked to broader structural changes in the United States. In the colonial period, adolescent sexuality was linked to debates about religion and labor; in the nineteenth century it was linked to slavery, urbanization, industrialization, and immigration; in the twentieth century it has been linked to feminism, the sexual revolutions, and gay rights as well as to hot-button issues such as child sexual abuse, out-of-wedlock pregnancy, single-parent households, and welfare. Further, such discourses have keyed into multiple anxieties about race, class, ethnicity, gender, nation, and sexuality, which have played out through the site of adolescent sexuality and the adolescent body.

Adolescent Sexuality is the first comprehensive, historical, and multidisciplinary account of how discussions about adolescent sexuality are about far more than just the biological ages of the young people engaged in some form of sexual activity. It is composed of three parts; part I consists of five original essays, each of which covers a different aspect of the history of adolescent sexuality. The first, "Sex in Adolescence," by Vern Bullough, gives a broad demographic overview of major trends in adolescent sexuality over more than two thousand years as well as some of the major studies that have influenced how we think about adolescent sexuality. Carolyn Cocca's "16 Will Get You 20" focuses on U.S. statutory rape laws criminalizing certain types of adolescent sexualities and how those laws reflect certain assumptions about gender, race, class, and age. James W. Reed and John C. Spurlock's "Young and Pregnant" discusses teens and contraception, pregnancy, abortion, and birth and the frequent disconnects between policies and popular culture representations of adolescent sexuality on the one hand and data about teen pregnancy and the teen birthrate on the other. "Facts of Life and More," by Susan Freeman, looks at the history of sex education targeted at teens in the United States and how its content has changed over time due to the push and pull of forces promoting different approaches to how much and how detailed information about sex should be for young people. David Considine's "Get Real" examines the history of representations of adolescent sexuality in television and film as well as societal reactions to those depictions; while depictions have become more graphic and nuanced overall, there are roots of today's portrayals in past works.

Part II consists of selected primary sources grouped into five categories: theories about adolescent sexuality and sex education, the age of consent and the protection of/proscription of teens from sex, teen pregnancy and abstinence, images of adolescent sexuality, and current statistics on adolescent sexuality and contraceptive use. These primary sources, either printed in full or excerpted, depending on the length of the original document, illuminate the themes in the essays and allow the reader to evaluate the presentation of information in the essays for him or herself. This and part III, which consists of an extensive bibliography of primary and secondary sources, provide a starting point for those seeking to engage in further research on the topic.

As a whole, this volume illustrates that adolescent sexuality has generally been constructed as problematic in order to serve a variety of political agendas that have changed over time. But adolescents are not monolithic; neither is sexuality. This book seeks to provide a more balanced, nuanced, and data-grounded view of the subject of adolescent sexuality, thereby providing readers with a fact-based overview that should stimulate further inquiry on the topic.

Carolyn Cocca

I Essays

1 Sex in Adolescence: Trends and Theories from Ancient Greece to the Present

Vern Bullough

A dolescents have always been sexually active. But juvenile experimentation has often coexisted uneasily with public morals about the nature of sexuality (particularly those of the Judeo-Christian tradition) as well as with prevailing theories about the nature of childhood itself. This chapter provides an overview of sex in adolescence and studies of sex in adolescence from ancient Greece to the present.

DEFINING ADOLESCENCE

Though all individuals go through the biological changes that occur with reproductive maturation, it is not clear that there is an adolescent social stage common across cultures. Anthropological studies of preindustrial societies seem to find that there is a social stage intervening between childhood and adulthood but that the length of such a period is highly variable: it may be as short as one year or, as in modern society, last for much longer periods. Despite many similarities, there are gender differences in length of adolescence, and that of boys is usually longer than that of girls.

One of the particular difficulties of studying adolescence in the past is the lack of source materials. Historically, most of what we know is based on the upper classes and is derived from literary sources written down much later. These literary sources are mostly about elite individuals, kings, nobles, and Christian saints, and they tell us much more about males than females. Many of the accounts, such as those of the lives of Christian saints, ignore reality in order to paint portraits of flawless characters who grew into holy icons of society, and their accuracy about incidents in childhood can be seriously questioned.

Another difficulty is that in almost all the literary references, what might be called the language of age is hopelessly vague; that is, childhood is not divided into separate parts, and we are never certain at what age events occurred. Put simply, past cultures did not share our obsession about ages and stages of childhood and early adulthood. They did, however, note biological changes, such as the onset of menses or growth of pubic hair, and these changes, in most past societies, established the age of consent. Traditionally and legally, this age was set between 12 and 14, although younger ages also appear (see chapter 2 in this volume). In many societies an adolescent period is almost nonexistent because young people, particularly girls, are married shortly after puberty, and while marriage itself might not make them adults, pregnancy and childbirth does. It is probably best, therefore, to think of adolescence as an ongoing process of reorganization rather than giving it an age date for completion.

SEX IN ADOLESCENCE IN ANCIENT GREECE

Not all sexual activities are heterosexual ones. Historically, for example, Greek society turned to homosexuality as a way of dealing with youthful male sexuality and the lack of resources to accommodate a burgeoning population. The Greeks, who began migrating into Europe from Asia at the end of the second millennium, rapidly grew in numbers after they had settled down. They first dealt with this rapid growth by establishing new colonies around the Mediterranean, but as this became more difficult, they also attempted to control the growth of their population by limiting family size and delaying marriage. The age of marriage for men was raised to 30 (although girls still married in their teens). The earliest literary references we have to these changes in practice are in the works of Hesiod (seventh century B.C.E.), who, both in his *Theogony* and in his *Works and Days*, not only counseled older people who had reached the age of 60 to drink hemlock juice (i.e., commit suicide) so they would not be a burden to society, but also encouraged males to marry late (at least 30 years of age).

One result of this raising of the age of marriage for men was the institutionalization of pederasty in many of the Greek city-states. Strabo, in his *Geography*, described it in Crete, where formal puberty for boys (determined by their ability to ejaculate) was regarded as taking place at 12. When he hit puberty, the boy was regarded as eligible for symbolic abduction by an older man, who made him his lover. After the young man returned from his "honeymoon," he was given a military uniform and an ox as well as other costly and numerous things by his friends, commemorating his coming of age. The young man then could decide whether he was pleased with his new lover or not; if he had been an unwilling participant, he could avenge himself by renouncing his kidnapper (Percy 1996, 65).

Other Greek city-states had similar practices, and as ephebophilia (i.e., sex between a young teenager and an adult) became institutionalized, the abduction part was dropped, and the youth was taken in hand to be educated by a person of 20 or so, who had a boy lover until he reached 30, the age at which he married, usually a young girl. The process was then continued by the young man when at 20 his protector left him, and he himself then took a 12-year-old boy under his wing. These were essentially aristocratic youths, and although some older lovers might have continued to be attracted by a beautiful pubescent youth, most men ultimately married and had a family, although their social lives were primarily with other men.

Girls, for their part, soon became mothers after they married, although there is an occasional hint that at least some had a female partner for a time. Most scholars believe that they did not and that their adolescence ended with an early motherhood, although some of the fragments of the poems by Sappho can be read as implying that at least some adolescents had adolescent lesbian love affairs (Percy 1996, 147–48). The only Greek city to officially provide for education for girls was Sparta. This education often involved learning and giving musical performances as well as athletic activities, and its purpose was to create mothers who would produce hoplites (soldiers) and mothers of hoplites (Pomeroy 2002).

In this time, in general, most people were either in hunting and nomadic societies or settled down in villages, and in both cases, people now deemed juveniles or adolescents were doing the work of adults. There were some larger cities, particularly of larger kingdoms or states, and in such areas, where specialty crafts emerged, young males served apprenticeships or, if they came from the nobility or ruling elite, learned the art of war. If they were not slaves, they could sign a contract after they reached puberty, get married (or in the case of Greece, take on a lover), have sex, and begin raising a family of their own. Obviously, customs differed widely among peoples and cultures, but in general, females married in their early teens, and while some economic or other barriers often encouraged males to delay starting a family, they still had sexual outlets with prostitutes or, as in certain classes in Greece, with a homosexual patron.

PREINDUSTRIAL EUROPE

Though we might lack some detail on sexual activities of adolescents during much of human history, we know that they (particularly the males) were sexually active. Most individuals had little privacy, and children learned early about sex since they had seen and heard their parents or siblings and had probably imitated them in sex play. Premarital sex was common, and pregnant brides were the norm in many areas of the world. Pregnancy, in fact, guaranteed that the woman was fertile, something that was deemed by many to be far more important than being a virgin on her wedding night, although it was assumed that the young people were committed to marriage if she became pregnant.

There was, however, in much of Europe, a tendency to recognize a period of sexual innocence in young children, and in Christian Europe, such innocence ended with confirmation, between the ages of seven and eight. Because a child was considered capable of expressing himself properly at these early ages, he could be betrothed, although it was not considered a binding marriage act until it was consummated. If it had not been consummated by age 12, the marriage vows were no longer valid. The recognition of a change in status with menarche or ejaculation was recognized by the Catholic Church in the way it treated confession. In Catholic countries, while young people were expected to confess and do penance for sexual sins after the period of innocence ended, the penance before puberty was lighter than afterward. In the United States, women generally married younger than in Europe, and as late at the 1950s, the age category with the largest number of brides was 17. It was only in the last part of the twentieth century that the age of brides began to rise significantly.

Surviving texts from Germany in the later medieval and early modern periods continued to emphasize the flexible thresholds between childhood and adulthood. While some people in the past lived to advanced age, all took on adult responsibilities early, and most died before they were 50. In Middle High German texts a person could become a knight as early as 11 and as late as 24, but mostly between 15 and 19. Girls married between 12 and 14, and their families began looking for a husband for their daughter as soon as she began to menstruate.

Education throughout most of history was limited, and most people were illiterate. In medieval society, schooling was sex segregated and was primarily a task for parents, meaning that tradition passed down from fathers to sons and mothers to daughters. Children in rural areas rarely went to school. In some of the larger villages, there might have been schools catering to the sons of the leading citizens; in the cathedral cities, there were all-male cathedral schools; and in the late medieval period, some noncathedral boarding schools for boys were established. Girls were less free to mingle in society and were generally tutored at home, often by a hired teacher (or governess), if they were allowed to learn anything at all.

But even the least of villages had its holidays, feast days, competitive contests, and other activities. Most teenage children traveled to nearby market towns, fairs, and other events, which might have brought them together with their peers. In the larger towns and in the city, there were more opportunities for advancement and change for the males, particularly if they could learn a trade. War offered an opportunity for change, to travel and to pillage, and, if they survived and their side was victorious, to better themselves.

Society in the past was not always stable, if only because there were mass movements of peoples periodically taking place. Inevitably, it was young people who were the most likely to move on and seek new settlements, and this meant that young people took on a great deal of responsibility, including families and whether they stayed and fought the invaders or joined with them to establish new settlements. In the newly founded United States, in the first part of the nineteenth century, for example, the average age of the population in most parts of the country was in the late teens or early twenties. Some of them, like the semilegendary Daniel Boone, had settled down and begun a family before reaching their middle teens.

THEORIES OF THE EIGHTEENTH AND NINETEENTH CENTURIES

Despite the ubiquity of adolescent sexuality and the fluidity of childhood-adulthood boundaries, theorists often debated the significance and implications of juvenile sex. Many such works, beginning with St. Augustine in the 300s, were focused on the moral dangers of nonprocreative and nonmarital sexual activities.

Were children capable of having sex? This was much debated in the eighteenth century. One view of children common in early America as well as elsewhere in Europe was that the child was naturally wicked, and hence the function of education was to teach a child to modify and control sexual or erotic proclivities. Hannah More (1745–1843), for example, wrote that it was a fundamental error to consider children as innocent beings since even their little weaknesses may want some correction. Instead, she held that children should be regarded as beings conceived with a corrupt nature and evil disposition, something which education had to rectify and change. On the other side of the equation was Jean-Jacques Rousseau (1712–78), who proclaimed the innocence of the child. He also believed that such innocence could so easily be destroyed that the only way to help them develop satisfactorily was by disciplining them. Both sides ended up with education and discipline as a key.

The great worry about juvenile sexuality in the nineteenth and early part of the twentieth centuries was the danger of masturbation. In the days before the germ theory of disease came to be accepted at the end of the nineteenth century, the loss of vital energy through masturbation was regarded as a main cause of disease. Adolescents were particularly susceptible to serious diseases, and parents had to always be on the lookout for the dangers. John Harvey Kellogg could write as late as 1884 that the recognizable signs of the masturbator included acne, sudden changes in disposition, fickleness, bashfulness, boldness, and many other descriptors that could apply to almost any adolescent at some time in their teens. One consequence of this belief was the growth of circumcision in the United States since this was believed to make it less likely that adolescent boys would masturbate. Some said one way to avoid the dangers of masturbation was to encourage early marriage and family responsibilities. Children might be innocent, but sex posed great danger, even to the innocent.

FREUD AND THE STUDY OF SEX: HIS CONTEMPORARIES AND HIS SUCCESSORS

Sexual innocence, however, was something to which the newly developing field of sex research in the nineteenth century did not subscribe (Bullough 1994). One of the founders of modern sex research, Richard von Krafft-Ebing (1894), recounted the story of a girl of eight who was "devoid of all childlike and moral feelings: because she had been masturbating from her fourth year." At the same time she consorted with boys of the ages of 10 or 12. He also included the case of a girl who began to masturbate at seven years of age, practiced lewdness with boys, and seduced her younger sister into masturbating as well.

It was, however, Sigmund Freud in the early twentieth century (1908) who gave the death knell to the concept of a sexually innocent childhood. In the process he redefined sexuality to include a large variety of behaviors that previously had not been included. He wrote that the parent who did not credit his or her children with having sexual feelings and expressions was a parent who had not taken the time or trouble to observe the children closely. Freud held that sexuality was a prime factor in human development and that sexual experiences during infancy influenced the development of adult personality. He hypothesized that children competed with the parent of the same gender for the sexual relationship with the parent of the other gender, a competition that he named the Oedipus complex (for boys) and the Electra complex (for girls).

Freud divided childhood sexuality into phases. The "oral stage" coincided with infancy and lasted to 18 months, and sensuality was expressed in sucking, touching, holding, bodily contact, and genital exploration. This was followed by the "anal stage," in early childhood, when the development of sphincter control, the ability in males to produce erection, the awareness of nongenital gender differences, and a developing gender identity took place. Next came the phallic, or "Oedipal/Electra," phase, which took place between three and five and resulted in deliberate pleasurable self-stimulation, curiosity about sexual and productive processes, and well-developed gender identity. This was followed from the 5th to the 11th years by the "latency period," which Freud equated with active sexual exploration, active desire for sex information, prepubescent surge in hormones, and growth of internal and external sexual organs. The final phase was adolescence, which he carried from 12 to 20 years of age and called the "genital stage." This involved the development of capacities to ejaculate and to menstruate, sexual maturation, seeking questions of self-identity, and intense romantic attachments.

Freud was the dominant force in the United States in the 1930s and 1940s and brought about a new focus on the importance of discussing sexuality. Many followed him, departing only in minor ways, while others openly challenged him. Erik Erikson (1968) accepted the age steps for the development of sexuality but also believed that things often went awry. He postulated eight stages of life, each of which involved a crisis for the individual and in which negative developments in one phase could be overcome in others. Other investigators, such as evolutionary and social biologists, emphasized the differences between the sexes, teaching that the way children approached sex was a result of evolutionary changes over time that emerged from the reproductive success of individuals who had greater adaptive skills than others (Symons 1979). Well-developed gross motor skills and aggressiveness in males probably would have greater value in ensuring evolutionary survival, whereas attachment bonds, sociability, and interpersonal sensitivity would have been favored in women (Rossi 1985). It was in this context that major research finally began to be carried out on juvenile sexuality. The problem was how to find out what juveniles were actually doing.

WHAT WE NOW KNOW: SEX IN ADOLESCENCE IN THE TWENTIETH CENTURY

Rather than encouraging inquiry, legislators, particularly in the United States, have made research into the topic more difficult. Laws that were enacted to protect children have been interpreted in ways to prevent any serious study of childhood sexuality involving direct questioning of them (Graupner and Bullough 2004). In general, there are four ways to conduct research on childhood sexuality. One is to ask adults to recall and describe their sexual feelings and behavior during childhood. Another is to ask children about their sex lives, and still another is to observe children's sexual behavior, while a fourth way is to obtain observations from their parents or from those who take care of children. All four methods have been used, but all have raised political controversy.

Before the enactment of the more restrictive laws Alfred Kinsey and his colleagues (Kinsey, Pomeroy, and Martin 1948) had done some research that provided evidence for much of what Freud had said about childhood sexual development. The Kinsey group asked adults as well as a handful of children about their youthful sexual activities. They found that 48 percent of the older males and 60 percent of the adolescent boys had engaged in homosexual activity; the mean age of contact was nine years. The problem is what is defined as homosexual activity, and Kinsey included exhibition of genitals, manual manipulation of genitalia, anal or oral contact with genitalia, and urethral insertions, some of which others would not define as homosexual. Childhood heterosexual sex play (inspection of each sex by the other, finger insertion in the vagina or handling of the penis by the opposite sex) began at a median age of 8 years and 10 months; genital insertions occurred slightly later. The team also reported that orgasms had been reported by other observers occurring as early as five months for boys and four months for girls. Preadolescent boys could reach a climax much faster than adolescent boys.

In the study of females (Kinsey et al. 1953), approximately 4 percent reported that they had been responding sexually by five years of age, whereas nearly 16 percent recalled doing so by 10 years and a total of 27 percent responding sexually before they were defined as being adolescent. Fourteen percent had achieved orgasm. Thirty percent reported preadolescent sexual play, and much of the play was due to curiosity about their partner's anatomy.

Robert Sorenson (1973) interviewed and questioned American teenagers about their personal values and sexual behaviors. He found that 33 percent of the boys and 12 percent of the girls had begun to masturbate before the age of 11. Boys had been told about or shown masturbation by their peers, whereas girls tended to learn about it through self-discovery. Since the Sorenson study, American law has changed, making it more difficult, if not almost impossible, to question students. Human use committees at research institutions are particularly hesitant to encourage research, fearful that it would violate the rights of individual students. It is still possible to question teenagers, but there are limits about what can be asked; there is also a reluctance of researchers to be involved for fear of being charged with committing a sex crime.

Many researchers, stymied by American law, looked to Europe for answers. One of the first comprehensive examinations of sexual development was that by the Austrian Ernest Borneman (1994), who believed that the retroactive method used by Kinsey and others was not valid for early childhood and that direct observation and questioning of children was essential. Borneman found that the sex lives of children are more complicated in earlier phases of development than in later ones, that they have much more in common with adult sex lives than with any animal model, that childhood sex is not necessarily having coitus, and that no real understanding of adult sexual life is possible without first knowing about their children. Still, Borneman, even in Austria, was denounced for doing such research and was accused of pedophilia. Even if a researcher succeeded in studying childhood or adolescent sex, there was a reluctance by many publishers to publish the findings. Floyd Martinson (1973), for example, who arrived at many of the same conclusions that Borneman did, had to turn to self-publishing to get his material out.

Whatever difficulties researchers might have, and even with federally sponsored abstinence-only programs handicapping sex education, young people learn about sex (see chapter 4 in this volume). Research consistently has shown that by age 18, most young males and females in the United States and Canada have engaged in coitus and a variety of other activities (DeLameter and MacCorquodale 1979; King et al. 1988). Recent research has often focused on social influences, particularly on teens, and the effect of such influences on sexual behavior. The findings indicate that sexual activities tend to start earlier among children who are from lower socioeconomic levels, probably because this is the norm in the communities in which they live (Brewster, Billy, and Grady 1993). Sexual activity tends to start later among children who are religiously observant and of higher intelligence, although it is not clear whether it is the religion or the higher intelligence that is most influential (Halpern et al. 1994, 2000). Initiation into sexual activity is more likely to occur earlier if the person has a significantly older boyfriend or girlfriend than her or his peers (Van Oss et al. 2000). We also know that indicators of nonconforming sexual behavior, such as homosexuality or gender-challenged activities, tend to begin fairly early in childhood, even before adolescence (Green 1987).

In a study that encompassed countries outside the United States, Canada, and Europe, Schlegel and Barry (1991) examined anthropological reports of 173 contemporary, preindustrial societies for boys and 175 for girls. Most girls were married early, within a year or two of menarche, while boys remained single longer. Most of the societies they examined were tolerant about sexuality, although usually only about sexual activities within peer groups. Only a small number tolerated widespread promiscuity. In general, we have more information about heterosexual activities than about homosexual or solitary sex (i.e., masturbation).

Some societies were and still are very restrictive; others are not. In many Middle Eastern villages, for example, girls cannot speak to males outside their families after puberty. At the opposite end of the spectrum are more permissive Polynesian societies, where, during festivals that involve special baths, the donning of scents, and adornment with flowers, the youths "strut" about and then "troop" to a neighboring village for festivities that end in sexual activity. Other cultures also have special ceremonies. The Muria, a tribe in central India, for example, has adolescent dormitories set aside for youths for courting and sexual intercourse (Elwin 1968).

Despite these recent gains in knowledge, in many ways, studies of and discussions about sexuality are still politically and socially restricted. What seems clear from this brief overview, however, is that the onset of puberty, and the period we now call adolescence, has always been one of sexual experimentation and that society has often been reluctant to recognize and deal with this.

WORKS CITED

Borneman, Ernest. 1994. *Childhood Phases of Maturity: Sexual Developmental Psychology*, trans. M. Lombardi-Nash. Amherst, NY: Prometheus Books.

Brewster, K. L., J.O.G. Billy, and W. R. Grady. 1993. "Social Context and Adolescent Behavior: The Impact of Community and the Transition to Sexual Activity." *Social Forces* 71: 713–40.

Bullough, Vern L. 1994. *Science in the Bedroom: A History of Sex Research.* New York: Basic Books.

DeLameter, John, and Patricia MacCorquodale. 1979. *Premarital Sexuality: Attitudes, Relationships, Behavior.* Madison: University of Wisconsin Press.

Elwin, Verrier. 1968. *The Kingdom of the Young.* London: Oxford University Press.

Erickson, Erik H. 1968. *Identity, Youth, and Crisis.* New York: Norton.

Freud, Sigmund. 1908. "On the Sexual Theories of Children." In J. Strachey and A. Freud, eds. *The Standard Edition of the Complete Psychological Works of Sigmund Freud*, Vol. 9. London: Hogarth Press, 1962.

Graupner, Helmut, and Vern L. Bullough, eds. 2004. *Adolescence, Sexuality and the Criminal Law: Multidisciplinary Perspectives.* Birmingham, NY: Haworth Press.

Green, Richard. 1987. *The "Sissy Boy" Syndrome and the Development of Homosexuality.* New Haven, CT: Yale University Press.

Halpern, C. T., et al. 1994. "Testosterone and Religiosity as Predictor of Sexual Attitudes and Activity among Adolescent Males: A Biosocial Model." *Journal of Biosocial Sciences* 26: 217–34.

Halpern, C. T., et al. 2000. "Smart Teens Don't Have Sex (or Kiss Much Either)." *Journal of Adolescent Health* 26: 213–25.

Kellogg, John Harvey. 1884. *Plain Facts for Old and Young.* Burlington, Iowa: I. F. Segner.

King, A.J.C., R. P. Beazley, W. K. Warrren, C. A. Hankins, A. S. Robertson, and J. L. Radford. 1988. *Canada Youth and Aids Study.* Ottawa: Federal Centre for Aids Health Protection, Branch, Health and Welfare Canada.

Kinsey, Alfred C., Wardell B. Pomeroy, and Clyde E. Martin. 1948. *Sexual Behavior in the Human Male.* Philadelphia: W. B. Saunders.

Kinsey, Alfred C., Wardell B. Pomeroy, Clyde E. Martin, and Paul Gebhard. 1953. *Sexual Behavior in the Human Female.* Philadelphia: W. B. Saunders.

Martinson, Floyd. 1973. *Infant and Child Sexuality: A Sociological Perspective.* St. Peter, MN: Book Mark, Gustavus Adolphus College.

More, Hannah. 1799. *Strictures on the Modern System of Female Education.* London: A. Strahan.

Percy, William A. 1996. *Pederasty and Pedagogy in Archaic Greece.* Urbana: University of Illinois Press.

Pomeroy, Sarah B. 2002. *Spartan Women.* New York: Oxford University Press.

Rossi, Alice S. 1985. *Gender and the Life Course.* New York: Aldine.

Rousseau, Jean-Jacques. 1911. *Émile, l'education*, trans. B. Foxley. London: Dent.

Schlegel, Alice, and Herbert Barry III. 1991. *Adolescence: An Anthropological Inquiry.* New York: Free Press.

Sorenson, Robert C. 1973. *Adolescent Sexuality in Contemporary America: Personal Values and Sexual Behavior, Ages Thirteen to Nineteen.* New York: World Publishing.

Symons, D. 1979. *The Evolution of Human Sexuality.* New York: Oxford University Press.

Van Oss, M. B., et al. 2000. "Older Boyfriends and Girlfriends Increase Risk of Sexual Initiations in Young Adolescents." *Journal of Adolescent Health* 27: 409–18.

von Krafft-Ebing, Richard. 1894. *Psychopathia Sexualis, with Especial Reference to Contrary Sexual Instinct: A Medico-Legal Study,* trans. C. G. Chaddock from the 7th German ed. Philadelphia: F. A. Davis.

2 "16 Will Get You 20": Adolescent Sexuality and Statutory Rape Laws

Carolyn Cocca

At what age is a person capable of making an informed decision about whether or not to engage in sex? Would it be 7, 10, 12, 13, 14, 15, 16, 17, 18, or 21? Would it be different in different time periods, or different states, or different countries? Over the last 300 years, all the ages listed above were thought to be that magic age at which one could make such a decision, and all the ages listed above have, at various times, been inscribed into law as the age of consent to sex.

Statutory rape laws criminalize sexual activity with an unmarried person who is under the age of consent. Today, this age still varies depending on the country in which one lives; in the United States it varies across the states. In practice the laws have always been a double-edged sword. They can punish someone who has taken advantage of or harmed an underage person or perhaps deter people from engaging in potentially coercive, unequal, manipulative, or predatory relationships. But they can also punish consensual sexual activity simply because the two people are not married to one another. The laws contain a number of contradictions vis-à-vis whom they protect and whom they punish. This is because the laws have never been considered in isolation; rather, they have been repeatedly intertwined with and used as a symbol of larger issues, such as changes in marriage rates; the growth of women's power, both within and outside the home; the economic and social dislocations of immigration and urbanization; and the increasing visibility of nonmarital relationships and sexualities (Cocca 2004). This chapter examines these intersections as it details changes made to statutory rape laws from colonial times to the present.

THE EARLY UNITED STATES THROUGH THE 1800s

Statutory rape laws were originally gender-specific. The crime was defined as sexual penetration of an underage female by a male. England codified its statutory rape law in the Statute of Westminster of 1275, setting the age at 12 (Statute of Westminster I, 1275, 3 Edw., c. 13). It was lowered to 10 in 1576: "… if any person shall unlawfully and carnally know and abuse any woman-child under the age of ten years, every such unlawful and carnal knowledge shall be a felony" (1576, 18 Eliz., c. 7 §4).

Following this, the colonies chose either 10 or 12 as the age of consent. The laws at that time were less about the female's ability to consent and more about protecting her chastity—a valuable commodity. Virginity made a female marriageable and perhaps would even bring her father a monetary gift from her future husband on their marriage. Thus "statutory rape was a property crime" (Eidson 1980, 767; Fuentes 1994) because it was the theft of an unmarried female's virginity. This is why the laws stated (as they still do today) that no crime has been committed if the two people are married.

This, in practice, only applied to white females. African American females were generally formally enslaved, and for a variety of political, economic, social, and cultural reasons their sexuality was not deemed to be in need of legal protection. This manifested itself in several myths about the "natural" state of black female sexuality as being the opposite of the "natural" state of white female sexuality. While the latter was considered chaste, pure, and passionless, the black female was promiscuous, impure, and lascivious—justifying white men's sexual abuse of black women (Cott 1978; Roberts 1997).

STATUTORY RAPE LAW REFORM IN THE LATE NINETEENTH AND EARLY TWENTIETH CENTURIES

The ways in which the laws operated in the late nineteenth and early twentieth centuries are vital to understanding the ways in which the laws operate today. Beginning in the 1880s, statutory rape laws were changed in virtually every state. Anxieties over the numerous social, economic, and political dislocations of the times, such as increasing immigration; fears of "race suicide" as white middle-class women were viewed as having too many abortions; women gaining some power in the public sphere; and perhaps most importantly, urbanization and industrialization. Young, unmarried females, often of immigrant descent, began to work on their own in the cities, earned a meager amount of economic independence from their families, and engaged in activities at which they could mingle unchaperoned with unmarried males.

First-wave feminists, white working-class men's organizations, and religious conservatives worked together to raise the age of consent. White middle-class women were very concerned about the public morality of working-class males and females and the quite visible nature of the latter's leisure time activities in the cities—these women viewed young males and females going to the pub, or to the movies, or to dances together as symbols of disorder and moral decay. These social purity reformers sought to portray a hearth-oriented married life as the ultimate goal to which a decent and moral woman should aspire. Unmarried female sexuality was viewed as being akin to prostitution as young urban females who dated were often "treated" to dinner, dancing, or a movie and then had sex with their dates. They were unable or unwilling to accept that some of these young females may have chosen to engage in sexual activities and perhaps experienced pleasure through them. Thus they sought to "uplift" the working girls' morals so that they might aspire to take on middle-class values (DuBois and Gordon 1984; Kunzel 1993; Langum 1994; Larson 1997; Odem 1995; Peiss 1986; Stansell 1987; Walkowitz 1980, 1992).

At the same time, as Victorians, these reformers were concerned with the potential for young, vulnerable females to be abused by predatory males, both within and outside of their families. Like casual dating, this could lead to one's becoming a so-called fallen woman, looked down on by society and unable to marry. Thus the reformers' second major concern was with the sexual double standard that demanded female chastity before marriage yet allowed men access to those above age 10 or 12 without much fear of repercussion. They fashioned a particular narrative, in which affluent males tricked or forced young working females into sexual situations. They wanted society at large to acknowledge sexual coercion and sexual danger, at least that facing white females (Odem 1995). Indeed, some began to use the language of the popular narrative of "white slavery"—that young, white females were being tricked or kidnapped and then forced into prostitution in the cities. Although there was little to no basis in fact for this concern, the U.S. government did, in 1910, pass the White-Slave Traffic Act (also known as the Mann Act), criminalizing transporting "women and girls" across state lines for "immoral purposes." Such language strengthened the efforts of statutory rape reformers in the 1880s, and after as well.

African American women's groups did support the idea of a single moral standard. But they worried that more stringent age of consent laws would be used to target black males, who were stereotyped as rapists of white women. Second, they were concerned that the white feminists did not take into account the kind of sexual danger faced by black women. The laws of the southern states generally didn't allow blacks to testify against whites, some rape laws specifically excluded black women, and cultural narratives constructed black females as undeserving of protection (Roberts 1997). The white female reformers went forward without them in the campaign to change statutory rape laws.

The image of the passive, white working-class victim did draw the support of white working-class men. One could also argue that workingmen were also concerned about the morality of those young working females (that is, that they were going out with young males unsupervised and possibly making "bad" decisions about dating or sex) and joined the age of consent movement out of social conservatism along with protectionist instincts. More conservative religious elements were drawn in in this way, and these forces became dominant in the reform movement. But they did not share the feminists' interest in uplifting working-class morals. They were more concerned with proscribing premarital sexuality, and particularly female sexuality (Kunzel 1993; Odem 1995; Olsen 1984; Walkowitz 1980).

Led by the Woman's Christian Temperance Union (WCTU), which had broadened its antialcohol/antipub stance to include combating what it saw as other types of immorality, the groups described above lobbied in each state to have "the age at which a girl can legally consent to her own ruin be raised to at least eighteen years" (Larson 1997). All states did raise the age to 16 or 18; at one point Tennessee raised it to 21.

Male legislators, though, did not take the protectionist ideals very seriously. Only a few years after this campaign, many states considered measures to roll back their ages of consent to prereform levels, although in most cases the women's groups were able to halt those efforts (Larson 1997, 57–58; Pivar 1973, 144–45). They were concerned that in an age in which marriage in one's teens was extremely common, young males who were expressing their "natural" sexual desires would be punished for engaging in activity with willing young females. They did three things: (1) they graded the penalties so that underage males would have more lenient sentences; (2) they required that female victims be "of previously chaste character," that is, virgins, for the crime to have occurred; and (3) they allowed a "mistake of age" defense—there could be no conviction if the perpetrator said he thought the victim was above the age of consent.

With these latter two requirements, statutory rape laws protected only a virgin, and only a virgin whose sex partner did not try to claim that he thought she was older. The laws thus became a means of preserving a particular conception of morality rather than punishing someone for taking advantage of an underage, unmarried female (Oberman 1994). One could argue that this was in line with the original purpose of the laws—to punish a male for stealing a young female's chastity. But this served few young females well. It was particularly problematic for young black females, who, as noted, were already constructed as unchaste. The "previously chaste character" requirement remained in effect in some states until quite recently; Mississippi was the last to remove that language, in 1998.

In effect, the raising of the age of consent and the codification of the "chaste character" defense made what was a crime about "stealing" the virginity of a female of 10 or 12 into a crime about stealing the virginity of a female of 16 or 18. Thus began an interesting anomaly, in which one could be of age to choose to marry and thus have sexual intercourse legally, but not of age to consent to unmarried sex. Indeed, even today, thousands of underage teens marry each year because although in most states one must be 18 to marry on one's own, one can do so at a younger age with parental or judicial permission, and in some states the couple does not need such permission if the female is pregnant or has already given birth (Posner and Silbaugh 1996). But in the Victorian Era in particular, many, if not most, young males and females were married and had children before they reached the new, higher ages of consent.

After the turn of the century, activities centered around statutory rape laws began to take a more conservative and punitive turn. Three things changed. First, middle-class women reformers had begun to discover that many working-class females were willing participants in sexual activity and sought to "rehabilitate" them through reformatories and maternity homes. Second, male police, prosecutors, and judges were more prone to subscribe to the notion of the female as a vixen rather than a victim and would often sentence the male defendant to probation while sentencing the female on delinquency charges and sending them to the previously mentioned reformatories. Third, families began to use the laws to try to control their "incorrigible" and "delinquent" daughters, and young females were unable to stop the prosecutions. These young women were far more often than not poor and of immigrant descent or status (Alexander 1995; Kunzel 1993; Larson 1997; Odem 1995; Schlossman and Wallach 1985; Stansell 1987).

There are many similarities between statutory rape politics in the late 1800s and statutory rape politics today. Class, race, and ethnicity still play a part in who is more often prosecuted. So does gender—even though all the states now have gender-neutral laws, the idea of male as aggressor and female as victim pervades the discourse as well as the prosecutions (Cocca 2004). Strange political bedfellows (e.g., some feminists and religious conservatives) sometimes agree on the necessity of using the laws against males. Last, the laws as implemented at the turn of the nineteenth and at the turn of the twentieth centuries have both protected and punished adolescents engaged in sexual activity.

FEMINIST REFORMS OF THE LATE TWENTIETH CENTURY

Statutory rape reform was part of a larger program of forcible rape reform begun by second-wave feminists in 1973. They saw statutory rape laws less as protective and more as punitive, less as empowering and more as infantilizing. They felt that the nineteenth-century feminists had served in some measure to codify patriarchal notions of female sexuality and mental incapacity into law and to reinforce stereotypes of gender by prohibiting sex with an underage female only. They also felt that the language used by first-wave feminists was restrictive in its advocacy for passivity and chastity and its implication that sexuality be confined to heterosexual marriage.

But these feminists also felt that the shortcomings of forcible rape law showed the necessity of statutory rape law to prosecute coerced or manipulated sex with the underaged that fell short of the legal definitions and cultural conceptions of forcible rape. For instance, in the 1970s and, to some extent, still today, juries were likely to feel that the crime of rape required an armed male stranger as the perpetrator and that a victim resist the force of her attacker and prove that that resistance had occurred. In a statutory rape case the prosecution has to prove only that the victim was underage and that the two people were not married when the sexual act occurred. Statutory rape is simply easier to prosecute than is forcible rape.

Liberal feminists thus sought to restore some agency and formal equality to young women while also safeguarding them from sexual coercion. Specifically, they lobbied for gender-neutral language, which would treat males and females equally by protecting both as victims and charging both as perpetrators. Thus young male victims would not be neglected, and the crime would be based solely on the age of the victim, not both age and gender. They also lobbied for age-span provisions which mandated that the perpetrator be a certain number of years older than the victim so that sex between similarly aged teens would go unprosecuted. The idea here is that a young person, particularly a teen whose self-esteem tends to decline and who is perhaps more easily swayed by peer pressure, could be easily taken advantage of by someone who was older and thus more experienced in manipulating sexual situations. Along with gender-neutral language and age spans, their other goals for statutory rape laws included eliminating the "promiscuity" clause that dismissed cases if the young female was not a virgin and eliminating the "mistake of age" defense, in which the perpetrator could claim he thought the victim was above the age of consent (Bienen 1980, 177–80; Searles and Berger 1987, 25–27).

This is not to say that all feminists were united in their support of statutory rape laws. Radical feminists argued that for socially constructed reasons, men and women were simply not similarly situated in modern society, that a female was always the less powerful party in heterosexual relationships, and that a young female's nonconsent may manifest itself in a way not recognized in forcible rape laws (see, e.g., MacKinnon 1991). Sex radicals, sometimes called prosex feminists, were on the opposite side of the debate from the radical feminists. While they acknowledged that statutory rape laws had a protective function, they were concerned that the laws punished potentially consensual unmarried sex, painted all young people, and particularly young females, as incapable of making decisions about their own bodies, and sent a message that nonmarital sex and female sexual agency in and of themselves were wrong and harmful (see, e.g., Duggan and Hunter 1995; Rubin 1984). They also feared that the gender-neutral language would enable the prosecution of homosexual couples already suffering from other forms of legalized discrimination based on their sexuality. Indeed, until the last few years, many European countries maintained two different sets of ages of consent: one for male-female sex and one for male-male sex (Shvartsman 2004).

With these potential problems in mind the reformers moved forward. The drive for gender-neutral language was successful in all states by 2000. A law that formerly read that "a male commits the crime of statutory rape if he engages in sexual intercourse with a female not his wife and under the age of consent ..." today would read "a person commits the crime of statutory rape if he or she engages in sexual intercourse with a person not his or her spouse under the age of consent...." Although the gains made have been noteworthy, they are incomplete: gendered inequalities cannot be changed overnight as can the legal language, and feminist reformers (like their counterparts in the nineteenth century) have had little control over the implementation of the laws.

More cases can be prosecuted with gender-neutral language, thus potentially protecting more young people. There has been a disproportionate increase in cases involving male perpetrators and male victims, and that perpetrator is often labeled a pedophile and excoriated. Yet cases involving female perpetrators and male victims are often framed differently; more often than not, the young male is assumed not to have been harmed, and the older female is assumed to have been in love. To quote one district attorney describing the types of comments many people would make about his prosecutions of older women, "'Oh, well, he's a boy and it's probably the greatest thing that ever happened to him.'" He continued, "[But when] it's a young girl, it's clear to people that it's a molest" (Moody 1993). In cases of older women who have become pregnant by underage males, those males have been forced to pay child support—the cultural assumption that he should be a provider apparently outweighs whatever criminal harm may have been done to him (Cocca 2004).

Age-span provisions have been adopted by all but seven states, and the spans themselves vary from two to six years across the states. Table 2.1 shows current ages of consent across the 50 states as well as the age spans in each state (Cocca 2004). Table 2.2 shows current ages of consent in other countries.

The age spans have accomplished the goals sought by some feminist reformers but also live up to the fears expressed by others. Age spans leave a swath of vulnerable teens unprotected, open to coercion that is not recognized as meeting the legal definitions of forcible rape. But their implementation has, in most counties, concentrated resources on instances of sexual intercourse most likely to be coercive, that is, those in which the parties are far apart in age or in which one is in a supervisory position over the other. Some states do not have age spans, and many that do prosecute same-age perpetrators at the misdemeanor (instead of felony) level. So, depending on the state, both the 16-year-old in a relationship with a 15-year-old and the 50-year-old stranger who molests a 5-year-old may be required to register as sex offenders; both may be subject to confinement and/or psychiatric treatment to "cure" such urges as part of their prison terms, paroles, or probations. Both may be considered perpetrators of statutory rape.

Table 2.1
Ages of Consent, 1885–2005, and Age Spans in the 50 States

State	1885	1890	1920	2005	Age Span (Years)
AL	10	10	16	16	2
AK	NA	NA	16*	16	3
AZ	12	14	18	18	2
AR	10	10	16	16	5
CA	10	14	18	18	3
CO	10	10	18	15	4
CT	10	14	16	16	2
DE	7	15	16	16	4
FL	10	10	18	18	6
GA	10	10	14	16	3
HI	10*	NA	NA	16	5
ID	10	10	18	18	5
IL	10	14	16	17	5
IN	12*	NA	16	16	3
IA	10	13	16	16	4
KS	10	10	18	16	0
KY	12	12	16	16	6
LA	12	12	18	17	2
ME	10	14	16	16	5
MD	10	10	16	16	6
MA	10	14	16	16	0
MI	10	14	16	16	0
MN	10	10	18	16	2
MS	10	10	18	16	3
MO	12	14	18	17	5
MT	10	15	18	16	3
NE	10	15	18	16	4
NV	12	14	18	16	6
NH	10	10	16	16	0
NJ	10	16	16	16	4
NM	10	10	16	17	4
NY	10	16	18	17	5
NC	10	10	16	16	4

(continued)

Table 2.1

(continued)

State	1885	1890	1920	2005	Age Span (Years)
ND	10	14	18	18	5
OH	10	10	16	16	4
OK	NA	14*	NA	16	3
OR	10*	NA	16	16	3
PA	10	16	16	16	4
RI	10	13	16	16	3
SC	10	10	16	15	0
SD	10	14	18	16	3
TN	10	10	18	18	4
TX	10	10	18	17	3
UT	10	13	18	16	4
VT	10	14	16	16	0
VA	12	12	16	15	3
WA	12	12	18	16	4
WV	12	12	16	16	4
WI	10	14	16	16	0
WY	10	14	16	16	4

Source: Adapted by the author from state statutes. For 1885, 1980, and 1920, data are from Odem (1995, 14–15, 30, 199).
*Data drawn from Bienen (1980, 190).
NA = not available.

Again, such difficulties illuminate the dual nature of statutory rape laws as well as the shortcomings of legal language in trying to encompass a continuum of forcible to coercive to manipulated to consensual sexual relationships.

CONSERVATIVE REFORMS IN THE LATE TWENTIETH CENTURY

In the late 1990s, statutory rape laws were amended in several states. But, different from the other two sets of amendments to statutory rape laws, this was a policy initiative most pursued by conservative forces, who, as in the nineteenth century, were able to exert more control over the policy's implementation.

In 1981 the Supreme Court heard its only case dealing with statutory rape laws, *Michael M. v. Superior Court of Sonoma County* (450 U.S. 464–502 (1981)). The majority of the court held that gender-specific statutory rape laws, in which only males were considered perpetrators, were constitutional because they served to deter the "epidemic" of teenage pregnancy. Young

Table 2.2
Ages of Consent, Various Countries, 2005

Country	Age of consent	Country	Age of Consent
Albania	14	Israel	16
Australia	16-17	Italy	14
Austria	14	Japan	16/18
Belgium	16	Luxembourg	16
China	14	Netherlands	12/16
Croatia	14	Norway	16
Czech Republic	15	Poland	15
Denmark	15	Portugal	14/16
Finland	16	Romania	15
France	15	Russia	14/16
Germany	14/16	Serbia	14
Great Britain	16	Spain	13
Greece	15/17	Sweden	15
Hungary	14	Switzerland	16
India	18	Turkey	15/18
Ireland	17	United States	15–18

Source: Data are drawn from http://www.avert.org/aofconsent.htm, http://www.interpol.int/ Public/Children/SexualAbuse/NationalLaws/Default.asp, and http://www.ageofconsent. com/ (accessed June 12, 2005).

females were, or should be, deterred from sex by the threat of pregnancy, and young males would be deterred from sex by the fear of prosecution. Statutory rape laws, then, would serve to reduce teen pregnancy. In making this much-criticized argument the court explicitly linked teen pregnancy, statutory rape, and adolescent sexuality.

At the same time a broader backlash was taking place. Reacting to longer-term changes in the social structure and mores of the United States that had begun in the 1960s and 1970s, conservatives in the 1980s became focused on the rising numbers of nonmarital sexual relationships and out-of-wedlock births and on the concurrently rising percentage of women and children in poverty who required public assistance. Indeed, conservatives linked these two elements together in a cultural argument against welfare state liberalism, as they saw it: the lax morals and single-parent families of the poor, particularly people of color, were responsible for the rising numbers of such families requiring welfare and the rising costs of supplying that welfare (see, e.g., Murray 1984). The liberalism that allowed such things to occur, they argued, would result in nothing less than the destruction of so-called American values and the American way of life. What the Supreme Court had said in 1981 dovetailed with the movement described above vis-à-vis sexuality, pregnancy, and the economy, making the 1980s and 1990s ripe for new policy initiatives aimed at reclaiming so-called traditional American economics and morality. These would include cutting income taxes, reducing welfare benefits, promoting marriage, encouraging sexual abstinence by teens, and restricting funding for and access to abortion.

The discourse about and the activities specifically surrounding statutory rape vis-à-vis teen pregnancy and teenage births intensified beginning in 1995, when the nonpartisan Alan Guttmacher Institute released a study on teen pregnancy called *Sex and America's Teenagers*. It found that 65 percent of teen mothers had children by men who were 20 or older and that not infrequently, the younger the mother, the larger the age gap between her and the baby's father. That study itself as well as subsequent studies also showed (1) that about 60 percent of these teen mothers were 18 or 19 with partners of 20 or 21, and many of them were married; (2) that about 50 percent of the 15- to 17-year-old mothers had a same-age partner, with another 30 percent having a partner within three to five years of their age, and many of them were married; and (3) that therefore only about 8 percent of all 15- to 19-year-old girls who gave birth were in a relationship with someone of five or more years older and were unmarried (see, e.g., Saul 1999; Urban Institute 1997). These nuances were ignored, and calls for stemming the tide of teen pregnancy grew louder. Vital to doing so, according to this view, would be to get tough on statutory rape. Further, some argued, severe punishment for violating statutory rape laws would result in fewer unmarried teen births and thus reduce the public assistance rolls.

The following year, the newly Republican-controlled Congress was legislating welfare reform in the Personal Responsibility and Work Opportunity Reconciliation Act of 1996 (PRWORA) (Public Law 104-193, 110 Stat 2105). The first sentence of the PRWORA is "marriage is the foundation of a successful society." Shortly thereafter, it says, "The increase in the number of children receiving public assistance is closely related to the increase in births to unmarried women…. The increase of teenage pregnancies among the youngest girls is particularly severe and is linked to predatory sexual practices by men who are significantly older…. Available data suggests that almost 70% of births to teenage girls are fathered by men over age 20…." Ostensibly, Congress's source for this figure was the Alan Guttmacher Institute study mentioned above. But they did not note the subtleties within that "almost 70%" figure.

The welfare reform act then challenges each state to submit plans on how it will "prevent and reduce the incidence of out-of-wedlock pregnancies, with special emphasis on teen pregnancies, and establish numerical goals for reducing the illegitimacy ratio of the State … [and provide] education and training on the problem of statutory rape so that teenage pregnancy prevention programs may be expanded in scope to include men" (Public

Law 104-193, 110 Stat 2105, § 402 (a) (1), (v), and (vi)). Up to five states each year can receive bonuses of up to $100 million if they have the highest rates of decrease in both illegitimate births *and* abortions. And so with federal PRWORA resources to back them, and in response to conservative lobbying, a number of states (California, Connecticut, Delaware, Florida, Idaho, Pennsylvania, Tennessee, Texas, Virginia, and Wisconsin) quickly passed laws allotting millions of dollars to targeting the partners of pregnant teens. These states increased their number of statutory rape prosecutions in three ways: by linking statutory rape and child abuse, thereby requiring teachers and others to report suspected cases; by requiring those who apply for Medicaid to identify their partners in order to receive assistance; and by requiring health care providers to report to state authorities any suspicions of statutory rape. They have also, along with others, such as Arizona, Georgia, Maryland, Michigan, Mississippi, Nevada, and New York, created task forces on statutory rape and out-of-wedlock pregnancy. Some have spent millions conducting outreach campaigns consisting of Web sites, pamphlets, and billboards with gender-specific messages, such as "So when I saw my buddy going after this young girl, I knew I couldn't just sit there. Isn't she a little young?" (Virginia) and "You didn't bring her up to let an older man bring her down. She's your kid. Protect her" (New York) (http://www.varapelaws.org; http://www.notmenotnow.com).

Not noted was the fact that only about 1 percent of mothers receiving public assistance are under 18; or that today's teen birthrate is less than half that of the twentieth century's peak in 1957; or that the married teen birthrate is about 10 times higher than the unmarried teen birthrate; or that two-thirds of teen mothers are 18 or 19; or that most unmarried mothers are women in their twenties who do not require public assistance. Reinvigorating statutory rape laws, therefore, could not get at the vast majority of relationships resulting in out-of-wedlock children, nor impact teen pregnancy, nor reduce the welfare rolls, nor reduce poverty in the United States (Cocca 2004).

While some feminists and liberals supported the targeting at first as a means by which to collect child support and protect young women from exploitative relationships, they became wary of the fervent support from religious conservatives and backed away from the issue (Maynard 1999). Groups such as the National Organization for Women protested the welfare reform bill; Planned Parenthood and the American Civil Liberties Union, among others, testified repeatedly at the state level against the new construction of the crime. While little noted in the media, these groups expressed a number of concerns about the potentially adverse effects of the implementation of the laws: (1) that a pregnant teen in a consensual relationship would be deterred from seeking prenatal care in fear that her partner might be incarcerated during his child's infancy or have to register as a sex offender if he is convicted at the felony level, even if he intended to support the child and remain in a relationship with the mother; (2) that a pregnant teen in a nonconsensual relationship would similarly be deterred because she feared physical or other retribution from the father; (3) that a pregnant teen wishing to receive an abortion might be more prone to seek an illegal one so as to avoid a judicial bypass requirement in which she might have to name the father; and (4) that the law would tell males that coercive relationships would go unpunished as long as they didn't culminate in pregnancy. In other words, these groups argued, same-age relationships that do not result in pregnancy might be nonconsensual, and age-differentiated relationships that do result in pregnancy might be consensual and long term—but the newly revised laws would not catch the first instance and would punish the second (Cocca 2004; Donovan 1997; Elders and Albert 1998).

The link forged between statutory rape, the rate of births to teen mothers, and public assistance expenditures served to reinvigorate funding and prosecutorial efforts toward the crime, while also undermining the gender-neutral language of the laws by focusing on young women as victims. But as in the nineteenth century, the implementation of the laws tends to have mixed results that please few and do not serve to deter adolescent sexuality.

CONCLUSION

Statutory rape laws have undergone numerous constructions and reconstructions over the last 100 years in particular, illustrating their double-edged nature as being both protective (if, indeed, a young female is being abused) and punitive (if the relationship is a consensual one) toward adolescent sexuality and illustrating the way in which the subject has been shaped and reshaped to reflect some Americans' fears about broader political, economic, social, and cultural change and uncertainty. In the 1800s, statutory rape laws were focused on preserving the chastity of white females for marriage, but African American women were not so safeguarded; in the 1900s the laws centered on reforming the sexual behavior of immigrant working-class girls in the cities so that they would aspire to middle-class values and family structures; in 2000 the laws disproportionately prosecute gay men and also target a population coded as both immoral and as nonwhite: teens who give birth out of wedlock and require public assistance (Cocca 2004).

The laws also contain a number of contradictions. As they specifically state that the perpetrator and the victim be unmarried to one another, as homosexual couples have been charged disproportionately, as perpetrators the same age as their victims have been charged at both the misdemeanor and felony levels and have had to register as sex offenders, and as many states retain the "mistake of age" defense dismissing the charges if the perpetrator says he or she thought the victim to be of age, they reveal themselves to be more about marriage and sexuality than about age. Statutory rape laws purport to be about protecting those under a certain age from sexual intercourse, but marriage laws allow those under the age of consent to marry. Almost all states allow young people under their ages of consent to marry with judicial or parental approval, and several states allow marriage at any age if the female is pregnant or if the two prospective spouses are already parents of an out-of-wedlock child (Posner and Silbaugh 1996). Married teens are not necessarily less vulnerable than their unmarried counterparts—but married teens in coercive relationships will go unprosecuted, while unmarried teens cannot prevent prosecutions of their sex partners.

While it is no longer true in every state that having sex with someone who is 16 will get you 20 years in jail, the catchphrase remains part of our culture and the laws part of our system. The question remains as to how to protect the vulnerable without essentializing all young people as victims and how, at the same time, to leave those who are choosing to engage in particular activities to their privacy.

WORKS CITED

Alan Guttmacher Institute. 1994. *Sex and America's Teenagers*. New York: Alan Guttmacher Institute.

Alexander, Ruth. 1995. *The "Girl Problem": Female Sexual Delinquency in New York, 1900–1930*. Ithaca, NY: Cornell University Press.

Bienen, Leigh. 1980. "Rape III: National Developments in Rape Reform Legislation." *Women's Rights Law Reporter* 6 (3): 170–213.

Cocca, Carolyn. 2004. *Jailbait: The Politics of Statutory Rape Laws in the United States*. Albany, NY: State University of New York Press.

Cott, Nancy. 1978. "Passionlessness: An Interpretation of Victorian Sexual Ideology, 1790–1850." *Signs* 4 (Winter): 219–36.

Donovan, Patricia. 1997. "Can Statutory Rape Laws Be Effective in Preventing Adolescent Pregnancy?" *Family Planning Perspectives* 29 (1): 30–34.

DuBois, Ellen, and Linda Gordon. 1984. "Seeking Ecstasy on the Battlefield: Danger and Pleasure in Nineteenth Century Feminist Sexual Thought." In *Pleasure and Danger: Exploring Female Sexuality*, ed. C. S. Vance, 31–49. 2nd edition, 1992. New York: Pandora.

Duggan, Lisa, and Nan D. Hunter, eds. 1995. *Sex Wars: Sexual Dissent and Political Culture*. New York: Routledge.

Eidson, Rita. 1980. "The Constitutionality of Statutory Rape Laws." *UCLA Law Review* 27: 757–815.

Elders, M. Jocelyn, and Alexa Albert. 1998. "Adolescent Pregnancy and Sexual Abuse." *Journal of the American Medical Association* 280 (7): 648–49.

Fuentes, Luisa. 1994. "Note: The Fourteenth Amendment and Sexual Consent: Statutory Rape and Judicial Progeny." *Women's Rights Law Reporter* 16: 139–52.

Kunzel, Regina G. 1993. *Fallen Women, Problem Girls: Unmarried Mothers and the Professionalization of Social Work, 1890–1945*. New Haven, CT: Yale University Press.

Langum, David J. 1994. *Crossing over the Line: Legislating Morality and the Mann Act*. Chicago: University of Chicago Press.

Larson, Jane. 1997. "'Even a Worm Will Turn at Last': Rape Reform in Late Nineteenth Century America." *Yale Journal of Law and the Humanities* 9 (Winter): 1–71.

MacKinnon, Catharine. 1991. "Reflections on Sex Equality under Law." *Yale Law Journal* 10: 1281–328.

Maynard, Roy. 1999. "The End of Innocence." *World* (30 January): n.p.

Moody, Lori. 1993. "Underage Sex: A Double Standard? Those Closely Affected Want Rape Laws to Be Gender Neutral." *Los Angeles Daily News* (4 March): n.p.

Murray, Charles A. 1984. *Losing Ground: American Social Policy, 1950–1980.* New York: Basic Books.

Oberman, Michelle. 1994. "Turning Girls into Women: Reevaluating Modern Statutory Rape Law." *Journal of Criminal Law and Criminology* 85: 15–78.

Odem, Mary E. 1995. *Delinquent Daughters: Protecting and Policing Adolescent Female Sexuality in the United States, 1885–1920.* Chapel Hill: University of North Carolina Press.

Olsen, Frances. 1984. "Statutory Rape: A Feminist Critique of Rights Analysis." *Texas Law Review* 63: 387–432.

Peiss, Kathy Lee. 1986. *Cheap Amusements: Working Women and Leisure in Turn-of-the-Century New York.* Philadelphia: Temple University Press.

Pivar, David J. 1973. *Purity Crusade: Sexual Morality and Social Control, 1868–1900.* Westport, CT: Greenwood Press.

Posner, Richard A., and Katharine B. Silbaugh. 1996. *A Guide to America's Sex Laws.* Chicago: University of Chicago Press.

Roberts, Dorothy E. 1997. *Killing the Black Body: Race, Reproduction, and the Meaning of Liberty.* New York: Pantheon Books.

Rubin, Gayle. 1984. "Thinking Sex: Notes for a Radical Theory of the Politics of Sexuality." In *Pleasure and Danger: Exploring Female Sexuality,* ed. C. S. Vance, 267–319. 2nd edition, 1992. New York: Pandora. .

Saul, Rebekah. 1999. "Using—and Misusing—Data on Age Differences between Minors and Their Sexual Partners." In *The Guttmacher Report on Public Policy.* New York: Alan Guttmacher Institute.

Schlossman, Steven, and Stephanie Wallach. 1985. "The Crime of Precocious Sexuality." *Harvard Educational Review* 48 (1): 65–94.

Searles, Patricia, and Ronald Berger. 1987. "The Current Status of Rape Reform Legislation: An Examination of State Statutes." *Women's Rights Law Reporter* 10 (1): 25–43.

Shvartsman, Shulamit H. 2004. "Romeo and Romeo: An Examination of *Limon v. Kansas* in Light of *Lawrence v. Texas.*" *Seton Hall Law Review* 35: 359–401.

Stansell, Christine. 1987. *City of Women: Sex and Class in New York, 1789–1860.* Urbana: University of Illinois Press.

Urban Institute. 1997. "Tougher statutory rape laws expected to have limited impact on teen childbearing." Press release. April 15.

Walkowitz, Judith R. 1980. *Prostitution and Victorian Society: Women, Class, and the State.* New York: Cambridge University Press.

Walkowitz, Judith R. 1992. *City of Dreadful Delight: Narratives of Sexual Danger in Late-Victorian London.* Chicago: University of Chicago Press.

3 Young and Pregnant: Teenage Pregnancies in the United States

James W. Reed and John C. Spurlock

S ocial authorities have always sought to confine the sexuality of young women within established boundaries of procreation and marriage, and the sanctions imposed upon sexual deviants have included shunning and abandonment. Before the rise of the welfare state in the mid-twentieth century, the life prospects for a single woman with a child were poor because female wages usually fell below bare subsistence. Prostitution, practically the only work that might provide a living for a disgraced woman and her children, carried high risk of venereal infection, often leading to incapacity and death. The crucial determinants of the fate of pregnant young women were the levels of support provided by the fathers of their children, by their families and local communities, and by the state. Regardless of age, the fate of pregnant women without such support was likely to be grim. With the support of public opinion, pregnant but unmarried women successfully claimed aid from the fathers of their children, and many eventually wed the father of their children or found other supportive mates.

COLONIAL TIMES THROUGH THE MID-NINETEENTH CENTURY

In the 1970s, historical demographers discovered that premarital pregnancy rates ranging from 30 to 50 percent were salient social facts in many New England communities from the mid-eighteenth century through the Revolution. Rapid population growth put great pressure on an economy constrained by mercantilist regulations that limited credit, migration to fertile land, and occupational diversification. As a result, the customary supervision of the sexuality of young adults by family and village began to break down. Familial politics were transformed by rapid social change that included the decline of partible inheritance and the necessity for younger siblings to find economic opportunity outside the rural communities in which they were born. As young people of the Revolutionary Era pursued economic opportunity in new places and occupations, they asserted their right to choose mates on their own terms, but the new freedom posed dangers as well as opportunities for women, who might be freed from the close supervision of family and community only to fall victim to male sexual exploitation in the form of false promises or rape. Out of the ferment of political revolution and economic change, social advisers created a vast didactic literature to guide youth through the dangers and temptations of freedom. Young people who read newspapers, almanacs, and magazines learned the rules of a new sexual economy, in which premarital chastity was an essential asset. Old visions of sexually rapacious women were discarded for a new gender system, in which women were defined as the guardians of republican virtue and the essential managers of male libidos (Godbeer 2002). As the new morality won the imaginations of socially ambitious young adults, premarital pregnancy rates declined, and polite society managed its sexual tensions through hypocrisy and reticence.

Many young women failed to internalize the new sexual etiquette or fell victim to male exploitation. By the early nineteenth century, wealthy families might send wayward daughters away to give birth anonymously, while maintaining the fiction that they were acquiring refinement at a female academy. In the urban communities that marked the emergence of a market society in the early republic, alms houses and Magdalen societies provided temporary relief for the large populations of female servants and other wage earners who were likely to be dismissed if they could not work due to pregnancy. Before the late nineteenth century the age of the mother was not generally viewed as the issue in comparison to such matters as the identification of the father and the provision of support for mother and child. A developing economy needed the labor of young adults, so there was no period of extended dependency, as is typical of contemporary adolescence (see chapter 1 in this volume). In the social ecology of Jacksonian America a pregnant teenager was not a cause for concern as long as she had male support and did not impose an illegitimate child on her family or community. Until the twentieth century, the average age for menarche was much later than today, probably about 15. This later age of menarche, with the period of subfecundity that follows, limited the number of girls and women under 20 who became pregnant (Harari and Vinovskis 1993). A flourishing abortion trade also helped to limit illegitimacy.

By the closing decades of the nineteenth century, the sexuality of youth came to be perceived as problematic in new ways. Middle-class opinion leaders, such as Clark University psychologist G. Stanley Hall, began to see age-segregated schooling and extended dependency as a normal part of youth. In the same decades, concerned urbanites began to confront what they understood as the sexual problems in the cities. Purity crusaders attacked the circulation of smut and organized to suppress prostitution. Between 1840 and 1880, physicians successfully lobbied most state legislatures to criminalize abortion (Luker 1984; Mohr 1978). In the 1880s, national organizations, such as the Woman's Christian Temperance Union, began a campaign to change age of consent laws. By 1900, every state had revised statutory rape laws, increasing the age of consent from the common-law standard of 10 years old to 16 in most states (Cocca 2004; Odem 1995). Reformers, police, magistrates, and parents began to impose sterner controls on working-class girls who violated family and community standards (see chapter 2 in this volume).

The new cadres of social workers who emerged during the Progressive Era counted urban adolescent pregnancies among the pathologies that needed their attention (Nathanson 1991). The rate of adolescent pregnancy began to rise in the late nineteenth century, along with rates for illegitimacy. This trend was driven by the rapid rise in immigration to the nation's cities and the consequent loosening of traditional family and community controls related to youth and marriage. Pregnancy fit into the larger patterns of disorder and the flagrant sexuality of urban girls. Rural areas received less attention from reformers and policy makers, even though adolescent girls became pregnant in the countryside as readily as in the cities. In 1938, for instance, when unwed mothers made up 3.8 percent of all mothers, the figure was 5.8 percent for rural women (Gordon 1994, 21). Rural communities in the late nineteenth century probably experienced less relative disorganization than cities, and young people undoubtedly continued to use the strategy of avoiding illegitimacy by setting a marriage date. Many families, whether rural or urban, could afford to send a daughter away to have the child and then give it up for adoption. Abortion, even though illegal, also continued to serve as a remedy for pregnant women. Estimates of various populations in the early twentieth century placed the abortion rate at between 20 and 30 percent of all pregnancies. But one study found that 90 percent of all out-of-wedlock pregnancies had been aborted (Gebhard et al. 1958; Luker 1996, 49; Reagan 1997, 23).

Policies and initiatives concerning pregnancy, at least to the 1960s, generally targeted working-class white women. Middle-class women had greater access to birth control, and middle-class families typically had the resources to find an abortionist or to send a daughter away for the term of an unwanted pregnancy. African American girls tended to keep their children and found support from networks of kin. It was the girls who lacked family resources either to hide, abort, or accept an unwed pregnancy who came under the care of the institutional response to pregnancy.

LATE NINETEENTH CENTURY TO THE 1920s

Although immigrant girls in the industrial cities of the Gilded Age often worked to help support their families, the demands of family and Old World values competed with the attractions of the urban environment. Working girls saved pennies a week from their tiny wages to belong to clubs, dress well, and attend social functions (Peiss 1986). Often, these girls found companionship with other girls, and with boys, on the streets or in the cheap movie houses or amusement parks that grew rapidly in the era (Alexander 1995). They often depended on their dates to provide entrance fees or other gifts. The boys, in turn, pressed for greater physical intimacy. Most girls accepted this exchange as a way to have fun and socialize; others pressed beyond the boundaries of conviviality, "rustling" men for expensive gifts in exchange for sex (Ullman 1997). In either case, heterosexuality became a spectacle on the streets of big cities, a manifest of social disorganization and the loosening of family controls (Rhode 1993/1994).

In the early twentieth century those who viewed youthful pregnancy as a social issue typically turned their attention to illegitimacy. Although most people in the early twentieth century gave some credence to the religious view that sex outside of marriage was a sin, they had other concerns. A young woman with a child and without a husband or suitor lost much of her currency in the late nineteenth-century marriage market. Families with traditional values, whether homegrown or imported, might find the shame or sin of unwed pregnancy so great that they would reject a daughter. Or, even if they allowed her to stay at home with her child, a girl's parents might place such restrictions and demands on her that her life would become intolerable. By the late nineteenth century, a wide range of reformers and intellectuals had accepted the eugenic concern for inherited defects. In this light, illegitimate children swelled the population of the mentally defective and criminally inclined (Kline 2001).

Reformers, including magistrates, legislators, social work professionals, and religious leaders, often worked with the support of working-class parents in attempting to control the behavior of urban youth. Laws in New York City in the late nineteenth century (later expanded between 1900 and 1930) criminalized disobedience to parents and broadened the definition of prostitution to include sexual behavior not done in exchange for pay (Alexander 1995). Parents used the courts as a last resort to control recalcitrant or truant children, especially daughters. Five new reformatories for girls had been built each decade, 1850 to 1910, but from 1910 to 1920, 23 reformatories were constructed. Although boys presented problems for families as well as police, much of the behavior of adolescent males fit within the culture's double standard for behavior. Older boys and young men could act wildly and still seem to be on their way to becoming normal men. Wildness in young women was another matter entirely. Courts consistently treated girls more harshly than boys. For similar offenses, boys could receive probation, while girls were sent to state reformatories. Pregnancy was among the offenses that could land a girl in a reformatory (Schlossman and Wallach 1978).

Another response to the sexual disorder of the cities had its basis in religious concerns and private charity. In 1883 the first Florence Critten-ton Mission opened in New York City as a refuge and school to redeem young women. The Salvation Army began similar homes in the same de-cade, and Catholic institutions also grew up with the goal of saving young women from the city. These homes were established in the commercial centers of cities, close to the homes and the sources of downfall for the girls. By the close of the nineteenth century, the homes shifted from the general mission of redeeming the city's young women to sheltering and redeeming unwed mothers. These mothers-to-be were younger by the turn of the century (the average age fell from 22 in the 1880s to 15 by century's end) and far more likely to be immigrants or foreign born. Young women spent an average of two years in the home, giving birth and then learning to care for their children, and also learning the skills of domestic servants, the typical out-placement for women who finished their time in the homes (Kunzel 1993; Luker 1996; Sedlak 1983).

The missions existed to aid women of tarnished virtue. Direct government aid was reserved for the untainted. The only pregnant women or unwed mothers universally considered virtuous in the early twentieth century were widows. Between 1910 and 1920, growing concern for the plight of widows led 46 of 48 states to pass laws for deserving mothers, that is, widows. These Mothers' Aid Laws became the first widely established welfare program in the United States. The monies could not be extended to women with ille-gitimate children, but they established a state responsibility to at least some unmarried mothers (Gordon 1994).

JAZZ AGE AND DEPRESSION

Changes in attitudes, in demographic trends, and in institutional and policy responses to adolescent pregnancy began in the 1920s. None of these trends had the drama of the early twentieth-century campaigns to tame urban sexuality or of the shift in sexual behavior that came with World War II.

By the 1920s, flagrant heterosexuality had lost its power to shock and to inspire reform. When Denver juvenile court judge Ben Lindsey wrote *The Revolt of Modern Youth,* his description of teenaged boys and girls riding in cars, drinking, smoking, and exploring their sexuality together could have applied as much to middle-class as to working-class girls. More adolescents attended high school, and the growing population of boys in school pro-vided a basis for a "rating and dating" system. Even though dating had begun decades earlier, high school youth made it a normal part of American social practice (Lindsey and Evans 1925; Waller 1937). Although disobedience,

running away, and lewd behavior could still land a girl in a state reformatory, the range of immoral behaviors became smaller in the 1920s, and an
earlier generation's wickedness became the jazz age's acceptable fun.

In spite of the acceptance of casual sexual activity, there were no dramatic shifts in adolescent pregnancy. Dating inevitably included petting
by the 1920s, and this sexual exploration shortened the distance between
acquaintance and intercourse. During the decade the rate of premarital
intercourse for women rose rapidly to more than 50 percent, a level where
it would remain until the 1960s (Rhode 1993/1994, 640). For most women,
premarital intercourse was closely linked to courtship and marriage. This,
along with a drop in the age of marriage, meant that many premarital
pregnancies never led to illegitimate births.

The shifts in family organization and fertility are reflected in statistics
for the early decades of the century. At the turn of the century, 77 percent of unwed mothers had been widows. By 1930, only 55 percent were
widows. The others were divorced, separated, abandoned, or never married. Yet the percentage of mothers who were unwed had fallen, from 4.6
percent in 1900 to 3.8 percent by 1938 (Gordon 1994, 19–21). Diffusion of
contraceptive information accounts for part of the change in demograph-
ics. By the 1920s, birth control had been popularized by Margaret Sanger
and by vendors of feminine hygiene products and condoms (Reed 1978;
Tone 2001). As young adults gained confidence in their ability to manage
their fertility, companionship often trumped parenthood as the rationale
for marriage. The Depression of the 1930s saw an even sharper decline in
birthrates. Many couples postponed marriage, and even married couples
put off childbearing.

Even in the relatively freer atmosphere of the 1920s, a young, unmarried woman who was pregnant or the mother of a child faced social cen-
sure with little support and few options. One option that remained for
women who could neither hide nor abort an unwanted pregnancy was
the network of homes for unmarried mothers. The two most extensive
programs, the Florence Crittenton homes and the homes run by the Salvation Army, had evangelical roots and aimed at the moral and spiritual
redemption of the women who came to them. A shift in practices at the
homes began in the 1920s and transformed the institutions by the 1940s.
As support for the pregnancy homes shifted toward consolidated charity
organizations, the homes became subject to the scrutiny of social work
professionals. Charity organizations began to press for social work professionals as directors and to have the homes offer programs in line with
social science (Kunzel 1993; Sedlak 1983).

The shift in control of the homes had a variety of practical effects for
the pregnant girls and unwed mothers who lived there. Instead of evangelical programs, the homes moved toward recreational activities and education. The homes stopped preparing girls for work as domestic servants.
There was less need for domestics by the 1920s as the middle-class home

gained the benefits of labor-saving devices. Social workers also recognized that domestic service often led to more problems as male employers took advantage of the young women in their homes. Consequently, education in the homes attempted to prepare women for the rapidly growing, though ill paid, sector of pink collar occupations, such as the department store clerk and the switchboard operator.

Perhaps the most important change for the mothers within the homes was the shift in placement for the children born in the homes. Throughout the twentieth century, adoption, both legal and illegal, flourished in the United States. Even with declining family size, having a child remained a fundamental goal of most married couples. Until the 1920s, the homes encouraged women to keep their children. From the 1920s until the decline of the homes in the 1960s the directors and social workers urged young women to give up children for adoption. This change allied the pregnancy homes with the business of legal adoption (Solinger 1992).

While the pregnancy homes continued as the main recourse of young, unwed mothers, a policy development at the federal level in this period eventually led to new approaches. One of the New Deal programs of the mid-1930s was Aid to Dependent Children (ADC). This matched federal funds to state programs to offer help to children in need. This program gave federal support for the state Mothers' Aid Laws. Since these state programs typically kept funds out of the hands of unwed mothers, the federal program would have little initial impact. By 1939, ADC began to make some funds available to unwed mothers. State agencies, of course, could and did find ways to deny these funds to the unmarried women. But the rationale for federal and state aid to young women with children had at least been established (Solinger 1992).

WORLD WAR II AND POSTWAR

The most dramatic changes in the trends related to adolescent pregnancy, and in institutional and policy responses to those trends, came during the long postwar era in the United States, lasting from the late 1940s to about 1970. Demographic trends shifted dramatically during this period, attitudes that had remained consistent for decades went through fundamental changes, and well-established institutions disappeared to be replaced by newer approaches. Since about 1980, the United States has witnessed extraordinary public drama over the issue of teen pregnancy. But these discussions, to a large extent, deal with changes that had taken place during this earlier period.

Some demographic trends indicate changes in sexual behavior (Petigny 2004). The stable, slowly declining birthrate typical of the early twentieth century disappeared in the 1940s. Births per thousand American women had dropped below 20 after 1931 and remained there for the rest of the decade. During the war years, however, the rate rose above 20 and jumped sharply to 24.1 in 1946. That was the *lowest* birthrate per year until 1960, as Figure 3.1 illustrates. Illegitimate births also began to climb, increasing every year during the war and continuing to increase after the war and through the decade of the 1950s. The age of marriage declined as the rate of marriage increased. More than twice the proportion of 15- to 19-year-olds were married in 1960 as compared to 1940. The rapid growth of birthrates and the declining age of marriage meant that teenagers had a larger proportion of the children born in the baby boom years. The birthrate for teenagers peaked in 1957, its highest level of the entire century (U.S. Bureau of the Census 1975, v. 2).

The generally friendly attitudes toward marriage, even early marriage, and larger families meant that many young, pregnant women took their problems straight to the altar. The proportion of white women who were pregnant at marriage doubled in the 1950s (Coontz 1992). Also, with growing prosperity, childless couples were more likely to seek to adopt. Pregnancy homes played an important role in providing children for adoption. Following the war, the number of infants adopted rose by 80 percent (Solinger 1992, 154).

While the demographic trends for African American women matched trends for white women, the experience of pregnancy remained distinct. African American women made up a larger share of unwed mothers than their share of the general population. But the practice of keeping illegitimate children and raising them with the support of family and of kin net-

Figure 3.1
Live Births for 15- to 19-Year-Olds, Per 1,000, 1940–2000

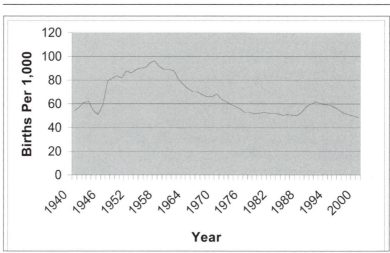

Source: George Thomas Kurian, *Datapedia of the United States 1790–2000: American Year by Year.* Various Editions. Lanham, MD: Bernan Press, 1994, 2001, and 2004.

works continued. There existed almost no demand in the adoption system for black children (Solinger 1992). As a disproportionate share of the unwed mothers, African American girls and young women became frequent targets of state laws that fined, jailed, or sterilized girls who had illegitimate children (Solinger 1992).

The rapid rise in the birthrate meant that American society would confront a huge cohort of teenagers in the 1960s and 1970s (Nathanson 1991). This translated into major changes in the sexual attitudes and practices of the young. Petting, and then going steady, made intimate sexual exploration ever more normal among American adolescents. Most American women had coitus before marriage, and the formal standard of abstinence before marriage would give way by the 1970s to permissiveness with affection (Reiss 1960, 158; Thompson 1995).

Another shift in attitude and behavior would have a major impact on the experience of teenage pregnancy. White women in the 1960s began to keep their illegitimate children (Solinger 1992). While this change remained muted in the 1960s, as it grew, it would have a huge impact on the availability of white infants for adoption. This also appears to have signaled a growing willingness of families to support pregnant daughters. These trends tended to undermine the usefulness of the pregnancy homes for unwed mothers and to undercut the role of the homes in the adoption market. As federal policy shifted in the direction of providing family planning services and infant care on an outpatient basis, the pregnancy homes lost more and more of their usefulness and began to disappear in the mid-1960s (Sedlak 1983).

The marketing of the birth control pill in 1960 made contraception more attractive; the federal "War on Poverty" made family planning services available in the late 1960s, and by the 1970s, physicians began to make birth control available to younger people (Luker 1996). In 1972 the Supreme Court established the precedent that the unmarried have a right to birth control. Teenage pregnancy came into the open as state laws banning pregnant women from high school were overturned in 1972 by the Supreme Court. The legalization of abortion in 1973 also aided women in their ability to control their fertility. By the early 1970s, the birthrate for the nation as a whole dropped to the levels of the early 1940s (Thompson 1995). Unwanted births declined by one-third between 1965 and 1972 (Luker 1996, 51). Consequently, even with the rise in the marriage age in the 1960s and the growing acceptance of premarital intercourse, the birthrate for teenagers began a long-term slide after 1957.

"AN EPIDEMIC OF TEENAGE PREGNANCY": 1970s TO 1990s

During the closing decades of the twentieth century, adolescent pregnancy per se was not increasing. By the 1970s, pregnancy rates for teenagers had been falling for almost two decades. The future seemed to promise a continued decline of adolescent pregnancies, especially unwanted ones, and a growing willingness of families and society to support the few pregnant girls who remained.

Rather than a period of growing acceptance and optimism, however, the closing decades of the century were widely experienced as a time of crisis. In spite of declining birthrates, the large number of children born immediately after World War II meant that the number becoming teenagers during the 1960s made up the largest cohort in the century (Nathanson 1991). It was this large population that practiced the mid-century shift toward permissiveness with affection. By the 1970s, the proportion of teenage girls 15 to 19 who were sexually active began to increase rapidly, from just over 27 percent in 1971 to 42 percent by 1979. Although these trends varied by race, the difference generally related to the age when teenage girls became sexually active. By age 19, 64 percent of girls were sexually active (Vinovskis 1988, 34–35). And, while there was a lower proportion of these girls becoming pregnant, this was mainly due to a rise in the age of marriage. As Figure 3.2 illustrates, the proportion of births to single mothers grew from 15 percent of all births in 1960 to 31 percent in 1970 (Nathanson 1991, 29). During

Figure 3.2
Illegitimate Live Births, Per 1,000, 1940–2002

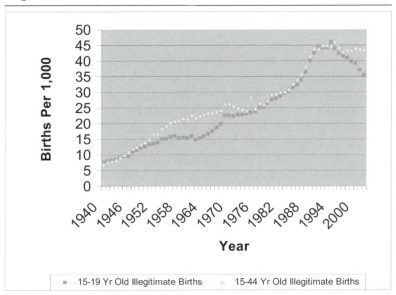

Source: George Thomas Kurian, *Datapedia of the United States 1790–2000:American Year by Year.* Various Editions. Lanham, MD: Bernan Press, 1994, 2001, and 2004.

about the same time frame (1960–77), out-of-wedlock births to teenagers increased 64 percent. By the 1990s, although teenagers gave birth to only about 12 percent of the children in the United States, they accounted for about one-third of illegitimate births (Luker 1996, 1). The "girl problem" of the early twentieth century had seemingly returned with a new look.

During the 1960s and early 1970s, health care and social work profession-als had treated teenage sexuality as a medical problem. Their approach was to offer more support in clinics and schools, programs for pregnant girls, birth control, and abortion (Nathanson 1991). By the late 1960s, however, conservative religious leaders and political activists had begun to mobilize around opposition to sex education in the schools (see chapter 4 in this volume). These groups would gain an important boost from the antiabor-tion movement that followed the 1973 *Roe v. Wade* decision. The presidency of Ronald Reagan during the 1980s indicated a shift in political power toward conservative groups such as evangelicals. Social issues, above all, abortion, became highly controversial, and often, the pregnant teenager was at the center of political rhetoric. Conservatives successfully limited access to abortion by passage of parental consent laws in many states and also undermined sex education programs in many school districts. Rather than teaching students how to control their fertility, the abstinence curric-ulum put forward by conservative groups urged teenaged girls to practice abstinence and denounced programs of "rational expressiveness" that ac-cepted sexual activity and informed students about contraception (Irvine 2002; Moran 2000).

Social problems, of course, reflect perceptions as well as social trends. Conservatives, liberals, and feminists all took up the rhetoric of pregnancy as an issue to garner support for their distinctive initiatives. By 1990, the media gave more attention to pregnancy, with more than 200 articles on the issues of teenage pregnancy (Luker 1996, 80). In 1992 Vice President Dan Quayle would object to a television program, *Murphy Brown*, that posi-tively portrayed a single woman's pregnancy. From the early 1970s, conser-vatives in Congress had decried teenage pregnancy, particularly black teen pregnancy, as a drag on the welfare system. But during the decade, liberals, such as Senator Edward Kennedy, would also raise the issue of teenage preg-nancy as a growing crisis in an effort to gain greater support for programs that would expand the resources that the federal government could provide poor families. In the mid-1990s Congress accepted the figures provided by the Alan Guttmacher Institute, the policy think tank associated with the Planned Parenthood Federation of America, that 65 percent of pregnant teens had been impregnated by men 20 or older. This played a vital role in the debate over welfare reform and the regulations for block grants to states (Cocca 2004). Conservatives and liberals alike could agree that young mothers would have few resources and so raise children ill suited to be-coming productive members of society. One phrase seemed to capture the essence of the policy crisis: "children having children" (Maynard 1997).

Regardless of their age, unmarried women with children lost their right to state support with the passage in 1996 of the Welfare Reform Act, which ended federal support of Aid to Families with Dependent Children and mandated both employment and limits on benefits for mothers on welfare (DeParle 2004).

Although a narrative of social disability continues to shape assumptions and policy related to pregnant girls, the narrative partially obscures the experience of teenage pregnancy. The large majority of teenage mothers are 18 or 19, hardly children (Luker 1996, 8), and studies of teenage mothers do not support the dire predictions that children of young mothers will inevitably drop out of school and become social liabilities. Teenage pregnancy generally rose during the 1980s, but then it leveled off and began to fall in the 1990s and continues to fall to the present. This contradicts the narrative of social disability. Nor does the decline in the pregnancy rate seem to result from programs stressing sexual self-control. Studies show that girls who sign abstinence oaths are less likely to use birth control when they have sex and so are more likely to become pregnant out of wedlock (Boonstra 2002).

Teenage pregnancy in the twentieth century should be understood in the broad context of the adolescent striving for identity and status in a changing society. Some young women discovered that heterosexuality offered them a realm of freedom outside family control. Others may have been victimized by rapid social changes that left them vulnerable to exploitation of older males in a culture that no longer provided adequate coming-of-age rites to guide youth through the challenges of a consumer culture in which ever more human relationships became commodities. Although unwanted pregnancies resulting from sexual freedom often disrupted the normative life course for young women, the rapid increase in teenage pregnancy in the late nineteenth century and at various periods of the twentieth century was but one of many signs of fundamental social change. Reformers and policy makers responded to these shifts in social structure without confronting the economic changes that determined dependency among adolescents and young adults, including a rigidly age-segregated economy and the growing scarcity of jobs for urban working-class youth. Narrow focus on pregnancy as *the* source of disorder led to moral panics, during which adolescent pregnancy became a so-called epidemic to be addressed by the health care system. The primary issue of how to integrate youth into an economy of self-sufficiency and productive labor remained unresolved.

WORKS CITED

Alexander, Ruth. 1995. *The "Girl Problem": Female Sexual Delinquency in New York, 1900–1930.* Ithaca, N.Y.: Cornell University Press.

Boonstra, Heather. 2002. "Teen Pregnancy: Trends and Lessons Learned." *The Guttmacher Report on Public Policy* 5 (February), http://www.guttmacher.org/pubs/tgr/05/1/gr050107.html.

Cocca, Carolyn. 2004. *Jailbait: The Politics of Statutory Rape Laws in the United States.* Albany, N.Y.: State University of New York Press.

Coontz, Stephanie. 1992. *The Way We Never Were: American Families and the Nostalgia Trap.* New York: Basic Books.

DeParle, Jason. 2004. *American Dream: Three Women, Ten Kids, and a Nation's Drive to End Welfare.* New York: Viking.

Gebhard, Paul H., Wardell B. Pomeroy, Clyde E. Martin, and Cornelia V. Chistenson. 1958. *Pregnancy, Birth and Abortion.* New York: Harper.

Godbeer, Richard. 2002. *Sexual Revolution in Early America.* Baltimore, Md.: Johns Hopkins University Press.

Gordon, Linda. 1994. *Pitied but Not Entitled: Single Mothers and the History of Welfare, 1890–1935.* New York: Free Press.

Harari, Susan E., and Maris A. Vinovskis. 1993. "Adolescent Sexuality, Pregnancy, and Childbearing in the Past." In *The Politics of Pregnancy: Adolescent Sexuality and Public Policy*, ed. A. Lawson and D. L. Rhode, 23–45. New Haven, Conn.: Yale University Press.

Irvine, Janice M. 2002. *Talk about Sex : The Battles over Sex Education in the United States.* Berkeley: University of California Press.

Kline, Wendy. 2001. *Building a Better Race: Gender, Sexuality, and Eugenics from the Turn of the Century to the Baby Boom.* Berkeley: University of California Press.

Kunzel, Regina G. 1993. *Fallen Women, Problem Girls: Unmarried Mothers and the Professionalization of Social Work, 1870–1945.* New Haven, Conn.: Yale University Press.

Lindsey, Ben B., and Wainwright Evans. 1925. *The Revolt of Modern Youth.* New York: Boni and Liveright.

Luker, Kristin. 1984. *Abortion and the Politics of Motherhood.* Berkeley: University of California Press.

Luker, Kristin. 1996. *Dubious Conceptions: The Politics of Female Teenage Pregnancy.* Cambridge, Mass.: Harvard University Press.

Maynard, Rebecca A., ed. 1997. *Kids Having Kids: Economic Costs and Social Consequences of Teen Pregnancies* . Washington, DC: Urban Institute Press.

Mohr, James C. 1978. *Abortion in America : The Origins and Evolution of National Policy, 1800–1900.* New York: Oxford University Press.

Moran, Jeffrey P. 2000. *Teaching Sex: The Shaping of Adolescence in the 20th Century.* Cambridge, Mass.: Harvard University Press.

Nathanson, Constance A. 1991. *Dangerous Passage: The Social Control of Sexuality in Women's Adolescence.* Philadelphia: Temple University Press.

Odem, Mary E. 1995. *Delinquent Daughters: Protecting and Policing Adolescent Female Sexuality in the United States, 1885–1920.* Chapel Hill: University of North Carolina Press.

Peiss, Kathy Lee. 1986. *Cheap Amusements: Working Women and Leisure in Turn of Turn-the of-Century the-Century New York.* Philadelphia: Temple University Press.

Petigny, Alan. 2004. "Illegitimacy, Postwar Psychology, and the Reperiodization of the Sexual Revolution." *Journal of Social History* 38 (Fall): 62–79.

Reagan, Leslie J. 1997. *When Abortion Was a Crime: Women, Medicine, and Law in the United States, 1867–1973.* Berkeley: University of California Press.

Reed, James. 1978. *The Birth Control Movement and American Society: From Private Vice to Public Virtue.* Princeton, NJ: Princeton University Press.

Reiss, Ira L. 1960. *Premarital Sexual Standards in America.* Glencoe, Ill.: Free Press.

Rhode, Deborah L. 1993/1994. "Adolescent Pregnancy and Public Policy." *Political Science Quarterly* 108 (Winter): 635–69.

Schlossman, Steven, and Stephanie Wallach. 1978. "The Crime of Precocious Sexuality: Female Juvenile Delinquency in the Progressive Era." *Harvard Educational Review.* 48 (February): 65–94.

Sedlak, Michael W. 1983. "Young Women and the City: Adolescent Deviance and the Transformation of Educational Policy, 1870–1960." *History of Education Quarterly* 23 (Spring): 1–28.

Solinger, Rickie. 1992. *Wake Up Little Susie: Single Pregnancy and Race Before* Roe v. Wade. New York: Routledge.

Thompson, Sharon. 1995. *Going All the Way: Teenage Girls' Tales of Sex, Romance, and Pregnancy.* New York: Hill and Wang.

Tone, Andrea. 2001. *Devices and Desires : A History of Contraceptives in America.* New York: Hill and Wang.

Ullman, Sharon R. 1997. *Sex Seen: The Emergence of Modern Sexuality in America.* Berkeley: University of California Press.

U.S. Bureau of the Census. 1975. *Historical Statistics of the United States: Colonial Times to 1970.* 2 vols. Washington, DC: U.S. Department of Commerce.

Vinovskis, Maris. 1988. *An "Epidemic" of Adolescent Pregnancy?: Some Historical and Policy Considerations.* New York: Oxford University Press.

Waller, Willard. 1937. "The Rating and Dating Complex." *American Sociological Review* 2: 727–34.

4 Facts of Life and More: Adolescent Sex and Sexuality Education

Susan K. Freeman

Adults have always instructed adolescents about sex and sexuality. Whether using such direct means as planned discussions, lectures, books, pamphlets, and movies or indirectly exhibiting sexual norms, values, and expectations, they have continuously communicated ideas about sex to young people. Parents, teachers, medical professionals, religious leaders, counselors, and writers are among those who have been most active in dispensing information about sexuality; however, these adult sex educators are not the sole contributors to sexuality education for youth. Over the past century, creators of popular media and young people themselves have played significant roles in shaping the sexual knowledge and attitudes of adolescents. The history of sex education includes both formal and informal education, and it encompasses a variety of pedagogical materials and methods. Developments in popular media and state regulation of sexual discourse contribute to the history of sex education as well.

In tracing the development of sex education for American adolescents during the twentieth century, this chapter examines sex education advocates and creators of sex education materials, their motivations, and the messages they convey in various formats. Popular reception of sex education and the contributions of young people warrant attention as well. Sex education concerns gender as much as it does sexuality, and therefore the chapter pays attention to the underlying gender and sexual ideologies—as well as understandings of adolescence and adulthood—that have shaped the history of sex education.

SOCIAL HYGIENE, 1900–1940

In the late nineteenth century, middle-class reformers and professionals organized a "social hygiene" movement, which sought to eliminate sex-related vice. These reformers addressed the social problems of prostitution, unwanted pregnancy, and sexually transmitted infection, then known as venereal disease, or VD. Social hygiene activists organized conferences, lobbied for legislative changes, supported medical research, and promoted sex education. Concerned as they were about public health, reformers advocated sex education in the interest of maximizing the physical health of adults and children. To achieve physical health and well-being, they believed, it was essential to confine sexual relationships to the marital bed. While the educated men (and, in smaller numbers, women) of the social hygiene movement viewed themselves as enlightened by science, their views on "hygiene" were as much about middle-class, Christian moral standards—and the ubiquitous racism and sexism of the era—as they were about scientific knowledge of disease.

The American Social Hygiene Association (ASHA) gained a place of prominence in the movement for sex education during the first half of the twentieth century. It helped publicize research and information about sexual vice and efforts to ameliorate it through the publication of newsletters and a monthly journal. Published between 1914 and 1954, the *Journal of Social Hygiene,* originally called *Social Hygiene,* demonstrated a growing commitment to adolescent sex education. Articles in the journal, combined with other materials from the first part of the twentieth century, reveal common concerns and disagreements among sex educators, who wished to convey the so-called truth about sex.

Most sex educators in the twentieth century have viewed their work as a form of "positive" sex education, which they have often contrasted with "negative" instruction about sexual disease and deviance. The desire to reduce VD rates led a subset of early twentieth-century sex educators deliberately to provoke fear of promiscuity in audiences of youth, characteristically lecturing and displaying images of deformed syphilitics. This so-called negative approach especially took hold within the military, and one historian has conceptualized it as "knowledge of contagion" (Carter 2001). Educators who rejected the emphasis on vice and disease in instruction for adolescents invoked a more affirmative view of sexuality as a creative life force, but not without eliminating negative topics. The supposedly positive perspective situated sexuality within eugenic marriages, or marriages which would maximize childbearing among white, native-born, and middle-class citizens and minimize births to people of color, immigrants, and the impoverished. "Knowledge of development" is another way to characterize what educators said was positive sex education in the first few decades of the twentieth century (Carter 2001). Both these frameworks for sex education—contagion and development—invariably prescribed self-control, reinforced racial and class hierarchies, and affirmed asymmetrical gender relations.

One of the earliest and most controversial efforts to teach about sex in the schools was a short-lived undertaking in the Chicago public schools. Ella Flagg Young, a white, 68-year-old school superintendent, launched an effort, in fall 1913, to bring instruction about sex to junior and senior high school students. She enlisted physicians to give lectures to students, separated by sex and matched with a medical doctor of the same sex. The lectures covered physiology, hygienic and moral advice about sexual anatomy and behavior, and sex-related social problems, including venereal disease. Well received by the students, the lectures encountered opposition from conservatives, among them Catholic officials and parents, who intervened to discontinue the program. Accusing Young of violating the Comstock Law of 1873 (which criminalized the mailing of "obscene" materials, including information about sexuality, birth control, and abortion), her opponents chipped away at the superintendent's authority and credibility. The failure of the experiment in Chicago was due primarily to politics; however, sex education advocates critiqued the method, which they called "emergency" lectures, as inferior to education that was integrated into the regular curriculum (Moran 2000).

Other sex education programs, especially those integrating units of instruction into existing courses, attracted less publicity and controversy. In March 1915, for example, a male and female instructor from Grand Rapids, Michigan, Central High School reported on their high school "sex hygiene" classes in the column "How Shall We Teach?" (1915). In a trend that would develop and persist throughout the century, presentations by medical professionals or other outside lecturers were rejected in favor of relying on students' usual teachers, who could integrate the information more seamlessly into the regular curriculum. In the case of Central High School, the physiology teachers—a man and a woman—instructed the two sexes separately. Over the course of two weeks the science instructors presented their sex education unit, beginning with brief coverage of plant and animal reproduction, followed by human sexual organs and their "hygiene" or care, and then they completed the unit with sex cells, fertilization, fetal growth, heredity, and eugenics.

Several aspects of early twentieth century sex education are exemplified by the report from Grand Rapids. First, the lessons were rooted in scientific discourse about reproduction: taught in a physiology class, the lecture commenced with propagation and procreation in the plant and animal world. Second, instructors advised students about the hygiene of sexual anatomy. Hygiene encompassed not simply matters of bathing, but also cleanliness in a metaphorical and moral sense. For example, morally acceptable sexual behaviors did not extend to sex play and masturbation. Although instructors knew these were not physically harmful activities, they urged restraint and self-control.

Two additional features of the report are characteristic of the era. Educators treated marital sexuality, like personal hygiene, as benefiting from the exercise of self-control. Although little was revealed about sex during marriage (and pleasure was obliquely, if at all, mentioned), heredity and eugenics—and the racist politics of procreation and population control—were among the facts imparted through high school sex education in the early twentieth century. Finally, lessons conveyed and reaffirmed gender stereotypes. Lessons for boys and girls often differed: with their male students, Central High teachers invoked boys' "respect and love for their ideal in the realm of womanhood—their mothers." Girls apparently required less coaxing to treat the subject of sexuality with reverence. In the end the teachers noted that "character development" was an intended outcome of the lessons: chivalry for boys and responsibility for girls (Ellis and Upton 1915). As one historian has suggested, early sex educators sought to reshape male sexuality more so than female because contemporary sexual thought granted men more sexual agency, license, and stronger sex drives; young men were threatened, it was assumed, by internal desires, whereas the risks for young women were social and external (Moran 2000, 59–60).

State officials from the government, military, and public health sectors also grew concerned about the sexual knowledge and behavior of youth in the 1910s and 1920s. This was an era of increasing urbanization, sexualized commercial amusements, the automobile, anticipated medical improvements in treating VD, and the popularization of sexology, including Freudian ideas. Adults were vying for influence over the hearts, minds, and sexual habits of the nation's young people, fighting against increased sexual explicitness, changing fashions, a rising subculture of sexual nonconformity, and other forms of youthful rebellion that historians have labeled the first sexual revolution.

Within the military, especially during the First World War, enlisted soldiers served as an audience for sex education and prophylaxis. Some of the nation's first sex education films originated within the military (Eberwein 1999). Growing awareness of young soldiers' sexual contacts, which in many cases had occurred prior to enlistment, prompted some government agencies to expand educational endeavors among civilians. Building on the momentum for social hygiene within the military, the Chamberlain-Kahn Act of 1919 funded the creation of a VD division of the U.S. Public Health Service and the introduction and expansion of VD education at universities around the country. Some inroads were made into the public schools because of the law, most prominently in the state of Oregon. Meanwhile, ASHA membership swelled during and after World War I, and more organizations serving youth, such as the YMCA and YWCA, and parent teacher organizations joined the movement for sex education (Moran 2000).

When researchers commissioned by the U.S. government assessed the extent of sex education in the public schools in 1922 and 1927, the published results suggested sex education was already occurring in nearly half of responding schools. However, that optimistic portrait of sex education's success was qualified by data that revealed that many topics dealing with human sexuality were omitted, that larger high schools did most of the teaching, and that the rate of response to the survey diminished between the first and second studies (Edson 1922; Usilton and Edson 1928; Moran 2000). Nevertheless, the reports suggested government interest in sex education and a greater amount of sex education occurring than most people had suspected.

Outside the schools, parents, doctors, and other concerned community members sought to educate young people about sexuality, but they found few suitable resources at their disposal. Disappointed by the lack of educational materials available in 1915, birth control advocate Mary Ware Dennett created a pamphlet for instructing her 14-year-old son about sex. After much library research, including social hygiene literature, Dennett wrote and illustrated an essay about puberty, sexual feelings, sexual intercourse, reproduction, menstruation, seminal emissions, masturbation, VD, and love. After receiving her son's assurance that the information was helpful, Dennett began loaning the pamphlet to friends for educating their children about sex; in the process she discovered a great appreciation and demand for such information. Although initially unsuccessful in finding a publisher for the essay, it appeared in print in February 1918 in *Medical Review of Reviews,* followed by publication in June 1918 in *Modern School.* Finally, in 1919, Dennett printed the pamphlets herself and sold them for 25 cents a piece (Chen 1996).

During the 1920s, moralists sought to restrict popular depictions of sexuality, regardless of the commercial or educational purposes for which they were intended. Some antiobscenity reformers combined conservative and liberal approaches to sexual vice and sex education. Catheryne Cooke Gilman, for example, from the Women's Cooperative Alliance in Minneapolis, made a distinction between sexually explicit commercialized entertainment, such as risqué vaudeville and burlesque shows, which she sought to restrict, and educational sex information, such as Dennett's writing, which she worked to promote (Wheeler 2004). "The Sex Side of Life: An Explanation for Young People," as Dennett's pamphlet was called, circulated among parents, physicians, schoolteachers, professors, and others who worked with youth through social services, religious institutions, and recreational organizations. Within a decade Dennett had distributed nearly 25 thousand copies of "The Sex Side of Life." Charged with violating the federal Comstock Law, Dennett was convicted in 1929. In the weeks following the verdict she was vindicated by her allies and by publicity in the popular media, much of which objected to the court's decision. A successful appeal reversed the verdict, and the pamphlet was eventually translated into 15 languages and went through 23 printings (Chen 1996).

American Social Hygiene Association affiliates kept close watch on the results of Dennett's trial. While a few took prominent roles in her defense, others sought to distance themselves from Dennett's controversial public persona. (Besides endorsing contraception, Dennett was a divorcée and an activist for women's suffrage.) Having learned from the failed Chicago experiment and Dennett's persecution and costly legal battle, social hygiene leaders typically guarded against publicity and controversy.

At conferences and in publications, social hygiene leaders consolidated their ideas about the best practices in sex education, drawing from their personal convictions, ambitions, and research. A professor at Columbia University's Teachers College, Maurice A. Bigelow, was a prominent ASHA spokesperson for sex education from the organization's inception. He, along with colleagues in biology and medicine, formed a committee and reported on "The Matter and Methods of Sex Education" in 1912, drawing from research, questionnaires, and correspondence with experts around the country (*Social Hygiene* 1916). First published in 1916, the position statement was revised on several occasions and reprinted in 1924 and 1933. Calling the document "The Established Points in Social Hygiene Education" and capitalizing on the visibility of the ASHA, Bigelow built his expertise as a sex education authority, and unlike Dennett, his legitimacy was not undermined by his marital status or political involvement.

The three versions of Bigelow's established points indicate minor shifts in thinking about sex education in the first three decades of the twentieth century; more striking is the continuity of ideological viewpoints presented as truths. Bigelow and others since have been quick to contrast their own positions with the supposed repression of the Victorian Era; they cast themselves as more modern and in possession of an open attitude toward sexuality but often retained many of their predecessors' values. Over time the "Established Points" drew greater attention to maintaining the monogamic family ideal as the motivation for offering sex education to the young. Revisions inserted prescriptions of ideal practices and minimized the explication of what to avoid. Discarded from the original version was the recommendation that texts omit illustrations of human anatomy, for example, as was the claim that "premature development of sex consciousness and sex feelings is harmful" (*Social Hygiene* 1916, 574). Likewise dropped was the notion that sex education should give different messages, at different times, to boys and girls. While sex-differentiated lessons on sex education fell from favor, the idea that sex education would be presented gradually to youth based on age and maturity endured. For instance, experts recommended "nature study," or examination of the "birds and bees," in the elementary grades; lessons on puberty and human reproduction in preadolescence and early adolescence; and discussion of marriage and adult sexual responsibilities in senior high school (*Social Hygiene* 1916; Bigelow 1924, 1933).

Even as sex education materials for youth relied less on medical authority over time, ethical and moral considerations dating back to the nineteenth century remained central to education about sex. Sex education gained in respectability as it attracted the support of government bodies, school officials, and other professionals. It gained visibility during the 1940s, as national polls began to measure public support and as features on sex education became more prominent in the popular media. And as the U.S. Surgeon General explained in 1939 in his foreword to a government study of sex education, secondary schools should focus their sex education curricula on the "psychological and social" rather than on medical needs, a message that found many adherents in subsequent decades (Gruenberg 1939).

FAMILY RELATIONS, 1940–1965

During the middle of the twentieth century, sex educators widely embraced the ideal of marriage as companionship and a source of mutual heterosexual pleasure for adults. Writers had articulated this view of marriage in prior decades through "marriage manuals," or sex advice books for adults; increasingly, the premise influenced sex education for the young. Although printed sex education materials for youth did not grow more explicit about sexual acts, discussion of sexuality expanded beyond procreation. Marriage and family relationships became the preferred framework for teaching youth about sex by the 1940s.

As sex and family life education expanded in the middle of the twentieth century, no federal standards governed the instruction, and rarely did any two schools design or deliver curriculum identically. Different constituents— students, parents, school administrators, and state lawmakers—fostered a variety of environments for initiating and teaching sex education. Whereas reformers, doctors, and scientists had orchestrated the social hygiene efforts of the early twentieth century, educators rose to prominence within the movement for sex education at mid-century. Educators brought with them a commitment to social science perspectives and student-centered instruction. These educators included sociologists, who taught college-level marriage courses; schoolteachers with ties to the Progressive Education movement; high school home economics teachers; school psychologists and guidance counselors; leaders of parent teacher organizations; and school administrators.

Educators who advocated for sex instruction in the mid-twentieth century had a lot in common with their social hygiene predecessors. They tended to be white, middle-class Protestants who were committed to discussing sexuality more openly but were not, on the whole, radicals or revolutionaries. The influence of these educators and their view of companionate marriage helped to undermine ideologies of male domination, female passivity, and the sexual double standard; yet mid-century sex education continued to reinforce white, middle-class notions of superiority and morality, even as it challenged sexism in certain ways (Freeman 2007).

While teaching about reproduction remained integral to the project of sex education, teachers paid more attention to gender norms, sexuality, and, with students in the upper grades of high school, decision making regarding romantic and sexual relationships. By the 1940s, teachers were conducting sex and family life education in small classroom settings, whether they taught mixed- or single-sex groups. Social sciences contributed to the content and pedagogy of the courses. Educators painstakingly emphasized that both sexes faced similar adjustments and concerns with regard to growing up, developing sexually, entering adulthood, and establishing and caring for families. Sexual satisfaction was presented as a privilege of married adults but one to which young people might look forward. Conversations about the role of sexuality in marriage could extend beyond procreation and evolution because contemporaries discussed sexuality as an arena of psychological adjustment and personal fulfillment.

Unlike the earliest sex educators, mid-century teachers guided students to think about human psychology as much or more often than the physiology of sex. As sex education expert Lester Kirkendall explained in 1944, educators sought to illuminate "much more than the sheer physical aspects of sex," such as "those relationships between men and women growing out of the many differences between the sexes," "emotional, social, and ethical aspects" of sex, and "the place of sex as a constructive, up-building force in successful marriage and satisfactory family life" (1944, 387). Accordingly, high school students discussed such questions as, Are petting and necking acceptable? Is it a good idea for boys and girls to go steady? As one teachers' guide advised instructors, when addressing questions about dating and morality, "Do more listening than talking! Keep ears and mind and heart open!" Young people, the authors continued, more readily accepted the standards of their peers than those of adults (Force and Finck 1949, 29).

A few materials for use in the schools took a surprisingly progressive perspective on young people and sexual desire, although it is difficult to know how often teachers reinforced such ideas in the classroom. Nevertheless, two such texts were widely reviewed and cited in bibliographies. *Life and Growth* stressed girls' capacity to experience sexual arousal and boys' responsibility for setting sexual limits, challenging the orthodoxy that boys were easily stimulated and that girls, not boys, were expected to draw the line (Keliher 1937). *Units in Personal Health and Human Relations,* a guide for teachers that included lecture materials, diagrams, class activities, and tests, gave information about the clitoris and female sexual desire. The authors revealed that the clitoris was a pea-sized sex organ of the female body, covered by a hood and surrounded by folds of skin, and described it as "equipped with very sensitive nerve endings" (Biester, Griffiths, and Pearce 1947, 138–39). Such attention to female desire and the clitoris was uncharacteristic of most sexuality education during the entire twentieth century and was absent from nearly all material produced for youth at mid-century (Fine 1988).

While local sex education programs retained distinctive features, the similarities are striking in an array of accounts, including those of junior high schools in suburban Connecticut; Arlington Heights, Illinois; and Los Angeles, California. These programs, originating in the mid-1940s, resembled one another in that health and physical education teachers or nurses met with single-sex groups of adolescents to provide information about human sexual anatomy and discuss students' concerns and questions about puberty and adolescence. Likewise, analogous programs emerged in Highland Park, Michigan; Council Grove, Kansas; and Corona, California. These high schools each offered a coed family living course to senior students in the mid-1950s, focusing a great deal of attention on dating and preparing for marriage (Freeman 2007).

A national dialogue about sexuality and family life contributed to unifying aspects of sex education around the country. In 1948 the publication of the first volume of Alfred Kinsey's sex research, *Sexual Behavior in the Human Male* (Kinsey, Pomeroy, and Martin 1948), made a media splash and prompted many to wonder about sex education for youth and assess its status in the schools. That same year, *Human Growth* (1947), a new sex education movie produced in Oregon, attracted popular media attention. Between February and May 1948, readers could find expositions of sex and family life education in the schools in popular periodicals of the day, including *Today's Woman, Time, Newsweek, Ladies' Home Journal, Parent's, Parade,* and *Life* magazines—many of them featuring *Human Growth.* Numerous editors during the late 1940s also commissioned articles discussing sex education for adults, parents, and children (Freeman 2007).

Human Growth was a favorite teaching tool of many educators from the late 1940s into the early 1960s. The movie introduced to boys and girls the topics of puberty, human development, and reproduction, and its creators intended it to be used in middle school classrooms, with students' usual teachers leading a discussion following the screening. Over 1,300 prints of the film were purchased, and more than two million students viewed the movie between 1948 and 1962. Parent teacher associations and the film distributors coordinated hundreds of screenings before parents, with parental approval nearly unanimously in favor of showing the movie to adolescents or even elementary school children. Twenty minutes in length, the movie featured four scenes, including a white, middle-class pupil's home on the evening prior to the sex education lesson; a classroom scene with students preparing to watch a film; an animated "film within a film," explaining human growth and reproduction; and the students asking their teacher questions following the animated film (Freeman 2007).

In addition to movies and popular articles about sex education, the 1940s and 1950s also saw a rise in radio programs and educational records designed to instruct about sexuality at home and in school. Some authors developed materials that reflected their religious outlook on sexuality, such as the "Christopher recordings" made in the 1940s, which instructed parents on sex education in the home according to Catholic principles. "Sex Guidance for Today's Youth" aired on Boston's WEEI radio station in the late 1940s, and other cities saw radio programming develop in a similar fashion. (The BBC in Great Britain had led the way with radio broadcasts of sex education earlier in the decade.) Medical doctor Bert Y. Glassberg broadcast lectures for youth about sex through a St. Louis, Missouri, Board of Education's radio station, and the public schools used these lectures during the 1950s as part of their sex education programs. Debates about whether to offer sex education aired on radio programs during the 1950s as well.

Like radio programs, records, and movies, books and pamphlets often addressed boys and girls simultaneously rather than separately, offering uniform information and advice for both sexes. A significant number of new sex education lesson plans implemented in mid-century schools were likewise not differentiated by sex; while single-sex instruction persisted in many places, especially for discussing puberty, coeducational sex education became more commonplace. Among the most prolific authors of popular books, articles, and instructional guides was Frances Bruce Strain. Her *Love at the Threshold* (Strain 1939) and *Teen Days* (Strain 1946) were widely publicized and circulated. Strain and other writers began in the 1930s to advocate for boys and girls learning about sex in a coeducational setting, so long as adults established a comfortable and wholesome environment. Many experts believed that "teenagers," as they were beginning to be called in the 1940s, stood to benefit from learning about sex with their peers. Youth, they thought, would become better able to communicate their goals and values to one another as a consequence of such courses and conversations.

Part of legitimizing sex education for mixed (boy-girl) audiences was to link sex with marriage, love, and procreation. Whereas Dennett had dared to describe intercourse and discuss sexual pleasure in her pamphlet for youth, most commercially published books and pamphlets for young people during this time employed a less direct approach to discussing sexual activity—especially if designed for children or younger adolescents. Originally published in 1928 and revised in 1947, the picture book for children, *Growing Up: The Story of How We Become Alive, Are Born and Grow Up*, by Karl De Schweinitz, illustrated these tendencies. *Growing Up* appeared in countless sex education bibliographies and was incorporated into school sex education programs in a number of locations, including the highly regarded program in San Diego (Freeman, forthcoming). Artistic renderings of animal and human babies, a crowing rooster, and a male peacock displaying his feathers demonstrated the ubiquity of sexual attraction and love in the world and attempted to instill in children wholesome thoughts about sex. The reference to sexual intercourse avoided mention of adult genitals and instead invoked sex cells and love: "Men and women know that when the sperm joins the egg a baby will start growing, and when they mate, each wants to mate with the person he or she loves" (De Schweinitz 1947, 88–89).

A number of health-oriented texts for youth began to show diagrams of male and female sexual anatomy in the mid-twentieth century. While many sex education books for youth, such as Strain's, gave advice about conduct and said little about the physical body, illustrations of reproductive organs did appear in some textbooks and movies for adolescents. However, illustrations rarely included much detail. *Life and Growth,* a book commissioned by the Progressive Education Association for use in the schools, was adopted around the country by a small number of educators. Rather than depicting the sex organs detached from human bodies, line drawings in *Life and Growth* illustrated organs and showed how they figured in mature adult bodies (Keliher 1938). By contrast, *Human Growth*'s rendering of male and female genitals even provided misleading imagery. When the animated portion of the film demonstrated menstruation, it depicted the flow of menstrual blood with white rather than red; when it discussed ejaculation of semen, it showed the white sperm moving through a non-erect penis.

An educational museum in Cleveland, Ohio, provided sex education for visitors through 100 life-size, three-dimensional models of female reproductive organs and fetal development. Acquired in 1945 and known as the Dickinson-Belskie models, the works of art were unveiled at the 1939 World's Fair in New York and moved to the Cleveland Health Museum for permanent display. Not only were the models useful for teaching obstetrics to medical students as originally intended, but they became an educational resource for expectant parents and even adolescents and children. Local and regional schools sent elementary and high school students to view the exhibit, and replicas, filmstrips, and lantern slides of the sculptures were made available to educators (Gebhard 1948).

Books and pamphlets explaining puberty to adolescents grew in number in the mid-twentieth century. Many targeted girls and boys separately; for example, *So Youth May Know* addressed young men, while *The Questions Girls Ask* addressed young women (Dickerson 1948; Welshimer 1949). These texts were likely to discuss sexual anatomy along with the physical and emotional changes that accompany puberty. Mid-twentieth-century authors identified adolescent interest in the opposite sex as a normal part of growing up, whereas same-sex attraction was typically described as a temporary phase or psychological disturbance. In her Charlotte, North Carolina, high school family life education classes, one teacher explained, "A study is made of how the affections grow and develop from infancy through the homosexual stage to the transfer to heterosexuality" (Masten 1953, 107). Same-sex romantic or sexual relationships did not appear as so-called normal possibilities for adolescents in sex education materials of the mid-twentieth century; rather, the texts and lessons embodied the professional and popular views of homosexuality as mental illness or deviance prevalent throughout most of the twentieth century (Freedman 1987).

Pamphlets and movies about menstruation specifically for girls became more popular in the post–World War II era, prompted by the growth in commercially available hygiene products (Brumberg 1997). These films and pamphlets also dealt with anatomy but were often evasive about sexual activity and primarily focused on menstrual hygiene, conduct, and emotions (Martin 2004). Most famous among the motion pictures was the Disney-illustrated *Story of Menstruation* (1946), a 10-minute film sponsored by Kimberly-Clark, the makers of the menstrual hygiene products known as Kotex. Like *Human Growth,* the color picture depicted menstrual blood as white. Most of the time was spent in the movie discussing how girls felt while menstruating and reassuring girls that they could have fun while on their periods—but not too much fun!

Although some authors of general sex education texts drew parallels between menstruation for girls and seminal emissions, or wet dreams, for boys as indications of their budding sexuality, the two manifestations of sexuality had limited parallels. First, menstruation was always discussed in conjunction with girls' reproductive potential and hygiene, whereas boys' spontaneous erections and ejaculation were explained as a natural buildup of sexual tension and release. Sexual pleasure was not discussed with girls, and hygiene was not discussed with boys. Second, while seminal emissions could be briefly mentioned in a film, no educational films, books, or pamphlets were devoted specifically to helping boys cope with their changing bodies.

Young people sought and found information about sexuality outside of adult-sanctioned educational materials. They snuck copies of the 1956 novel *Peyton Place* (Metalious 1956), which included racy passages about the sexual lives and intrigues of a small New England community, or copies of *Playboy* magazine, a sexually titillating men's magazine that first appeared in the 1950s. Some found pulp fiction novels, including those with lesbian themes, at newsstands and drug stores. Others accessed tomes in the library, sometimes having to request librarians' permission to use the materials for their schoolwork, seeking answers to complex questions of sexuality. While Hollywood movies were scrutinized and edited to eliminate sexual explicitness, youth learned about romance and discovered sexual themes and subplots on the silver screen. And finally, many adults were scandalized as young people—girls in particular—became captivated by the sexual innuendo and imagery of rock and roll music, including Elvis Presley and his gyrating hips.

COMPREHENSIVE SEXUALITY EDUCATION, 1965–1980

The latter decades of the twentieth century saw continued efforts to teach sex education. "Sexuality education," as many preferred to call it, signaled a broader set of sexual issues beyond sex, which has often been used as shorthand for heterosexual intercourse. Instructional materials became more explicit about sexual activity and birth control after the 1960s, as some educators responded to the changing sexual behaviors of teenagers. The advent of the birth control pill, the availability of contraception for unmarried individuals, and the growing acceptance of sexual relations outside marriage drew media attention to what commentators began to call another sexual revolution in the 1960s. More explicit sexual speech was apparent in the popular media, especially as the courts further chipped away at obscenity provisions (Moran 2000). In the mid-1960s, physician and former Planned Parenthood director Mary Steichen Calderone helped form the Sex (later Sexuality) Information and Education Council of the United States (SIECUS), an organization whose founders included a physician, an educator, a lawyer, a businessman, and a minister. From 1964 to the present, SIECUS has worked to promote "comprehensive" education about sexuality that is realistic and frank. By the late 1960s, the women's liberation and gay and lesbian liberation movements were launching additional challenges to sex education orthodoxies, which eventually led to the production of their own educational materials.

Conservative evangelicals likewise joined forces to shape sex education. Members of Religious Right organizations, such as the John Birch Society and the Christian Crusade, employed smear campaigns to discredit SIECUS and like-minded educators in the 1960s and 1970s, in many cases making accusations of sexual deviance, atheism, and communism. Polemics appeared with such titles as *Is the School House the Proper Place to Teach Raw Sex?* (Drake 1968) and *Raping Our Children: The Sex Education Controversy* (Lentz 1972). Religious extremists began to produce their own sex education materials as well, although primarily marketed to adults, explaining sexuality through the lens of biblical fundamentalism (Irvine 2002).

Not all religious-based sex education presented fundamentalist and conservative values, and in fact, religious leaders had been part of the social hygiene movement and the family life education effort for many decades. In the late twentieth century, one example of a church-based sex education program was the Unitarian Universalist curriculum "About Your Sexuality," a candid program for youth that discussed such issues as masturbation and same-sex relationships without condemnation. However, with conservative opponents drawing attention to the liberal program, Unitarians in the 1990s ended their three-decades-old "About Your Sexuality" classes and replaced them with a less explicit program called "Our Whole Lives" (Levine 2002).

Clergy and other adults to whom youth turned for advice gained greater awareness of the sexual confusion that young people confronted in their daily lives during the 1960s. Syndicated advice columnist Ann Landers received hundreds of queries weekly from young people who sought information and guidance about their sexuality. Young people's letters to advice columnists were not new in the 1960s, but they were delving into explicitly sexual topics with less reticence than previously. For instance, *Senior Scholastic* magazine, distributed through schools, offered an advice column during the mid-twentieth century called "Boy Dates Girl," which focused on dating etiquette and only discussed sexual behavior in veiled terms (Bailey 1988). Landers's correspondents in the 1960s more bluntly inquired about sexual topics. In 1963 she published *Ann Landers Talks to Teenagers about Sex.* While Landers demonstrated some sympathy for those outside the norm (for instance, gay and lesbian teens) and was quick to admit that youth were sexual beings, the author prescribed conformity to sexist gender norms. Without condemning masturbation, she recommended, for example, that boys could channel their sexual energy into football, whereas girls might become more domestic: "Housework, particularly floor-scrubbing, is not only great for the female figure, but it's good for the soul. And it will help take the edge off your sex appetite. Cooking, baking, and sweeping will prepare you for homemaking. Energy siphoned off into these construc-tive channels will leave less energy for preoccupation with erotic fantasies" (Landers 1963, 54–55). Such extreme gender stereotypes were unusual in secular post–World War II sex education curricula; however, stereotyping based on gender and sexuality has persisted over time in materials produced by authors affiliated with Religious Right organizations (Irvine 2002).

The sex education program in Anaheim, California, established in the 1960s, illustrated ascendant approaches to discussing sexuality with youth; it also prompted one of the bigger controversies in the backlash against comprehensive sex education. The Anaheim public schools taught units on sexuality to coed groups, and teachers talked about controversial subjects with the seventh- through ninth-grade students—such topics as hetero-sexual intercourse, masturbation, sexual intimacy on dates, homosexuality, and VD, among other subjects. Teacher Sally Williams, who later became a consultant for SIECUS, also led students in discussions and critiques of conventional gender roles in her sex education classes. In the end a highly motivated and mobilized right-wing protest resulted in the termination of Anaheim's progressive curricula in the late 1960s (Cook 1972; Moran 2000; Irvine 2002).

Even with setbacks such as the one in Anaheim, sex education programs were gaining a foothold in U.S. public schools. Oftentimes, though, writers and educators were so convinced about their innovations that they overlooked or denied longer histories of sex education. One late 1960s assessment of the status of sex education across the United States noted that state legisla-tors passed sex education laws in Illinois, Maryland, New York, Michigan, and Ohio. The author made no mention of earlier legislative and state-wide efforts that occurred throughout the century. More states and school districts, she did note correctly, had begun developing policies and guide-lines (Gudridge 1969). While some of these policies and laws limited rather than expanded permissible topics in sex education, they collectively added legitimacy to some teaching about sex in the schools. In addition, sex education gained greater professional resources. Through workshops and degree programs at universities around the country, sex educators were able to create and implement a wider variety of instructional approaches. Specialized materials, such as those dealing with mentally and physically disabled youth, were a significant development of the 1970s (Brown 1981).

ABSTINENCE, 1980–2000

Religious conservatives began to wield greater influence over sex education in the early 1980s, when, during the administration of Ronald Reagan, they helped pass the Adolescent Family Life Act (AFLA). AFLA funded commercially produced, morality-based education. Religious perspectives have gained even greater prominence in sex education since the 1996 welfare reform law that supplied more money for so-called abstinence-only sex education programs, or those curricula that teach that abstinence from sexual activity is the only appropriate choice for teenagers (Irvine 2002). Funding for religious-based abstinence-only curricula skyrocketed under the administration of George W. Bush, an outspoken conservative on sexuality education.

With the discovery of HIV and AIDS in the 1980s, sex educators had to confront new and difficult questions about sex education. By 1989, laws in 28 states and the District of Columbia required teaching about HIV and AIDS. (The Helms Amendment complicated this teaching by requiring that programs receiving federal money essentially condemn homosexuality and drug use.) New York State, for example, adopted an *AIDS Instructional Guide,* a handbook for teachers of grades K–12. While attention to the virus and disease was important for dealing with an alarming health and social problem, critics noted that the curriculum's emphasis on morality, chastity, and abstaining from sex limited its relevance to young people's varied sexual lives and realities. Often, "sex" turned out to mean heterosexual vaginal intercourse, complicating discussion of risky behaviors and safer sexual activity. Also, the use of condoms to protect against virus transmission has been a controversial subject, and laws and school policies often prevent teachers from discussing their effectiveness when used properly (Mayo 2004).

In the 1980s and 1990s, educators attempted to address multiculturalism in sex education curricula and throughout the schools more generally, although the attempts to be more inclusive and respectful of differences, specially racial and ethnic differences, have had mixed results (Irvine 1995). Some gay and lesbian activists argued that multiculturalism should encompass gay and lesbian communities, and, in New York City, conflict arose over the city's Rainbow Curriculum, which attempted to educate children to be inclusive and accepting of gays and lesbians (Mayo 2004).

What many sex educators and critics have neglected to notice in creating policy and designing curricula is how sex education functions in practice.

Instead, they concentrate on written words, like curriculum guides, rather than on the dynamics of the sex education classroom or the gender and sexual organization of the schools altogether. Young people learn about sexuality not only through sex education classes, but also through informal school practices, such as pep rallies, proms, gossip, teasing, bullying, and sexual harassment (Trudell 1993).

A majority of U.S. adults favor teaching about sexuality, including condoms and some explicit information, yet there is agreement that abstinence should be highlighted as the best choice for young people (National Public Radio et al. 2004). Alternative viewpoints to the message that youth should abstain from sexual activity, or at least sexual intercourse, during adolescence have been largely silenced. Even liberal organizations, such as SIECUS and Planned Parenthood, have taken up the mantle of abstinence for young people. The Internet has facilitated young people's access to other points of view, from young people, feminist and queer educational resources, and also commercial pornography. Eve Ensler's play, *The Vagina Monologues,* has been performed and read by people of all ages, helping to eliminate body shame and acknowledging the possibilities of pleasure (and the realities of painful subjects, such as rape and clitoridectomies) for girls and women (Ensler 2001). In *Harmful to Minors* Judith Levine claims that children do not need to be protected from sex and that it is not necessarily healthy for youth to abstain from sexual activity, but hers is a viewpoint that few parents and professionals embrace (Levine 2002).

In December 2004 a scathing critique of federally funded abstinence-only programs found rampant and disturbing problems with the curricula. The report, commissioned by U.S. Representative Henry A. Waxman, concentrated on errors and distortions in many of the programs receiving government funds. The most egregious errors related to the effectiveness of contraceptives, the risks of abortion, the timing of conception, and HIV transmission. Moreover, the report documented how sexist and limiting gender stereotypes are presented as facts, including girls' alleged lack of ambition and weakness and boys' supposed sexual aggressiveness. The "Sexual Health Today" curriculum, published in 1999 by the Medical Institute for Sexual Health, for example, makes the preposterous claim that "touching another person's genitals 'can result in pregnancy'" (Committee on Government Reform 2004, 12).

Many of today's sex education programs derive either from the liberal tradition of SIECUS and comprehensive sex education or from the conservative bent of religious fundamentalist perspectives on sex, which convey the message "just say no." The ways that sex education has developed in the past century reflect not only the motivations of experts and the perspectives and demands of young people, but also the ideas and resources of the broader culture. The univocal celebration of abstinence for youth that is prevalent today may seem old-fashioned, but its contradictions should be more closely examined. The government-funded, widespread promotion of sexual abstinence also must be understood as historically specific and related to the practices and discourses of contemporary culture. Over time, sex education has sought to influence not just the knowledge, but also the attitudes and behavior of young people. More than the facts of life, sex instruction attempts to mold how adolescents think, feel, and live their lives. Sex educators have only been marginally successful in achieving their goals as in the end, formal education is only one part of how young people learn to inhabit their genders and sexual identities as they enter adulthood.

WORKS CITED

Bailey, Beth L. 1988. *From Front Porch to Back Seat: Courtship in Twentieth-Century America.* Baltimore, MD: Johns Hopkins University Press.

Biester, Lillian L., William Griffiths, and N. O. Pearce. 1947. *Units in Personal Health and Human Relations.* Minneapolis: University of Minnesota Press.

Bigelow, Maurice A. 1924. "The Established Points in Social Hygiene Education, 1905–1924." *Journal of Social Hygiene* 10 (January): 2–11.

———. 1933. *The Established Points in Social Hygiene Education.* Rev. ed. New York: American Social Hygiene Association.

Brown, Lorna, ed. 1981. *Sex Education in the Eighties: The Challenge of Healthy Sexual Evolution.* New York: Plenum Press.

Brumberg, Joan Jacobs. 1997. *The Body Project: An Intimate History of American Girls.* New York: Random House.

Carter, Julian B. 2001. "Birds, Bees, and Venereal Disease: Toward an Intellectual History of Sex Education." *Journal of the History of Sexuality* 10: 213–49.

Chen, Constance M. 1996. *"The Sex Side of Life": Mary Ware Dennett's Pioneering Battle for Birth Control and Sex Education.* New York: New Press.

Committee on Government Reform. 2004. *The Content of Federally Funded Abstinence-Only Education Programs.* Prepared for Rep. Henry A. Waxman. United States House of Representatives. http://www.democrats.reform.house.gov/Documents/20041201102153-50247.pdf.

Cook, Paul W. 1972. "A Great Experiment in Sex Education—The Anaheim Story." *Journal of School Health* 42: 7–9.

De Schweinitz, Karl. 1947. *Growing Up: The Story of How We Become Alive, Are Born and Grow Up.* Rev. ed. New York: Macmillan.

Dickerson, Roy E. 1948. *So Youth May Know: Sex Education for Youth.* Rev. ed. New York: Association Press.

Drake, Gordon V. 1968. *Is the School House the Proper Place to Teach Raw Sex?* Tulsa, Okla.: Christian Crusade Publications.

Eberwein, Robert T. 1999. *Sex Ed: Film, Video, and the Framework of Desire.* New Brunswick, NJ: Rutgers University Press.

Edson, Newell W. 1922. *Status of Sex Education in High Schools.* Washington, DC: Government Printing Office.

Ellis, Grace F., and T. Dinsmore Upton. 1915. "Sex Instruction in a High School." *Social Hygiene* 1: 271–72.

Ensler, Eve. 2001. *The Vagina Monologues.* New York: Villard.

Fine, Michelle. 1988. "Sexuality, Schooling, and Adolescent Females: The Missing Discourse of Desire." *Harvard Educational Review* 58: 29–53.

Force, Elizabeth S., and Edgar M. Finck. 1949. *Family Relationships: Ten Topics toward Happier Homes, a Handbook for Administrators and Teachers Who Use the Accompanying Study Guide.* Elizabethtown, PA.: Continental Press.

Freedman, Estelle B. 1987. "'Uncontrolled Desires': The Response to the Sexual Psychopath, 1920–1960." *Journal of American History* 74: 83–106.

Freeman, Susan Kathleen. 2007. *Up for Discussion: Girls and Sex Education in Mid-Twentieth Century Schools.* Urbana: University of Illinois Press.

Gebhard, Bruno. 1948. "More Information Please." *Hygeia* 26: 545–47, 574–76.

Gruenberg, Benjamin C. 1939. *High Schools and Sex Education.* With the assistance of J. L. Kaukonen. Washington, DC: Government Printing Office.

Gudridge, Beatrice M. 1969. *Sex Education in Schools: A Review of Current Policies and Programs for the Guidance of School Board Members, Administrators, Teachers, and Parents.* Washington, DC: National School Public Relations Association.

"How Shall We Teach?" *Social Hygiene* 1 (March 1915): 257-72.

Human Growth. 1947. Portland, Oreg.: E. C. Brown Trust and Eddie Albert Productions. Filmstrip.

Irvine, Janice M. 1995. *Sexuality Education across Cultures: Working with Differences.* San Francisco: Jossey-Bass.

———. 2002. *Talk about Sex: The Battles over Sex Education in the United States.* Berkeley: University of California Press.

Keliher, Alice V. 1938. *Life and Growth.* New York: D. Appleton-Century.

Kinsey, Alfred C., Wardell B. Pomeroy, and Clyde E. Martin. *Sexual Behavior in the Human Male.* Philadelphia: W. B. Saunders, 1948.

Kirkendall, Lester A. 1944. "Sex Education in 9 Cooperating High Schools, Part I." *Clearing House* 18: 387–91.

Landers, Ann. 1963. *Ann Landers Talks to Teenagers about Sex.* Englewood Cliffs, NJ: Prentice-Hall.

Lentz, Gloria. 1972. *Raping Our Children: The Sex Education Scandal.* New Rochelle, N.Y.: Arlington House.

Levine, Judith. 2002. *Harmful to Minors: The Perils of Protecting Children from Sex.* Minneapolis: University of Minnesota Press.

Martin, Michelle H. 2004. "'No One Will Ever Know Your Secret!' Commercial Puberty Pamphlets for Girls from the 1940s to the 1990s." In *Sexual Pedagogies: Sex Education in Britain, Australia, and America, 1879–2000,* ed. C. Nelson and M. H. Martin, 135–54. New York: Palgrave Macmillan.

Masten, Fannie B. 1953. "Family Life Education at Central High School, Charlotte, North Carolina." *Marriage and Family Living* 15: 105–8.

Mayo, Cris. 2004. *Disputing the Subject of Sex: Sexuality and Public School Controversies.* Lanham, Md.: Rowman and Littlefield.

Metalious, Grace. 1956. *Peyton Place.* New York: Julian Messner.

Moran, Jeffrey P. 2000. *Teaching Sex: The Shaping of Adolescence in the 20th Century.* Cambridge, MA: Harvard University Press.

National Public Radio, Kaiser Family Foundation, and Kennedy School of Government. 2004. *Sex Education in America.* http://www.kff.org/kaiserpolls/pomr012904oth.cfm.

Social Hygiene. 1916. "The Matter and Methods of Sex Education." 2: 573–81.

Story of Menstruation. 1946. Burbank, Calif.: Walt Disney Productions. Filmstrip.

Strain, Frances Bruce. 1939. *Love at the Threshold: A Book on Dating, Romance, and Marriage.* New York: D. Appleton-Century.

———. 1946. *Teen Days: A Book for Boys and Girls.* New York: D. Appleton-Century.

Trudell, Bonnie Nelson. 1993. *Doing Sex Education: Gender Politics and Schooling.* New York: Routledge.

Usilton, Lida J., and Newell W. Edson. 1928. *Status of Sex Education in the Senior High Schools of the United States in 1927.* Washington, DC: Government Printing Office.

Welshimer, Helen. 1949. *The Questions Girls Ask.* New York: E. P. Dutton.

Wheeler, Leigh Ann. 2004. *Against Obscenity: Reform and the Politics of Womanhood in America, 1873–1935.* Baltimore, Md.: Johns Hopkins University Press.

5   Get Real: Representations of Adolescent Sexuality in the Media

David M. Considine

Historically, depictions of teen sexuality in the media have generated controversy. From the early days, there were concerns about the way in which sexual media content contributed to offscreen sexual behavior and attitudes. These concerns remain with us today. As recently as 2004, for example, Collins and others (2004, e209) wrote in *Pediatrics* that "portrayals of sex on entertainment television may contribute to precocious adolescent sex." Such a perspective typically fails to take into account the context of the narratives and the complex ways in which young people select and process media messages. Studying and understanding images of adolescent sexuality in the media also includes an awareness of genre codes and conventions as well as distinguishing between depictions of adolescents in media made for young audiences and those targeting adult audiences.

Mixed messages may be dominant when it comes to mass media and human sexuality. Whether certain portrayals are aberrations or the norm can only be determined by serious analysis of the wider view of teenage sexuality as presented in the mass media. This chapter will consider the two dominant media of movies and television as it explores representations of sexuality, particularly teen sex, and their implications. It includes an emphasis on the changing depictions of teenagers and sex in relation to the era in which those media messages were both created and consumed. Sexuality will be considered not simply in terms of intercourse, foreplay, or intimacy, but also in terms of representation of gender roles and relationships.

SEXUALITY AND EARLY FILMS: THE 1890s–1920s

From its inception the film industry has been keenly aware of the value of sex at the box office. However, the way movies have represented sexuality has been controversial from their earliest years. In 1895, in Atlantic City, *Dolorita's Passion Dance* caused concern. The following year, *The Kiss* prompted complaints, as did *Courtship* in 1899. Nor was this restricted simply to adult fare. Describing the "Pickford teenager," Alexander Walker (1971, 27) wrote that "she is certainly not an obsessive flirt, but neither is she a passionless virgin."

Early concerns about inappropriate movie content led, in 1922, to the establishment of the Hays Office as an attempt at self-regulation by the film industry. Hays declared that "the industry must have towards that sacred thing, the mind of a child, the unmarred slate, the same responsibility, that same care about impressions made upon it, that the best clergyman or most inspired teacher would have" (Forman 1933, 121). Despite such concerns, it was evident even then that young people were both accessing and processing movie messages about sex. Published in 1929, *Children and the Movies* contained the following comment from a 16-year-old girl: "Those pictures with hot love-making in them, they make girls and boys sitting together want to get up and walk out, go off somewhere you know. Once I walked out with a boy before the picture was even over" (Mitchell 1929). Four years later, Herbert Blumer's *Movies and Conduct* documented the case of a 19-year-old girl who told researchers, "Ever since I saw Joan Crawford use her eyes to flirt with people, I caught that trick and used it to good advantage" (1933, 54).

SEX, YOUTH, AND FILM: THE 1930s AND 1940s

Although many might assume that adolescent sexuality first came to the screen during the so-called sexual revolution of the 1960s, in reality it can be located 30 years earlier. In the years prior to the introduction of the Production Code Administration (1934), several films included sexually active adolescent characters. Typically, these individuals were working class or lower middle class. Typically, they lived in fractured families, supported only by a mother or a surrogate mother, such as an older sister. The sexual aggressor or initiator in these relationships, more often than not, was the female. When sexual activity did take place, it was often, but not always, accompanied by death or mutilation, a convention that teen horror films would utilize decades later.

The presence of sex on the screens of the nation was controversial from the very start of the 1930s. In the first month of 1930, the *Christian Century* complained, "the movies are so occupied with crime and sex stuff and are so saturating the minds of children the world over with social sewage that they have become a menace to mental and moral life of the coming generation" (1930).

The following Easter, Universal released *All Quiet on the Western Front*. As the movie opens, adolescent Paul sits in a classroom with a group of fellow high school students. Encouraged by their teacher, Paul and his companions enlist to fight for the fatherland. So begins their odyssey to adulthood and their initiation into a brutal and frightening masculine, military milieu. Set against this background of war and clearly associated with the deaths he witnesses, Paul becomes increasingly aware of his own sexuality. In a cottage in the French countryside the young man loses his virginity. Paul moves offscreen to a bedroom with the young woman. We do not see, yet we clearly understand, the action that has taken place. The camera concentrates instead on a record slowly turning on a phonograph. It is a device used by Robert Mulligan 40 years later for another wartime sexual initiation in *The Summer of '42*. Paul does not comment on his encounter. Yet his silence testifies to his disappointment. In the book he observes, "I cannot trust myself to speak. I am not in the least happy" (Remarque 1928, 93). Sex, an act of procreation and regeneration, becomes meaningless within the context of war.

The following year, RKO released *Are These Our Children?*, which the *New York Times* (1931) regarded as an accurate depiction of contemporary life in big-city America. It was a cautionary tale of wayward youth and the consequences of their actions. As the film's prologue put it, "Youth, love and happiness—these make the world go around. To all, each day, comes choice—every hour we must decide. One way leads to shadows, the other into peace and light" (*Are These Our Children* 1931). The film begins romantically, with two high schoolers, Eddie and his girlfriend, Mary, framed inside a pulsating heart. When Eddie loses a speech contest at school, his bitter disappointment triggers a shift in behavior. Drawn by the allure of jazz, he enters the world of the Orient Club and the young women who frequent it—women without curfews and homework.

The club scenes represent some of the frankest depictions of adolescent sex throughout the era. Not until the 1950s and 1960s do teen characters express themselves in such earthy language. One girl announces that she doesn't have to be home until 3:00 A.M. After dancing, another says that she's hot. "I'll say you're hot," says Eddie. The girl proceeds to take his hand and run it across her breasts. The young people consume alcohol and tell dirty jokes. Flo makes her intentions clear. "You don't wear undershirts, do you?" she asks the boy. "No, I'm the big outdoor type," he replies. "I'll say. You've got the stuff that gets them, boy." Flo finds herself increasingly attracted to Eddie: "I'm hot for that guy." One night, after the club, she invites him home. Her mother is in the back room, but Flo says she won't hear them. Eddie's drunk and loud music plays as the screen turns into a swirling spiral.

Audiences were left with little doubt that the couple had engaged in intercourse. The impact upon Eddie is immediately obvious. He angrily dismisses his grandmother's scolding: "I want to live my own life. I don't want anyone waiting up for me and bothering about what I do ... I don't want anybody babying me. You're making a sissy out of me. I'm a man now!" Eddie's behavior becomes increasingly out of control. He kills a man, and although only 18, he is ultimately executed. It remains a rare example in American cinema of a teenager condemned to death and executed by the state. This movie gave audiences another example of the connection between sex and death.

The war and the impact of the Production Code would limit depictions of teen and adult sexuality throughout much of the 1940s. Emphasis was put upon patriotic, all-American imagery and values. One example of this form of storytelling was the successful Andy Hardy series, developed by MGM in the late 1930s and popular throughout the early forties. From today's perspective this vision of small-town American life appears naïve and idealized. At the time, however, it was viewed as a realistic representation. In her study, *America at the Movies,* Margaret Thorp (1939) wrote that this image of family life was carefully researched, promoted, and maintained. The studio attempted to shelter the public from the real-life romantic entanglements of Mickey Rooney, who played young Andy. Rooney has said himself that "there was no connection between what you saw on Andy Hardy on the screen and what was the reality of Mickey Rooney off camera" (1965, 94).

In *You're Only Young Once* (1938) Andy finds himself attracted to a girl who announces that "I want to have been everywhere and done everything by the time I'm 18." The judge warns his son that the girl is mentally, morally, and spiritually poisoned. Andy initially rejects and resents his father's advice: "I'm old enough to choose my own friends and if I can't I'm not going to live at home." In another example of the girl as sexual initiator, Andy accompanies her to a house she has arranged, where they can be alone. Just when it appears that he might succumb to her advances, he walks out on her, reinforcing his father's words: "You can't beat society. You can't beat a code of convention hammered out for years." But Judge Hardy's conventions were middle-class mores. Studies during the era documented sexual activity among the nation's young people, and the war would continue to change social attitudes, conventions, and behavior. William Foot Whyte's (1943) "A Slum Sex Code" and the *National Parent Teacher's* (1943) "Sex Guidance in Wartime" both acknowledged the sexual curiosity and experimentation of the nation's young people.

Despite the offscreen sexual activity of real American adolescents, their screen counterparts, for the most part, engaged in little more than hand-holding and a peck on the cheek as movies concentrated on the emergence of the bobby-soxer and the impact of this character on middle-class family life. Films like *High School* (1940), *Her First Beau* (1941), *Miss Annie Rooney* (1942), *Janie* (1944), *Junior Miss* (1945), *Cynthia* (1948), and *A Date with Judy* (1949) all depicted the teenage subculture, where physical contact was sublimated by crushes, corsages, proms, and malt shops. It was this period that also began to see the term "adolescent" creep into popular use. A review for *Miss Annie Rooney* prepared by the Library of Congress described it as "basically adolescent with their jitterbugging, first dates, romances and heartbreaks" (Department of War Information 1942).

Movies of the era typically defined adolescents as middle class, moral, and chaste. One striking aberration was the Oscar-winning film noir vehicle *Mildred Pierce*. Veda is self-centered and positively predatory. A *Commonweal* review greeted her as "the nastiest brat that ever broke a mother's heart" (1945). Her mother spells it out: "She's 17 years old and spoiled rotten. I'm losing her. She's starting to drift away from me. She hardly speaks to me anymore except to ask for money or poke fun at me in French because I work for a living." It is, in fact, Mildred's successful career and financial independence that is the catalyst for the calamity that befalls the family. Her marriage breaks up, her youngest child dies, and Veda murders her mother's second husband. Veda also traps a wealthy boy into marrying her. Claiming she is pregnant, she forces a financial settlement and then has the marriage dissolved. Sex is just one other weapon in her arsenal.

While Veda represents a rare image of a sexually active adolescent in 1940s American cinema, the real issue in the film is gender. Mildred's attempt to be more than a mother, to build a career for herself by moving beyond the home and the kitchen, has damaging consequences. Her husband worries, "There's something wrong. I don't know what. I'm not smart that way. But I know it isn't natural." There is little doubt that dialogue and the mise-en-scène construct Mildred as a threat to patriarchal order.

SMALL-TOWN AND SUBURBAN SEX:
THE 1950s AND 1960s

A decade later, screen images of adolescent angst reached their zenith with the James Dean vehicles *East of Eden* (1954) and *Rebel without a Cause* (1955). In the latter Dean plays Jim Stark, the product of a dysfunctional, middle-class, suburban family. The disturbance in the Stark household is clearly sexual in nature. Like *Mildred Pierce,* the narrative suggests that crazy, mixed-up kids are the result of inadequate parenting in general and the undermining of the patriarchy in particular. "How can you grow up in a circus like this?" Jim asks a juvenile officer. At the heart of Jim's problem is his need to understand, "What can you do when you have to be a man?" Henpecked by his wife, Jim's father can offer little in the way of meaningful advice. Repeating an image from *Mildred Pierce,* director Nicholas Ray outfits the father in one scene in a frilly apron, then to make the point unmistakably clear, he positions him on his hands and knees.

By the end of the film, as with *Mildred Pierce,* the patriarchy will be restored as father and son learn to stand up for each other. The gender disturbance in the Stark household was repeated with the two other teen characters in the movie. Sal Mineo plays the ill-fated Plato, who has been abandoned by his father and spends most of the movie looking for a male role model, whether in the presence of his new friend Jim or in the picture of Alan Ladd (as Shane) that he keeps in his locker. Natalie Wood plays 16-year-old Judy, a girl who loves her father and needs his love but finds it increasingly denied. Her relationship with her father is full of sexual tension. One evening, at the dinner table, she attempts to kiss him. She is tersely told, "You're getting too old for that kind of stuff, kiddo." Confused and upset, she tries to brush off the rebuff. She bends over and kisses her father. When she does so, he angrily strikes her. His reaction is clearly one of revulsion for the feelings his daughter's kiss awakens within him.

One of the dominant characteristics of adolescent sexuality in cinema of the 1950s and 1960s was the fact that sex was now a battleground between teens and their parents. In part, much of this was a response to the shifting motion picture audience. *Variety* (1949, 5) documented an industry report from Audience Research Incorporated. The analysis told the industry that "teenagers are the most frequent and faithful theater goers," and they encouraged the industry to "spend coin and extra steam, pitching to the natural, easy-to-get group." While their parents stayed at home with the new novelty called television, teenage children escaped to the drive-ins ("passion pits"), where movies targeting them typically showed them trying to grow up with little positive support from their hapless parents.

Fathers who were incapable of listening to or talking to their sons about sex were portrayed in a number of films. Robert Anderson's controversial play *Tea and Sympathy* came to the screen in 1956. It is the story of Tom Lee ("sister boy"), a sensitive 17-year-old whose behavior and mannerisms raise suspicions about his sexuality. The boy is constantly questioned and goaded by his father, who wonders, "Why isn't he a regular fella?" and who insists that his son "learn to run with the rest of the horses." When Bud Stanford tries to talk to his father about his feelings for Deenie in *Splendor in the Grass* (1961), the only advice he gets is to find a "different kind of girl" and "get a little steam out of the system." *Blue Denim* (1959), based on the play by James Leo O'Herlihy, introduces audiences to high school students Janet and Arthur, who become sexually active with little awareness of precautions. The consequence, of course, is that Janet becomes pregnant. While the boy tries to arrange an abortion, standards at the time required a happier ending, and the film closes with the concerned parents providing a toaster and a car for the young couple to start their married life.

Adolescent females fared no better with their mothers when it came to communicating about sex. As Molly, Sandra Dee was the victim of a sexually repressed mother in *A Summer Place* (1958). "She makes me ashamed of having a body," the girl complains. At one point, when her mother suspects she has had sex, she calls in a doctor and tells her daughter, "I want you to take off every stitch you've got on and let him examine you." While Molly is falling hopelessly and romantically in love with Johnny, her mother's advice is cold and calculating: "You've got to play your cards right. You can't let him think your kisses come cheap. You have to play a man like a fish; that's what's cheap, wanting a man." As was becoming common in films of the era, Molly becomes pregnant, and she and Johnny do "the right thing" and get married. In *Splendor in the Grass,* Wilma Deen gets similar negative advice and guidance from her mother on the subject of sex. "Boys don't respect a girl they can go all the way with…. Your father never laid a hand on me until we were married and then I just gave in because a wife has to. A woman doesn't enjoy these things the way a man does." Written by William Inge, the film was one of a small but growing number of movies to seriously address human sexuality, including teen sex. The *New York Times* (1961, 37) called it "one of the best films about children and parents that we have seen," adding that the movie was an expression of "youthful tensions and repressions as a result of misguided, misplaced adult dominance and deceit, showing the stark and sad effects of parental domineering and evasion in matters of sex."

A Summer Place also represented a more complex and sophisticated depiction of human sexuality. While Molly's mother is decidedly repressed and unsympathetic, her father is hot blooded, outspoken, and understanding. He criticizes his wife for trying to "de-sex" their daughter and bitterly complains that "you label young love-making as cheap, wanton and disgusting. Must you persist in making sex itself a filthy word?" Repressed mothers damaging the healthy sexual development of their offspring were also in *All Fall Down* (1962) and *Five Finger Exercise* (1962), written by Peter Shaffer. If Judy's father *(Rebel Without a Cause)* was uncomfortable about his own sexuality, Molly's father is clearly sympathetic with the urges he knows his daughter and Johnny are experiencing. "It's not so easy for them; they're so intense and in love…. So were we at their age and we didn't settle for a walk on the beach. What advice can I give her? To be a half virgin? I can't tell her to be half good. I'd feel like a hypocrite."

For the most part, however, few adults in films of the era are comfortable talking to teens about sex. While this typically is presented in the form of problems with parents, *Where the Boys Are* (1960) located the conflict in the classroom. On the eve of spring break and a trip to Fort Lauderdale we find Merritt Andrews sleeping during her freshman courtship and marriage class. The elderly female professor observes that "for many freshmen women, college provides their first experience in adult heterosexual society," providing "unrestricted contact with members of the opposite sex." As a result, she notes, it creates problems that she identifies as "random dating" and "premature emotional involvement." When Merritt wakes up, she tells the instructor that she finds their textbook "a little old-fashioned." Challenged to defend her claim, she points out that "in this day and age if a girl doesn't become a little emotionally involved on her first date, it's going to be her last." Pressed further by her teacher, she tries to defend herself by referencing Kinsey, only to find herself deeper in trouble. "We're not discussing Dr. Kinsey. We're discussing interpersonal relationships." "Well, what could be more interpersonal than backseat bingo?" she retorts, to the laughter of her classmates. When Merritt says she believes that a girl should "play house" before she is married, she is sent to the dean for being "overly concerned about the problem of sex."

GOING ALL THE WAY: THE 1970s AND BEYOND

Despite the spate of cinematic teen pregnancy and much discussion about adolescent sex, for the most part, throughout the 1950s and 1960s, sex was implied and alluded to rather than actually shown. There were exceptions, including Franco Zefferelli's 1968 version of *Romeo and Juliet*, which cast youthful actors (Leonard Whiting and Olivia Hussey) as the star-crossed lovers and included nudity and a bedroom scene. *You're a Big Boy Now* (1966) was that rarity of a film that touched on the subject of impotence and dealt with sexual initiation as neither conquest nor consummation, but rather a humiliating failure. *The Sterile Cuckoo* (1969) introduced Liza Minnelli as the lonely and awkward Pookie Adams, who forces her attention on a naïve freshman.

The so-called sexual revolution of the sixties and challenges to the regulation of film content resulted in a series of films that were much more sexually explicit than their predecessors. They included *Who's Afraid of Virginia Woolf* (1966), *The Graduate* (1967), *Easy Rider* (1969), *Bob and Carol and Ted and Alice* (1969), *Midnight Cowboy* (1969), *The Boys in the Band* (1970), *A Clockwork Orange* (1971), *Carnal Knowledge* (1971), *Klute* (1971), and *Last Tango in Paris* (1973). Although only one of these films included teenage characters throughout the narrative *(A Clockwork Orange),* they created the climate in which franker, though not always more representative, images of adolescent sexuality could be depicted.

The Male Perspective and Portrayals of the Sensitive Male

One of the earliest and finest films of the era to address this subject matter was Peter Bogdanovich's *The Last Picture Show* (1971). In many ways the movie broke new ground with its representation of human sexuality, including teen sex. It included partial nudity, bedroom scenes, and impotence. Shot in black and white, the movie won multiple Oscars and included outstanding performances from its young cast (Cybill Shepherd, Jeff Bridges, and Timothy and Sam Bottoms), while also garnering Oscars for Cloris Leachman and Ben Johnson. Set in the small town of Anarene, Texas, in the early 1950s, *The Last Picture Show* portrays two high school seniors, Sonny Crawford and Duane Jackson, who experience adolescence with little parental guidance, looking instead to football, movies, and Sam the Lion for direction. Ben Johnson was the veteran actor who played Sam the Lion, a crusty old-timer who owns the local pool hall, café, and movie house. His death in the film symbolically ends the old west and the myths of manhood that accompanied it.

The football coach berates his team of losers, telling them that they are out of shape and jack off too much. He, however, is apparently a failure in the bedroom. Lonely and desperate, his wife turns to young Sonny for both physical and emotional affection. At the opposite end of the scale is Lois Farrow. She tells her daughter Jacy that she scared her husband into getting rich. The fact that the radio is playing "A Fool Such as I" during the scene is a less than subtle commentary on the mother's cold, calculating ways. Anyone familiar with the mothers of *Rebel without a Cause, All Fall Down,* and *A Summer Place* will instantly recognize Lois Farrow. Acknowledging her daughter's sexual curiosity, she tells her bluntly, "There's nothing magical about sex and you'll find that out. Everything gets old if you do it often enough, so if you want to find out about monotony real quick, marry Duane."

While several characters in the film lose their virginity and have sexual experiences, none of them are satisfactory or fulfilling. Sonny's girlfriend Charlene refuses to go all the way and breaks up with him by saying, "You ain't good-looking enough. You ain't even got a ducktail." Jacy goes to a skinny-dipping party, intent on giving herself to Bobby Sheen, whose family has money. She finds herself rebuffed. "You a virgin?" he asks. "Yes I am. But I don't want to be, though." "Too bad. Come back and see me when you're not," he tells her. Jacy then falls back on Duane, and the couple head to the Cactus Motel, while their classmates wait outside in the parking lot to learn about their accomplishment. Unfortunately for Duane, he is unable to perform. "Well, get off me. You might just fall and mash me," Jacy tells him dismissively. Some days later, when they do finally consummate the relationship, the girl once again puts him down. "Oh, quit prissing. I don't think you did it right anyway."

The same year that *The Last Picture Show* was released, another major movie and another Oscar winner also used the past as the setting for another male coming-of-age story. *The Summer of '42* was a tender, touching, and at times humorous account of three boys and their sexual awakening during World War II. It was perhaps the first movie about adolescence to focus almost exclusively on the sexual curiosity and identity of its central characters, including, in two instances, their loss of virginity. It also introduced what has since become a staple scene in teen sex comedies: the requisite trip to the drug store and the awkward attempt to buy condoms for the first time. Asked by the pharmacist if he knows what they're for, Hermie says, "Sure, you fill them up with water and throw them off the roof." Yet despite this and numerous humorous moments, the film has a bittersweet mood, mostly to do with 15-year-old Hermie's infatuation with Dorothy. Hermie will lose his virginity to Dorothy in a very romantic scene that returns to the familiar nexus of sex and death. It takes place on the day Dorothy learns that her young husband has been killed in the war.

Although *The Last Picture Show* and *The Summer of '42* are both examples of a more honest portrayal of adolescent sex in all its awkwardness, it is equally true that both films reflect a male perspective. Nancy Schwartz criticized them at the time as examples of "the sexism implicit in the genre dealing with the search for manhood…. The women characters in both films are examples of the classic stereotypes of women…. The genre dealing with becoming a man, in its perpetuation of masculine mythology, is in and of itself an obstacle to raising the sexual-political consciousness of the film industry" (1972, 35).

Yet the young men in these films are frequently vulnerable and insecure about their own sexuality. While Hermie's friend Oscy openly brags about his conquests and exhibits a devil-may-care attitude ("I'll bring the marshmallows, you bring the rubbers"), Hermie is considerably more introspective about his own sexual development. In part, this grows out of his respect for Dorothy. Yet it is also part of his inability to find words to express his new feelings. In that sense his postcoital silence aligns him with Paul's loss of his virginity in *All Quiet on the Western Front*. Exactly this type of confusion and ambiguity can be found in the award-winning 1980s TV series, *The Wonder Years*. Most episodes focused on the lives of Kevin Arnold and Winnie Cooper as they progressed from middle school to high school. But the first character to lose his virginity was Kevin's conservative friend, Paul. The episode in which Paul tells Kevin of the unexpected event is a perfect example of just how confusing sex can be for the immature. While Kevin needs "the low down" on how "it happened," Paul struggles to find words: "It was dark and confusing." The event marks a psychological separation between the boys who have "always gone through everything together before." Finally, Paul unburdens himself: "It's awful. It's horrible. How am I supposed to handle this thing? How am I supposed to feel? I mean, did she like me or not? Was I ok? Or is she laughing at me? It all happened so fast."

This depiction of male sensitivity and insecurity was repeated the following decade in *Party of Five*. The episode "Grown Ups" dealt with 11-year-old Claudia's first period and 16-year-old Bailey's first experience of intercourse. As was the case with Paul, Bailey's first time is with a girl who is the initiator or sexual aggressor. Unlike *The Wonder Years*, *Party of Five* shows the couple in bed. Jill tells Bailey to "slow down," and he says, "Tell me what to do." Like Paul, Bailey finds his response to sex considerably different than what he had expected. His brother Charlie had told him earlier, "The sex, that's the easy part. You'll figure out what to do. It's everything else that's hard." Bailey finds himself in a situation where he has sex but finds it meaningless and empty. "It seems like every time we see each other," he tells Jill, "we only do one thing. I just wish we talked more. It feels bad because it just feels like kind of nothing."

In 2004, *Jack and Bobby* repeated the image of the female as sexual initiator. Despite, or perhaps because of, her father's profession as a man of the cloth, Missy assertively tells Jack she wants to do it the first time with him. When the relationship is consummated, it is in her father's church. Talking to his mother after the incident, Jack expresses remorse and regret. While the episode was called "Tonight I Am a Man," Jack's expectations were never realized.

Changing Portrayals of Gay and Lesbian Youth

This new, more sophisticated character development was not restricted to heterosexual relationships. In 1976 Billy Joe *(Ode to Billy Joe)* had to kill himself because of a drunken homosexual encounter with an older man. It is, he confesses, "a sin against nature, a sin against God." But as the 1980s opened, *Happy Birthday Gemini* depicted a son struggling with his sexuality and a supportive father who tells him, "It doesn't matter what you are and what you aren't.... I love you ... you're the best thing I've ever done. Be yourself." The Stonewall riots, gay pride, AIDS, and other factors would make gays and, to a lesser extent, lesbians more visible in society and mass media. British influences included *My Beautiful Laundrette* (1985), which successfully addressed race, class, and gender prejudice in modern-day London. *Another Country* (1984) and *Maurice* (1987) were both period pieces that looked at youthful homosexuality among England's privileged class.

In the United States, gay and lesbian characters appeared in important films, were played by high-profile stars, and won both critical and commercial acclaim, though frequently as a result of independent productions. Some of the important titles include *Silkwood* (1983), *My Own Private Idaho* (1999), and the Oscar-winning *Boys Don't Cry* (1999). Gay writer and actor Harvey Fierstein created *Torch Song Trilogy* (1988), which was both a successful play and then a successful movie. It included the character of a gay high school student adopted by a drag queen and his lover. On Broadway Matthew Broderick had played the son. By the time the film was made, Broderick was an established film star with successful credits, including *War Games* (1983) and the teen classic *Ferris Bueller's Day Off* (1986). His willingness to play the gay character in the *Torch Song Trilogy* film speaks to his own courage plus the changing climate in Hollywood and society.

In *Common Ground, Home Improvement* heartthrob Jonathan Taylor Thomas plays Toby Anderson, a high school swimming star from a small town. Set in the 1970s, the story addresses the boy's confusion about his own sexuality and the climate of hate he faces from his classmates and ultimately his teammates. Harking back to *The Loneliness of the Long Distance Runner,* the narrative has the boy deliberately lose a race he is capable of winning. He will suffer a savage beating and ultimately be raped in the locker room. Asked if he thought young people today were more enlightened about homosexuality than earlier generations, Thomas told *The Advocate,* "I think people are becoming more accepting, partly because it's more prevalent in the media. Part of what *Common Ground* does is express the humanity of these people. It's difficult to have animosity if you recognize that on so many levels, they're exactly the same as you" (Hensley 2000).

During the 1990s, gay and lesbian characters moved from being occasional guests in established series to main recurring characters, who for the most part were presented in a positive light. "Their potential as role models or transmitters of politicized messages seems to have been recognized by liberal drama writers, series producers, and television executives" (Davis 2004, 134). *My So-Called Life* introduced viewers to Rickie Vasquez, generally regarded as the first gay teen regular cast member in U.S. television history (Davis 2004). *Party of Five* included the gay character Elliot. *Buffy the Vampire Slayer* regularly featured story lines about Willow Rosenberg and her girlfriend, Tara Maclay. *Dawson's Creek* built major episodes around Jack McPhee's sexuality, including a painful scene when the boy tells his father he is gay.

An equally angry and painful encounter between a father and his gay son was the subject matter in *Queer as Folk,* a series that displayed more condoms, dildos, and lubricants in one season than in the entire history of television. It also was notable for two other elements. One was the casting of a gay actor (Randy Harrison) to play the character of 16-year-old Justin Taylor. But in a nod to U.S. conservatism, the character of Justin was made a year older than his character in the original British series. The other notable element about Justin's sexuality was the graphic and explicit sex scenes from the first episode, in which he goes home with a complete stranger and engages in anal sex for the first time. Aware of his potential influence on young, questioning audience members, Harrison said, "I hope that seeing a gay teen portrayed on television will be comforting and empowering to other gay teenagers" (*Planet Out,* n.d.).

Teen Sexual Relationships with Adults

In the 1970s, there were changes in the legal concept of age of consent (see chapter 2 in this volume). British films like *Deep End* (1971), *The Go-Between* (1971), and *Friends* (1972) set the stage for the emergence of stories of young love and the increasingly younger nature of the adolescent characters. The American industry's response included *Jeremy* (1973), *The Little Girl Who Lives Down the Lane* (1977), *Rich Kids* (1979), and *Manhattan* (1977), in which Mariel Hemingway plays a high school student having a relationship with an older man (Woody Allen).

The contemporary cinematic origins for such representations were established in the 1950s and 1960s. In 1956 Elia Kazan brought Tennessee Williams's *Baby Doll* to the screen. The story of infantile eroticism quickly won the condemnation of the Legion of Decency and was attacked by *Time* magazine as the "dirtiest" American movie ever exhibited legally. Six years later, Stanley Kubrick independently produced *Lolita* in England. Based on the controversial novel by Vladimir Nabokov, the story centered on a middle-aged man's obsession with a young girl.

The "Lolita," or young nymph, syndrome was also evident in critically acclaimed films like *Taxi Driver* (1976) and *Pretty Baby* (1976), which featured Jodie Foster and Brooke Shields as prostitutes, respectively.

At the same time, TV series *(Eight Is Enough, Family, White Shadow)* and made-for-TV movies *(Anatomy of a Seduction)* also depicted teenagers (both male and female) involved with older individuals. One of the most controversial programs was *James at 15*. On January 26, 1978, NBC screened "Star Crossed Lovers," an episode in which the young hero lost his virginity to a foreign exchange student. Responding to the depiction of sexual initiation in *James at 15*, one critic commented, "James' television plunge planted the anxiety provoking notion in the mind of the adolescent viewer that he was sexually lagging behind not only the precocious kid down the block, but the Average American Boy character of James" (Hawley 1978, 55). The writer of the episode left the program soon afterward because the network would not allow characters to use or discuss birth control.

TODAY'S COMPLEX REPRESENTATIONS OF ADOLESCENTS

Teen sex became a box office and ratings staple by the late 1970s. The industry became more and more provocative. The advertising campaign for *Foxes* (1980) employed the slogan "Daring to Do It." *The Last American Virgin* used the slogan "See It or Be It." *The Blue Lagoon* used a full-page ad in *The New York Times* to sell its idyllic tale of youthful love: "When their love happens it is as natural as the sea itself and as powerful. Love as nature intended it to be." The same period saw the emergence of the teen sex comedy, most notably the *Porky's* series of the 1980s, which ultimately ushered in the *American Pie* series of the 1990s. But while many of the movies could rightly be categorized as sexploitation and stereotypical, it is still possible to look at the era from the 1970s to today and identify growth, maturity, and complexity in media representations of teenage relationships.

> I came to sex late. I was 10. That was when my friend Mark Watkins told me how babies are made.... Fortunately at secondary school we were given the facts.... So that was sex. Simple really! Just find someone to do it with. Find somewhere to do it and just do it. The thing is when you're my age it just isn't that simple and as for falling in love. Well, nothing prepares you for that.
>
> *(17-year-old Steven Carter in Get Real (1999))*

Well received at the Sundance Film Festival, *Get Real* continued the trend, long ago developed in the United Kingdom, of treating adolescent sexuality in a more realistic and sensitive way than most American movies.

A more gritty realism was present in the American cinema's depiction of heterosexual teens, as evidenced by Larry Clark's controversial movie, *Kids* (1995), which depicted the callous and casual sexual encounters of a group of New York City youth. Like *Get Real*, the film opens with the voice-over narration of the central character, Telly. For Telly, sex is the only thing going. It's not about companionship or empathy or affection. It's about conquest—the younger the better, regardless of consequences. As he tells us at the end of the film:

> When you're young not much matters. When you find something that you care about, then that's all you got. A lot of time fucking is all you have. When you go to sleep at night you dream of pussy. When you wake up it's the same thing. It's there in your face, in your dreams, you can't escape it. Sometimes when you're young the only place to go is inside. That's just it. Fucking is what I love. Take that away from me and I really got nothing.

A less than idealized image of sexuality and human nature is also evident in *American Beauty* (1999), which won the Academy Award for best picture. As the film opens, we see a reclining teenage girl. Jane is framed by her boyfriend, Ricki, who is videotaping her. The camera is a distancing device for both teens, who move through much of the film with a cool, alienated sense of detachment, observing their parents and the other adults around them with a sense of disdain. The first line in the film is delivered by Jane: "I need a father who's a role model, not some horny geek boy who's going to spray his shorts whenever I bring a girlfriend home from school." From there the film includes masturbation, intercourse, adultery, homophobia, homosexuality, obsession, and, depending on one's interpretation of it, pedophilia. Casey McKittrick has argued that the movie "facilitated public discourse about social taboos and the moral and aesthetic implications of their representation in mainstream film" (2001, 3).

The overly articulate adolescents of *Dawson's Creek* offer something for every teen (with perhaps the exception of minorities, who are clearly un-derrepresented in the series) on the subject of sexuality—a cornucopia of mixed messages. The characters of Joey and Dawson, in particular, reflect at length about the physiological and psychological changes they experi-ence, starting from their first season as 15-year-olds. This television series has been described as "an attempt to powerfully revalue discourses of the teenager ... by stressing teen agency and articulacy" (Hills 2004, 54). The show was criticized from both the left and the right and included characters who proudly declared their virginity as well as sexually active heterosexual teens and the increasingly visible presence of one or more gay characters.

The highly acclaimed yet short-lived series *Jack and Bobby* was another example of the mixed messages contemporary media often send about sex. Jack consummates his relationship with Missy, who then gets pregnant. The portrayal of Jack's emotions about the encounter is sensitive and complex.

But the treatment of Missy's pregnancy seems like a return to cinema of the 1950s. Killing her off in a car accident may have gotten rid of the problem of addressing abortion—a remaining television taboo—but it also came awfully close to being a punishment for sexual activity.

Somewhere between Steven Carter's confusion, Telly's callousness, the cool detachment of Jane and Ricki, and the angst of Dawson and Joey exists the middle ground of adolescent sexuality, at least in terms of the way movies, television, popular music, advertising, and other media depict it. Somewhere between the sensitive representation of Jack and the killing off of Missy lies the increasing nuance of portrayals of teens, along with skittishness about some topics.

CONCLUSION

Television and other mass media can function as teachers. But media literacy research also suggests that the power of mass media to teach is greatly enhanced by adults, functioning as coviewers and intermediaries, helping children and teenagers alike to contextualize the media messages they encounter.

There is no doubt that media representations about sex have changed dramatically, both qualitatively and quantitatively. We have entered an era in which waves crashing on a beach, cannons firing, and other cinematic symbols for sex are no longer necessary. Nor is it now necessary for sexual references to be coded and concealed in literature, as they were in Frances Hodgson Burnett's 1911 classic, *The Secret Garden* (Davies 2001).

Whether we like it or not, today's adolescent audience can hear and see people their own age talking about sex, thinking about sex, and sometimes having sex, both straight and gay. Yet access to such media messages in and of itself should not be regarded as sex education. In many ways the preponderance of such messages our teenagers encounter in the media landscape still represents mixed messages, especially when compared to the dominance of politicized abstinence-only sex education in schools and the continued discomfort too many parents continue to have recognizing their children as sexual beings (see chapter 4 in this volume).

Like so much in contemporary America, media messages, including media messages about sex, have become part of the so-called culture wars. One's reaction to such representations would tell much about personal and political values and ideology. In the cable series *Huff,* for example, 14-year-old Byrd tells his parents that he attended a "rainbow [blowjob] party." While some people will regard such a story line as an honest, realistic, and even healthy development, others would no doubt regard it as evidence of moral decline, worrying about the influence and effects such messages might have on the young. British researchers David Buckingham and Sara Bragg challenge such worries when they write, "The question of whether sex in the media is good or bad for children is one that, in our view, has no absolute or meaningful answer. The fact is that children are already sexual: the media do not make them sexual, and we cannot stop them being sexual" (2004, 16).

WORKS CITED

Are These Our Children? 1931. Hollywood, CA: RKO Radio Pictures, Inc.

Blumer, Herbert. 1933. *Movies and Conduct.* New York: Macmillan.

Buckingham, David, and Sara Bragg. 2004. *Young People, Sex, and the Media: The Facts of Life?* New York: Palgrave Macmillan.

Christian Century. 1930. January.

Collins, L., et al. 2004. "Watching Sex on Television Predicts Adolescent Initiation of Sexual Behavior." *Pediatrics* 114 (3): 280–89.

Commonweal. 1945. 5 October.

Davies, Maire Messenger. 2001. "A Bit of Earth: Sexuality and the Repression of Childhood in Text and Screen Versions of *The Secret Garden*." *Velvet Light Trap* 48: 48–57.

Davis, G. 2004. "Saying It Out Loud: Revealing Television's Queer Teens." In *Teen TV: Genre, Consumption and Identity,* ed. G. Davis and K. Dickinson, 127–40. London: BFI Publishing.

Department of War Information. 1942. "Miss Annie Rooney, review." Washington, DC: Library of Congress.

Forman, Henry James. 1933. *Our Movie Made Children.* New York: Macmillan.

Hawley, R. 1978. "Television and the Adolescent: A Teacher's View." *American Film,* October.

Hensley, D. 2000. "Uncommonly Grounded." *The Advocate,* 1 February.

Hills, M. 2004. "*Dawson's Creek:* Quality Teen TV and Mainstream Cult?" In *Teen TV: Genre, Consumption and Identity,* ed. G. Davis and K. Dickinson, 54–70. London: BFI Publishing.

McKittrick, Casey. 2001. "I Laughed and Cringed at the Same Time: Shaping Pedophilic Discourse around *American Beauty* and *Happiness*." *Velvet Light Trap* 47: 3–14.

Mclean, D., and W. Helfrich. 1943. "Sex Guidance in Wartime." *National Parent Teacher,* October.

Mitchell, Alice Miller. 1929. *Children and the Movies.* Chicago: Chicago University Press.

New York Times. 1931. "Review: Are These Our Children?" 14 November.

New York Times. 1961. "Review: Splendor in the Grass." 13 October.

Planet Out. n.d. "Starstruck—Randy Harrison." http://www.planetout.com/.

Remarque, Erich Maria. 1928. *All Quiet on the Western Front.* Greenwich, CT: Fawcett. 93.

Rooney, M. 1965. *i.e. An Autobiography.* New York: G. P. Putnam and Sons.

Schwartz, Nancy. 1972. "Coming of Age: A Masculine Myth." *Velvet Light Trap* 6: 33–35.

Thorp, Magaret Farrand. 1939. *America at the Movies.* New Haven, CT: Yale University Press.

Variety. 1949. "Teenagers Road to BO Most Faithful Theater Goers." 31 August.

Walker, Alexander. 1971. *Stardom.* Melbourne: Penguin Books.

Whyte, William Foote. 1943. "A Slum Sex Code." *American Journal of Sociology* XLIX: 24–31.

II Documents

6 Theories of Adolescent Sexuality and Education about Sex

1. Sigmund Freud held that sexuality was a factor in human development from infancy. He divided childhood sexuality into phases, with oral and anal phases in early childhood leading to the genital phase beginning with puberty and continuing through the teen years. He writes below about these phases as well as about his views on girls' versus boys' erogenous zones and on what he sees as the dangers (particularly for girls) of remaining too attached to one's parent of the opposite sex.

THE INFANTILE SEXUALITY

It is a part of popular belief about the sexual impulse that it is absent in childhood and that it first appears in the period of life known as puberty. This, though a common error, is serious in its consequences and is chiefly due to our present ignorance of the fundamental principles of the sexual life. A comprehensive study of the sexual manifestations of childhood would probably reveal to us the existence of the essential features of the sexual impulse, and would make us acquainted with its development and its composition from various sources....

THE SEXUAL LATENCY PERIOD OF CHILDHOOD AND ITS INTERRUPTIONS

... It seems certain that the newborn child brings with it the germs of sexual feelings which continue to develop for some time and then succumb to a progressive suppression, which is in turn broken through by the proper advances of the sexual development and which can be checked by individual idiosyncrasies. Nothing is known concerning the laws and periodicity of this oscillating course of development. It seems, however, that the sexual life of the child mostly manifests itself in the third or fourth year in some form accessible to observation.

The Sexual Inhibition. It is during this period of total or at least partial latency that the psychic forces develop which later act as inhibitions on the sexual life, and narrow its direction like dams. These psychic forces are loathing, shame, and moral and esthetic ideal demands....

THE MANIFESTATIONS OF THE INFANTILE SEXUALITY

... Thumbsucking, which manifests itself in the nursing baby and which may be continued till maturity or throughout life, consists in a rhythmic repetition of sucking contact with the mouth (the lips), wherein the purpose of taking nourishment is excluded.... The pleasure-sucking is connected with an entire exhaustion of attention and leads to sleep or even to a motor reaction in the form of an orgasm. Pleasure-sucking is often combined with a rubbing contact with certain sensitive parts of the body, such as the breast and external genitals. It is by this road that many children go from thumb-sucking to masturbation....

THE MASTURBATIC SEXUAL MANIFESTATIONS

... The Activity of the Anal Zone. Like the lip zone the anal zone is, through its position, adapted to conduct the sexuality to the other functions of the body. It should be assumed that the erogenous significance of this region of the body was originally very large....

Children utilizing the erogenous sensitiveness of the anal zone can be recognized by their holding back of fecal masses until through accumulation there result violent muscular contractions; the passage of these masses through the anus is apt to produce a marked irritation of the mucus membrane. Besides the pain this must produce also a sensation of pleasure.... Real masturbatic irritation of the anal zone by means of the fingers, evoked through either centrally or peripherally supported itching, is not at all rare in older children.

The Activity of the Genital Zone. Among the erogenous zones of the child's body there is one which certainly does not play the main role, and which cannot be the carrier of earliest sexual feeling which, however, is destined for great things in later life. In both male and female it is connected with the voiding of urine (penis, clitoris), and in the former it is enclosed in a sack of mucous membrane, probably in order not to miss the irritations caused by the secretions which may arouse the sexual excitement at an early age. The sexual activities of this erogenous zone, which belongs to the real genitals, are the beginning of the later normal sexual life....

It can only help towards clearness if I state that the infantile masturbation should be divided into three phases. The first phase belongs to the nursing period, the second to the short flourishing period of sexual activity at about the fourth year, only the third corresponds to the one which is often considered exclusively as onanism of puberty....

THE INFANTILE SEXUAL INVESTIGATION

Inquisitiveness. At the same time when the sexual life of the child reaches its first bloom, from the age of three to the age of five, it also evinces the beginning of that activity which is ascribed to the impulse for knowledge and investigation. The desire for knowledge can neither be added to the elementary components of the impulses nor can it be altogether subordinated under sexuality....

The Castration Complex. This conviction is energetically adhered to by the boy and tenaciously defended against the contradictions which soon result, and are only given up after severe internal struggles (castration complex). The substitutive formations of this lost penis of the woman play a great part in the formation of many perversions.

The assumption of the same (male) genital in all persons is the first of the remarkable and consequential infantile sexual theories. It is of little help to the child when biological science agrees with his preconceptions and recognizes the feminine clitoris as the real substitute for the penis. The little girl does not react with similar refusals when she sees the differently formed genital of the boy. She is immediately prepared to recognize it, and soon becomes envious of the penis; this envy reaches its highest point in the consequentially important wish that she also should be a boy....

The Phases of Development of the Sexual Organization. As character-istics of the infantile sexuality we have hitherto emphasized the fact that it is essentially autoerotic (it finds its object in its own body), and that its individual partial impulses, which on the whole are unconnected and independent of one another, are striving for the acquisition of pleasure. The end of this development forms the so-called normal sexual life of the adult in which the acquisition of pleasure has been put into the ser-vice of the function of propagation, and the partial impulses, under the primacy of one single erogenous zone, have formed a firm organization for the attainment of the sexual aim in a strange sexual object....

Pregenital Organizations ... Organizations of the sexual life in which the genital zones have not yet assumed the dominating role we would call the pregenital phase. So far we have become acquainted with two of them which recall reversions to early animal states.

One of the first of such pregenital sexual organizations is the oral, or if we wish, the cannibalistic.... As a remnant of this fictitious phase of organization forced on us by pathology we can consider thumb-sucking.

Here the sexual activity became separated from the nourishment activity and the strange object was given up in favor of one from his own body.

A second pregenital phase is the sadistic-anal organization. Here the contrasts which run through the whole sexual life are already developed, but cannot yet be designated as masculine and feminine, but must be called active and passive. The activity is supplied by the musculature of the body through the mastery impulse; the erogenous mucous membrane of the bowel manifests itself above all as an organ with a passive sexual aim, for both strivings there are objects present, which however do not merge together. Besides them there are other partial impulses which are active in an autoerotic manner. The sexual polarity and the strange object can thus already be demonstrated in this phase. The organization and subordination under the function of propagation are still lacking....

THE TRANSFORMATION OF PUBERTY

With the beginning of puberty the changes set in which transform the infantile sexual life into its definite normal form. Hitherto the sexual impulse has been preponderantly autoerotic; it now finds the sexual object. Thus far it has manifested itself in single impulses and in erogenous zones seeking a certain pleasure as a single sexual aim. A new sexual aim now appears for the production of which all partial impulses cooperate, while the erogenous zones subordinate themselves to the primacy of the genital zone. As the new sexual aim assigns very different functions to the two sexes their sexual developments now part company. The sexual development of the man is more consistent and easier to understand, while in the woman there even appears a form of regression. The normality of the sexual life is guaranteed only by the exact concurrence of the two streams directed to the sexual object and sexual aim. It is like the piercing of a tunnel from opposite sides.

The new sexual aim in the man consists in the discharging of the sexual products; it is not contradictory to the former sexual aim, that of obtaining pleasure; on the contrary, the highest amount of pleasure is connected with this final act in the sexual process. The sexual impulse now enters into the service of the function of propagation; it becomes, so to say, altruistic. If this transformation is to succeed its process must be adjusted to the original dispositions and all the peculiarities of the impulses....

THE PRIMACY OF THE GENITAL ZONES
AND THE FORE-PLEASURE

... The most striking process of puberty has been selected as its most characteristic; it is the manifest growth of the external genitals which have shown a relative inhibition of growth during the latency period of childhood. Simultaneously the inner genitals develop to such an extent as to be able to furnish sexual products or to receive them for the purpose of forming a new living being. A most complicated apparatus is thus formed which waits to be claimed.

This apparatus can be set in motion by stimuli, and observation teaches that the stimuli can affect it in three ways: from the outer world through the familiar erogenous zones; from the inner organic-world by ways still to be investigated; and from the psychic life, which merely represents a depository of external impressions and a receptacle of inner excitations. The same result follows in all three cases, namely, a state which can be designated as "sexual excitation" and which manifests itself in psychic and somatic signs. The psychic sign consists in a peculiar feeling of tension of a most urgent character, and among the manifold somatic signs the many changes in the genitals stand first. They have a definite meaning, that of readiness; they constitute a preparation for the sexual act (the erection of the penis and the glandular activity of the vagina)....

DIFFERENTIATION BETWEEN MAN AND WOMAN

It is known that the sharp differentiation of the male and female character originates at puberty, and it is the resulting difference which, more than any other factor, decisively influences the later development of personality. To be sure, the male and female dispositions are easily recognizable even in infantile life; thus the development of sexual inhibitions (shame, loathing, sympathy, etc.) ensues earlier and with less resistance in the little girl than in the little boy. The tendency to sexual repression certainly seems much greater, and where partial impulses of sexuality are noticed they show a preference for the passive form. But, the autoerotic activity of the erogenous zones is the same in both sexes, and it is this agreement that removes the possibility of a sex differentiation in childhood as it appears after puberty. In respect to the autoerotic and masturbatic sexual manifestations, it may be asserted that the sexuality of the little girl has entirely a male character. Indeed, if one could give a more definite content to the terms "masculine and feminine," one might advance the opinion that the libido is regularly and lawfully of a masculine nature, whether in the man or in the woman; and if we consider its object, this may be either the man or the woman.

... The Leading Zones in Man and Woman. Further than this I can only add the following. The chief erogenous zone in the female child is the clitoris, which is homologous to the male penis. All I have been able to discover concerning masturbation in little girls concerned the clitoris and not those other external genitals which are so important for the later sexual functions. With few exceptions I myself doubt whether the female child can be seduced to anything but clitoris masturbation. The frequent spontaneous discharges of sexual excitement in little girls manifest themselves in a twitching of the clitoris, and its frequent erections enable the girl to understand correctly even without any instruction the sexual manifestations of the other sex; they simply transfer to the boys the sensations of their own sexual processes.

If one wishes to understand how the little girl becomes a woman, he must follow up the further destinies of this clitoris excitation. Puberty, which brings to the boy a great advance of libido, distinguishes itself in the girl by a new wave of repression which especially concerns the clitoris sexuality. It is a part of the male sexual life that sinks into repression. The reenforcement of the sexual inhibitions produced in the woman by the repression of puberty causes a stimulus in the libido of the man and forces it to increase its capacity; with the height of the libido there is a rise in the overestimation of the sexual, which can be present in its full force only when the woman refuses and denies her sexuality. If the sexual act is finally submitted to and the clitoris becomes excited its role is then to conduct the excitement to the adjacent female parts, and in this it acts like a chip of pine wood which is utilized to set fire to the harder wood. It often takes some time for this transference to be accomplished; during which the young wife remains anesthetic.

This anesthesia may become permanent if the clitoris zone refuses to give up its excitability; a condition brought on by abundant activities in infantile life.... If the transference of the erogenous excitability from the clitoris to the vagina has succeeded, the woman has thus changed her leading zone for the future sexual activity; the man on the other hand retains his from childhood....

THE OBJECT-FINDING

... Incest Barriers. If the tenderness of the parents for the child has luckily failed to awaken the sexual impulse of the child prematurely, i. e., before the physical determinations for puberty appear, and if that awakening has not gone so far as to cause an unmistakable breaking through of the psychic excitement into the genital system, it can then fulfill its task and direct the child at the age of maturity in the selection of the sexual object. It would, of course, be most natural for the child to select as the sexual object that person whom it has loved since childhood with, so to speak, a suppressed libido.... In the phantasies of all persons the infantile inclinations, now reenforced by somatic emphasis, reappear, and among them one finds in regular frequency and in the first place the sexual feeling of the child for the parents. This has usually already been differentiated by the sexual attraction, the attraction of the son for the mother and of the daughter for the father. Simultaneously with the overcoming and rejection of these distinctly incestuous phantasies there occurs one of the most important as well as one of the most painful psychic accomplishments of puberty; it is the breaking away from the parental authority, through which alone is formed that opposition between the new and old generations which is so important for cultural progress. Many persons are detained at each of the stations in the course of development through which the individual must pass; and accordingly there are persons who never overcome the parental authority and never, or very imperfectly, withdraw their affection from their parents. They are mostly girls, who, to the delight of their parents, retain their full infantile love far beyond puberty, and it is instructive to find that in their married life these girls are incapable of fulfilling their duties to their husbands. They make cold wives and remain sexually anesthetic....

Freud, Sigmund. Originally published in German, 1905. *Three Contributions to the Theory of Sex* [translated by A. A. Brill. *1916, 2d ed. Nervous and Mental Disease Monograph Series No. 7].* New York: Nervous and Mental Disease Pub. Co.

2. *Many cite the publication of G. S. Hall's two-volume* Adolescence *in 1904 as constructing the concept of adolescence as consisting of the years between childhood and adulthood. He famously wrote of it as a period of "storm and stress," during which adolescents were not yet ready to take on adult responsibilities (as so many did at the time, working and/or raising families) but should be engaged in more age-appropriate activities. This excerpt is from chapter 17, "Adolescent Girls and Their Education," in which he stresses the differences between adolescent girls and boys, in particular, tying girls' differences to menstruation.*

I. *The Biological and Anthropological Standpoint.*—Our modern knowledge of woman represents her as having characteristic differences from man in every organ and tissue.... Her peculiar organs, while constituting a far larger proportion of her body than those of man, are hidden and their psychic reverberations are dim, less-localized, more all-pervasive. She works by intuition and feeling; fear, anger, pity, love, and most of the emotions have a wider range and greater intensity....

II. *The Medical Standpoint.*—Even the demands of the new-school hygiene now represented by so many experts, new journals, conferences, etc., have revealed no point of such wide divergence between doctors and current methods and ideals as in the education of adolescent girls....

Dr. Storer, one of the first and most sagacious American writers in this field, urged that girls should be educated far more in body and less in mind, and thought delicate girls frequently ruined in both body and mind by school. He was not only one of the first to urge that surgery should be performed at the uterine ebb which affected the system even during pregnancy, but to hold that education should be regulated throughout with reference to monthly changes....

Dr. F. C. Taylor presents some pertinent considerations as follows: Civilization is hard on woman, and constantly stimulates her beyond her strength, fires her with ambitions she can not realize, and robs her of the tranquility she needs. Imperfect sexual hygiene is a prolific source of evil to the individual woman and to the race. If the latter deteriorates it will be through the degeneration of woman. In her, sex and its wider irradiations overshadow all else during her ripening period, is an ever-present influence controlling mind and body, and in old age is the glory of the declining day of life. If the sexual life is lowered or suppressed, a tonic needed for vigor in all directions is lost. Owing in part to the fact that her organs are internal and therefore less or later known, they are less often consciously connected with impressions that are indirectly if not directly sexual, and there is greater convertibility of emotions. Women can remain in what is really a suppressed semi-erotic state with never-culminating feeling, so scattered in their interests and enthusiasms that they can not fix their affections permanently.... Unmarried women are, and ought to be, great walkers, but wives and mothers expend the same energy normally in other ways. Where the normal exercise of functions is unduly restrained, it finds, therefore, many other outlets. Dr. Taylor thinks, however, that the difference between boys and girls in learning self-abuse on account of the more obvious anatomy of the former is overestimated, and that the latter, more commonly than is thought, not only find their organs and use them improperly, but are more difficult to cure of this vice....

Henry T. Finck insists that women attach far too much importance to politics; that their sphere is domestic, ninety-four out of every hundred marrying; that they control the all-determining first five years of a child's life and manners, which are almost as important as morals. One of the great functions of motherhood, he says, is to find husbands for daughters. The latter are often neglected, and vanity, which prompts American girls to dress like heiresses, produces, in his opinion, nearly as much unhappiness as whisky. In great cities superfine dressing opens pitfalls of temptation.... Ten per cent more girls than boys are on the way to college in our high schools....

IV. *Nubility of Educated Women.*—Mrs. Howes found about one-fourth and Dewey concluded that 23 per cent of the graduates of women's colleges marry; 21 per cent go into the professions; 28 per cent of coeducation girls marry, and 12 per cent go into the professions. From coeducational colleges 48 per cent teach as against 42 from the women's colleges....Miss Shinn later studied the marriage-rate of the Association of Collegiate Alumna comprising fifteen leading colleges. Of 1,805 enrolled in 1895, only 28 per cent were married, the rate for the country at large for women over 20 being nearly 80 per cent; she concluded that "under 25 college women rarely marry," and "that but a small proportion of them have married." Of 277 of the latest three classes but 10 were married; taking only those graduates past 25, 32.7 per cent; after 30, 43.7; after 35, 49.7; after 40, 54 per cent were married. "The ultimate probability of a college woman's marriage, therefore, seems to be below 55 per cent as against 90 per cent for other women."

V. *Fecundity of Educated Women.*—Here the matter is worse yet for educated women....In a significant paper by Dr. Allen, on the New England family, which was the germ of American civilization, and where for two hundred years the homes were well-nigh models, it is shown how the birth-rate has steadily declined for half a century and that at a very rapid rate until it is lower than that of any European nation, France itself not excepted.... First among the causes of the decline, Dr. Ellis places physical and mental inability to bear and care for children, at the proper period, and secondly, he places unwillingness to sacrifice ease, freedom, and enjoyment involved in parenthood, the disposition to put pleasure in place of duty, the effeminacy of wealth, the new woman movement, and foeticide, and he pleads for domestic labor as one of the best correctives....

Herbert Spencer declared that "absolute or relative infertility is generally produced in women by mental labor carried to excess." This has probably been nowhere better illustrated than by college graduates....

VI. *Education.*—The long battle of woman and her friends for equal educational and other opportunities is essentially won all along the line. Her academic achievements have forced conservative minds to admit that her intellect is not inferior to that of man. The old cloistral seclusion and exclusion is forever gone and new ideals are arising. It has been a noble movement and is a necessary first stage of woman's emancipation....

We should ask, however, what is nature's way at this stage of life? Whether boys, in order to be well virified later, ought not to be so boisterous and even rough as to be at times unfit companions for girls; or whether, on the other hand, girls to be best matured ought not to have their sentimental periods of instability, especially when we venture to raise the question, whether for a girl in the early teens, when her health for her whole life depends upon normalizing the lunar month, there is not something unhygienic, unnatural, not to say a little monstrous, in school associations with boys when she must suppress and conceal her feelings and instinctive promptings at those times which suggest withdrawing, to let nature do its beautiful work of inflorescence. It is a sacred time of reverent exemption from the hard struggle of existence in the world and from mental effort in the school. Medical specialists, many of the best of whom now insist that through this period she should be, as it were, "turned out to grass," or should lie fallow, so far as intellectual efforts go, one-fourth the time, no doubt often go too far, but their unanimous voice should not entirely be disregarded....

While some differences are emphasized by contact, others are compromised.... In place of the mystic attraction of the other sex that has inspired so much that is best in the world, familiar *camaraderie* brings a little disenchantment. The impulse to be at one's best in the presence of the other sex grows lax and sex tension remits.... Thus, I believe, although of course it is impossible to prove, that this is one of the factors of a decreasing percentage of marriage among educated young men and women....

Without specifying here details or curricula, the ideals that should be striven toward in the intermediate and collegiate education of adolescent girls with the proper presupposition of motherhood, and which are already just as practicable as Abbotsholme or *L'École des Roches,* may be rudely indicated somewhat as follows

The first aim, which should dominate every item, pedagogic method and matter, should be health—a momentous word that looms up beside holiness, to which it is etymologically akin.... The health of woman is, as we have seen, if possible even more important for the welfare of the race than that of man, and the influence of her body upon her mind is, in a sense, greater, so that its needs should be supreme and primary....

Regularity should be another all-pervading norm. In the main, even though he may have "played his sex symphony too harshly," E. H. Clarke was right. Periodicity, perhaps the deepest law of the cosmos, celebrates its highest triumphs in woman's life. For years everything must give way to its thorough and settled establishment. In the monthly Sabbaths of rest, the ideal school should revert to the meaning of the word leisure. The paradise of stated rest should be revisited, idleness be actively cultivated; reverie, in which the soul, which needs these seasons of withdrawal for its own development, expatiates over the whole life of the race, should be provided for and encouraged in every legitimate way, for in rest the whole momentum of heredity is felt in ways most favorable to full and complete development. Then woman should realize that *to be* is greater than *to do;* should step reverently aside from her daily routine and let Lord Nature work....

Hall, Granville Stanley. 1904. *Adolescence: Its Psychology and Its Relations to Physiology, Anthropology, Sociology, Sex, Crime, Religion, and Education.* New York: D. Appleton.

3. Maurice Bigelow, a biology professor at Columbia University's Teachers College, was a prominent spokesperson for the American Social Hygiene Association. Below are excerpts from a series of lectures he gave in 1914 and 1915 on sex education.

THE MEANING, NEED, AND SCOPE
OF SEX-EDUCATION....

Sex-education in its largest sense includes all scientific, ethical, social, and religious instruction and influence which directly and indirectly may help young people prepare to solve for themselves the problems of sex that inevitably come in some form into the life of every normal human individual. Note the carefully guarded phrase "help young people prepare to solve for themselves the problems of sex", for, like education in general, special sex-education cannot possibly do more than help the individual prepare to face the problems of life....

In the broadest outlook, sex-education (or sex-instruction) includes;

sex-hygiene (personal, social)
biology (including physiology) of reproduction
heredity and eugenics
ethics and sociology of sex
psychology of sex....

It appears that however desirable home instruction regarding sex may be, the majority of parents are not able and willing to undertake the work, and so the public educational system and organizations for social and religious work should provide a scheme of instruction which will make sure that all young people will have an opportunity to get the most helpful information for the guidance of their lives.

THE PROBLEMS FOR SEX-EDUCATION....

It is important that the general public, especially the parents, should understand the reasons which have induced numerous physicians, ministers, and educators to become active advocates of systematic sex-instruction for young people.... Even intelligent parents are not yet convinced that their children need sex-instruction. This is due largely to the fact that the parents have not yet been shown the reasons why it is now, and always has been, unsafe to allow children to gain more or less sexual information from unreliable and vulgar sources. In fact, it is surprising to find many parents, especially mothers, who seem unable to grasp the idea that their "protected" children can possibly get impure information....

There are eight important sex problems of our times that offer reasons or arguments for sex-instruction, because ignorance plays a large part in each problem. I shall state them briefly here and discuss each... : (1) Many people, especially in youth, need hygienic knowledge concerning sexual processes as they affect personal health. (2) There is an alarming amount of the dangerous social diseases which are distributed chiefly by the sexual promiscuity or immorality of many men. (3) The uncontrolled sexual passions of men have led to enormous development of organized and commercialized prostitution. (4) There are living to-day tens of thousands of unmarried mothers and illegitimate children, the result of the common sexual irresponsibility of men and the ignorance of women. (5) There is need of more general following of a definite moral standard regarding sexual relationships. (6) There is a prevailing unwholesome attitude of mind concerning all sexual processes. (7) There is very general misunderstanding of sexual life as related to healthy and happy marriage. (8) There is need of eugenic responsibility for sexual actions that concern future generations....

First Problem for Sex-instruction: Personal Sex-Hygiene

Such individual disorders as masturbation and deranged menstruation concern personal health directly, while venereal diseases are clearly included in social sex-hygiene.

If there were no other reasons for sex-instruction, I believe that it would be worth while to teach such hygienic knowledge of self as sex-hygiene would guard young people against harmful habits and unfaithful care of their sexual mechanisms; and which, moreover, would guide them across the threshold of adolescence with some helpful understanding of the significance of the metamorphosis. Many men and women suffer from injured, if not ruined, health because they did not know, especially between ten and fourteen years, the laws of personal sex-hygiene, which concern health in ways not involving sexual relationship. Many boys and some girls are injured both physically and mentally by the habit of masturbation. Numerous girls are injured physically and many mentally because they have not learned in advance the nature and hygiene of menstruation.

Second Problem for Sex-instruction: Social Diseases

During the past decade the general public has received some astounding revelations concerning the enormous extent of illicit sexual promiscuity, which is immorality according to our commonly accepted code of vice and morals. Along with the evidence as to the existence of widespread promiscuity, has come the still more alarming information from the medical profession that sexual promiscuity commonly distributes the germs of the two highly infectious and exceedingly destructive diseases, syphilis and gonorrhea, known in medical science as venereal or social. When these are acquired by individuals guilty of sexual promiscuity, they seriously and often fatally affect the victim; but far greater social-hygienic importance is the medical evidence that they are very often transmitted to persons innocent of any transgression of the moral law, especially to wives and children....

In short, the alarming problem of the social diseases results from masculine promiscuity or the failure of men to adhere to the monogamic standards of morality. In other and familiar phrasing, there is widespread acceptance and practice of the so-called "double standard of sexual morality," a monogamic one for respectable women and promiscuity for many of their male relatives and friends....

Third Problem for Sex-instruction: The Social Evil

So far as the problems of sex-education are concerned, there is nothing to be gained by an extensive review of commercialized prostitution. It is generally accepted that the social evil of prostitution is increased by the common ignorance of young people of both sexes regarding the physical and social relations of sex....

The Fourth Problem for Sex-education: Illegitimacy

Most awful of all the results of the sexual mistakes of men and women are the unmarried mothers and their illegitimate children. Of course, I know that there are well-meaning people who argue that motherhood is the supreme fact and that the formality of a marriage ceremony is merely a medievalism in our laws and customs but the inexorable truth remains that our modern social system is centered around the home which is strictly regulated by church and state and public opinion. Whatever may be the philosophical rights and wrongs of individual freedom in sexual relationship, the facts of practical life are that an overwhelming majority of the most intelligent people are united in support of our established laws and customs demanding legitimacy of motherhood and birthright. As a result of this age-old stand for legitimacy, illegitimate mothers and children do not have a square deal at the bar of public opinion. Everybody knows that the vast majority of illegitimate children do not have a fair chance in the world's work....

Another point needs emphasis with the numerous young people, especially men, who are not controlled by moral laws, who know the probabilities of illegitimacy occurring, but who have acquired the popular impression that the order of nature is easily changed. Many physicians and social workers know girls who have gone down because they were persuaded to trust the efficiency of popular ways and means of avoiding the natural outcome of the sexual act. Hence, young people of both sexes should somehow learn that under the conditions that usually attend illicit union there is always a strong probability that the ways of nature cannot be easily circumvented. It is unlawful to explain, except to medical audiences, why this is so; but much illegitimacy will be prevented if it can be made widely known among young men and women that, according to reliable physicians, tragedies of illegitimacy are often due to misplaced confidence in popular methods of contraception.

There is yet another line of information that if widely known might have some bearing on the problem of illicit sexual relations: Physicians and social workers report that many operations, young men and some women know the possibility of illegitimate pregnancy, but feel safe because they know the addresses of doctors and midwives who will perform criminal operations. The great danger of the operation, especially at the hands of such third-class doctors as would attempt to terminate pregnancy criminally, should be widely known by the general public, which only now and then gets a hint in the newspaper reports of a tragedy involving some unfortunate girl....

The Fifth Problem for Sex-education: Sexual Morality

Sexual morality demands that sexual union be restricted to monogamic marriage, and conversely, that such sexual relation outside of marriage is immoral. Such a definition of sexual morality is accepted by church and state and the chief citizens in every morality-civilized country. It is the only practical definition which is satisfactory to the vast majority of educated American men and women, even to those who believe in freedom of divorce and in forgiveness for youthful transgressions of the accepted moral code. Sexual morality has had changeable standards, and in other times and countries custom has made polygamy and promiscuity acceptable as moral; but the monogamic ideal of morality now prevails in the world's best life....

The Sixth Problem for Sex-education: Sexual Vulgarity

Even a limited study of the prevailing attitude towards sex and reproduction convinces one that back of the greatest sexual problems of our times is the almost universal secrecy, disrespect, vulgarity, and irreverence concerning every aspect of sex and reproduction. Even expectant motherhood is commonly concealed as long as possible, and all reference to the developing new life is usually accompanied with blushes and tones suggestive of some great shame.... And I am not simply referring to the great masses of uneducated people, for the saddest fact is that a very large proportion of intelligent people have not an open-minded and respectful attitude concerning sex and reproduction.

Now, unless we can devise some way to counteract the prevailing narrow, vulgar, disrespectful, and irreverent attitude towards all aspects of sex and reproduction; unless we can make people see sexual processes in all their normal aspects as noble, beautiful, and splendid steps in the great plan of nature; unless we can substitute a philosophical and aesthetic view of sex relationship for the time-worn interpretation of everything sexual as inherently vulgar, base, ignoble, and demanding asceticism for those who would reach the highest spiritual development; unless we can begin to make these changes in the prevailing attitude towards sex and reproduction, we cannot make any decided advance in the attempt to help solve sexual problems by special instruction....

The Seventh Problem for Sex-instruction: Marriage

It is the consensus of opinion of numerous physicians, ministers, and lawyers that a very large proportion of matrimonial disharmonies have their foundation in the common misunderstanding of the physiology and especially of the psychology of sex. In the opinion of many students of sexual problems, this is the strongest reason for sex-instruction. It is certainly a line in which limited spread of information has already given some definite and satisfactory results.... Psychological and physiological knowledge will undoubtedly help the two married individuals in their progress towards the harmonious adjustment of their individualities; but there are many little, but often serious, problems that the physiology and psychology of sex cannot solve. They are problems that involve mutual affection, comradeship, sympathy, unselfishness, cooperation, kindliness, and devotion of husband and wife. Obviously, these can never be developed by any formal instruction....

The Eighth Problem for Sex-instruction: Eugenics

Eugenics, or the science of human good breeding, is just now the most popular of the problems concerning human sex and reproduction. In recent years, the biological investigators of heredity have published some startling facts which show that the human race must soon check its reckless propagation of the unfit and encourage reproduction by the best types of men and women.... Some of the chief facts of eugenics should be a part of every well-organized scheme of sex-instruction, and taught through biology. Probably no other topic in biology is so likely to make an ethical-social appeal, for the central point of eugenics is the responsibility of the individual whose uncontrolled sexual actions may transmit undesirable and heritable qualities and bring a train of disaster to generations of descendants....

At this point we digress to correct the widespread error in confusing sex-hygiene and eugenics.... Eugenics aims to select better parents who will transmit their own qualities genetically. Sex-hygiene in its personal and social aspects will make healthier parents able to give their offspring a healthier start in life, especially because the offspring is free from the prenatal effects of disease....

The teaching of heredity and eugenics is intended to develop a sense of individual responsibility for the transmission of one's good or bad inherited qualities to offspring. The teaching of sex-hygiene, either personal or social, looks towards improving personal health and preventing infection and injurious influence on the unborn next generation....

ORGANIZATION OF EDUCATIONAL ATTACK ON THE SEX PROBLEMS

As I now see in the large the sexual problems which scientifically organized education should attack, the educational aims may be grouped under four general headings as follows: First and most important, sex-education should aim to develop an open-minded, serious, scientific, and respectful attitude towards all problems of human life which relate to sex and reproduction.

Second, sex-education should aim to give that knowledge of personal hygiene of the sexual organs which is of direct value in making for the most healthful and efficient life of the individual.

Third, sex-education should aim to develop personal responsibility regarding the social, ethical, psychical, and eugenic aspects of sex as affecting the individual life in its relation to other individuals of the present and future generations; in short, sex-education should consider the problems of sexual instincts and actions in relation to society.

Fourth, sex-education should aim to teach briefly to young people, during later adolescence, the essential hygienic, social, and eugenic facts regarding the two destructive diseases which are chargeable to sexual promiscuity or immorality....

THE PAST AND THE FUTURE OF THE SEX-EDUCATION MOVEMENT

... Let me state my confession of faith in sex-education: It is certainly only one of several possible lines [of] attack on the alarming sex problems of our time; but it offers the most hopeful outlook towards improved sexual morals and health, both physical and psychical. However, we shall gain nothing of permanent value by extravagant claims or hopes as to the ultimate effect of sex-education. We must expect incomplete results....

In so far as each coming generation of individuals may be thus guided by the larger sex-education, the problems of sex will be pragmatically solved, for the social aggregate of human life will become better, happier, nobler, truer, more in harmony with the highest ideals of life, more like our vision of perfected humanity.

Bigelow, Maurice. 1916. *Sex-Education: A Series of Lectures Concerning Knowledge of Sex in Its Relation to Human Life.* New York: Macmillan.

4. With support from the YMCA, Anthony Comstock founded the New York Society for the Suppression of Vice in 1872. He drove the passage of the federal antiobscenity law, usually known as the Comstock Law (1873), that prohibited the mailing of obscene materials, including information about contraception or abortion. Below are excerpts from one of his works, Frauds Exposed, *detailing his crusade to eradicate obscene literature and protect young people from its dangers, particularly those of arousal and masturbation.*

PREFACE

Before my readers turn to the contents of this book, they are respectfully requested to first carefully consider the objects and aims of the writer, as well as the peculiar circumstances under which this book has been prepared.

I make no pretensions to literary excellence. My object is to expose the multitudinous schemes and devices of the sharper to deceive and rob the unwary and credulous through the mails; to warn honest and simple–minded persons; to shield our youth from debauching and corrupting influences; to arouse a public sentiment against the vampires who are casting deadly poison into the fountain of moral purity in the children; and at the same time expose to public indignation the infidels and liberals who defend these moral cancer–planters. With malice toward none, but with unbounded sympathy and charity toward the multitudes who each year are defrauded through the mails, or cursed in mind, body and soul by obscene matter, I present some of the devices to plunder, ruin, and debauch, which it has been my privilege and duty to overthrow and stop, during a seven years' experience as a Special Agent of the Post–Office Department of the United States, and Chief Agent and Secretary of the New York Society for the Suppression of Vice. Let it be remembered, that these facts have been gathered in the discharge of my duty under my solemn oaths of office. Many of these are the evidences upon which juries have convicted and courts sentenced....

No part of this book can be of greater interest, than those chapters that expose the Liberal Fraud, and the infamous conspiracies entered into by the Liberals, to repeal the laws against obscene literature. I regret it becomes necessary to refer to some of these creatures. But when a body of men unite to advance a cause, which promises a morality better than that offered by the Word of God, a system of government better than the grand institutions of Free America, a religion purer and nobler than that of our Lord Jesus Christ, a hereafter more glorious than the eternal heavens, it is well for the public to know their true character. "By their fruits ye shall know them." I have presented facts; I have drawn an indictment against this horde of blasphemers and revilers of the ever–living God, and I submit my evidence to sustain this indictment. Let every decent man read, and see what we have in our land, and then say if they will consent that our youth shall be inoculated with this virus. Let youth read it, and then say if, in all this ranting mob, there is a character worthy to be placed before that of our blessed Saviour as an exemplar for them....

It is a faithful record, written to head off the secret devices of the sharper—a shield to the poor, and a defence of the right. I have tried to avoid personalities, but oftentimes my indignation would get the better of me, and I have used strong words of condemnation against the scheme or conspiracy which I have been exposing. I have visited the offices and dens of these men. I am familiar with the manner in which their nefarious business has been conducted, and the extent of robberies thus perpetrated. I have had thousands of letters of their victims, which have been seized in the possession of the criminal, as well as hundreds of complaints from all classes, sent to me direct, showing youth debauched and ruined, and base wrongs perpetrated; and the reader must remember all these sad stories come back and ring their appeals anew in my ears, while they lay a heavy burden on my heart. I have again and again said these people shall not be robbed if I can prevent it; and by a seven years' conflict I have endeavored to raise a legal barrier between the youth and this hydra–headed monster of Obscenity. I have enforced the laws, by bringing many of these scoundrels to justice, and by laying before the Post–Office Department evidence of their nefarious traffic; and now, with all these facts refreshing memory, I have fought these battles over again. By a careful study of all the facts, I have concentrated the stories of some of the principal schemes between the covers of this book, in the hope of accomplishing a most needed object— arouse an enlightened public sentiment to sustain the enforcement of laws, and at the same time to warn the unwary.

I therefore place this book in the hands of the public, and appeal to them to extend a fair charity over its defects, while I vouch for its absolute and positive truthfulness as a record of facts.

There are those who cry, "there is no danger," but I am not of that number. There is great danger. This evil is found everywhere. Like the plagues of Egypt it has crept up into our homes; the mails were formerly literally loaded down with these devil–traps for the young....

We ought, in this enlightened country, to have enough of decency and moral courage to protect our youth from these contaminating influences, and enough Christianity to protect and sustain any organization engaging in such a noble crusade against the powers of darkness as has been waged by the officers and members of the New York Society for the Suppression of Vice. There ought to be enough honesty and fairness to protect a man, engaged in suppressing this monster evil, from being branded as a criminal, and maligned by insinuations and base charges, in reputable papers. No man outside of a very limited circle knows of the faithful and heroic conduct of the officers of the Society that has dared to confront this evil....

BOYS' PAPERS

The Board are deeply impressed with the importance of guarding the youthful mind from the debasing influence of what are called Boys' Papers. Facts that have come to our knowledge force us to do all that lies within our power to check this growing evil....

The following are a few facts that have been brought to the attention of the Society:

Our Agent arrested a young man 19 years of age, of advertising and sending through the mails, under about a dozen aliases, the most obscene matter. While searching for this vile trash in his sleeping room in his father's house, the Agent found a mass of these Boys' Papers piled up in onecorner. No sooner had they been discovered than the prisoner started back, exclaiming with great force, "There, there's the cause of my ruin—that has cursed me and brought me to this!"

... The effect of these publications is thus spoken of by professors in colleges and others. One writes:

> "The corrupting literature which you are so sedulously seeking to suppress, is a great curse in producing the ruinous habit of self–abuse among the youth of our country. From such meagre statistics as I have been able to gather, I am forced to the conviction that not less than 75 per cent of our youths from 12 to 18 years of age, are more or less the victims of this soul, mind and body destroying vice."

A prominent citizen of Cincinnati, speaking of the effects of these books and pictures on the mind of the youth, says:

> "Self–abuse is a thousand times worse where it is occasioned by obscene plates." "When the excitement is made on the mind by obscene plates, it is indelible, and the images remain through life. I cannot write out my feelings of disgust on those damnable creatures in human shape who vend or deal in obscene literature. Their infernal trade destroys the manhood and woman-hood of millions of our race, annually, over the earth."

The result of this literary poison, cast into the very fountains of social life, is found everywhere. It is infecting the pure life and heart of our youth. They are becoming weak–minded, vapid, sentimental, lustful, criminal. Parents are mourning over the distaste of their children for all that is sensible and use-ful. The teacher finds study to be irksome to them; romantic tales, narratives of love, lust, hate, revenge and murder are to their taste. They assimilate what they read, and so down, down our youth go, weaker and weaker in all the mental and moral elements of true manhood and womanhood.

Corrupt thoughts, desires and aims supplant native innocence. Virtue flies out of the window; vice flies in and takes full possession. We condemn the man who deals out liquid poison to the unhappy drunkard. He stands a nobleman far above the miserable miscreant who supplies the youth with the demoralizing venom contained in many dime novels, flashy periodicals, sporting newspapers and other obscene publications. Let fathers, mothers and teachers watch closely over the pockets, desks and rooms of their children. Be sure that the imagery and seeds of moral death are not in your houses and schools....

Comstock, Anthony. 1880. *Frauds Exposed: Or, How the People Are Deceived and Robbed, and Youth Corrupted. Being a Full Exposure of Various Schemes Operated through the Mails, and Unearthed by the Author in a Seven Years' Service as a Special Agent of the Post Office Department and Secretary and Chief Agent of the New York Society for the Suppression of Vice.* New York: J. H. Brown.

5. *Socialist, pacifist, suffragist, and birth control advocate Mary Ware Dennett was convicted in 1929 under the federal Comstock Law, which criminalized sending obscene materials through the mail. She had written the pamphlet in question, "The Sex Side of Life," a primer on sex education. The following contains excerpts from the opinion of the federal appellate court that in 1930 reversed the trial court's judgment.*

The statute under which the defendant was convicted reads as follows: 'Every obscene, lewd, or lascivious, and every filthy book, pamphlet, picture, paper, letter, writing, print, or other publication of an indecent character, and every article or thing designed, adapted, or intended for preventing conception or producing abortion, or for any indecent or immoral use; is hereby declared to be nonmailable matter and shall not be conveyed in the mails or delivered from any post office or by any letter carrier. Whoever shall knowingly deposit, or cause to be deposited, for mailing or delivery, anything declared by this section to be nonmailable, or shall knowingly take, or cause the same to be taken, from the mails for the purpose of circulating or disposing thereof, or of aiding in the circulation or disposition thereof, shall be fined not more than $5,000, or imprisoned not more than five years, or both.

The defendant is the mother of two boys. When they had reached the respective ages of eleven and fourteen, she concluded that she ought to teach them about the sex side of life. After examining about sixty publications on the subject and forming the opinion that they were inadequate and unsatisfactory, she wrote the pamphlet entitled 'Sex Side of Life,' for the mailing of which she was afterwards indicted.

The defendant allowed some of her friends, both parents and young people, to read the manuscript which she had written for her own children, and it finally came to the notice of the owner of the *Medical Review of Reviews,* who asked if he might read it and afterwards published it. About a year afterwards she published the article herself at twenty-five cents a copy when sold singly, and at lower prices when ordered in quantities.

Twenty-five thousand of the pamphlets seem to have been distributed in this way.

At the trial, the defendant sought to prove the cost of publication in order to show that there could have been no motive of gain on her part. She also offered to prove that she had received orders from the Union Theological Seminary, Young Men's Christian Association, the Young Women's Christian Association, the Public Health Departments of the various states and from no less than four hundred welfare and religious organizations, as well as from clergymen, college professors, and doctors, and that the pamphlet was in use in the public schools at Bronxville, N.Y....

The pamphlet begins with a so-called 'Introduction for Elders' which sets forth the general views of the writer and is as follows:

'In reading several dozen books on sex matters for the young with a view to selecting the best for my own children, I found none that I was willing to put into their hands, without first guarding them against what I considered very misleading and harmful impressions, which they would otherwise be sure to acquire in reading them. That is the excuse for this article.

'It is far more specific than most sex information written for young people. I believe we owe it to children to be specific if we talk about the subject at all.

'From a careful observation of youthful curiosity and a very vivid recollection of my own childhood, I have tried to explain frankly the points about which there is the greatest inquiry. These points are not frankly or clearly explained in most sex literature....

'I found that from the physiological point of view, the question was handled with limitations and reservations. From the point of natural science it was often handled with sentimentality, the child being led from a semi-esthetic study of the reproduction of flowers and animals to the acceptance of a similar idea for human beings. From the moral point of view it was handled least satisfactorily of all, the child being given a jumble of conflicting ideas, with no means of correlating them—fear of venereal disease, one's duty to suppress 'animal passion,' the sacredness of marriage, and so forth. And from the emotional point of view, the subject was not handled at all.

'This one omission seems to me to be the key to the whole situation, and it is the basis of the radical departure I have made from the precedents in most sex literature for children.

'Concerning all four points of view just mentioned, there are certain departures from the traditional method that have seemed to me worth making.

'On the physiological side I have given, as far as possible, the proper terminology for the sex organs and functions. Children have had to read the expurgated literature which has been specially prepared for them in poetic or colloquial terms, and then are needlessly mystified when they hear things called by their real names.

'On the side of natural science, I have emphasized our unlikeness to the plants and animals rather than our likeness, for while the points we have in common with the lower orders make an interesting section in our general education, it is knowing about the vital points in which we differ that helps us to solve the sexual problems of maturity; and the child needs that knowledge precisely as he needs knowledge of everything which will fortify him for wise decisions when he is grown.

'On the moral side, I have tried to avoid confusion and dogmatism in the following ways: by eliminating fear of venereal disease as an appeal for strictly limited sex relations, stating candidly that venereal disease is becoming curable; by barring out all mention of 'brute' or 'animal' passion, terms frequently used in pleas for chastity and self control, as such talk is an aspersion on the brute and has done children much harm in giving them the impression that there is an essential baseness in the sex relation; by inviting the inference that marriage is 'sacred' by virtue of its being a reflection of human ideality rather than because it is a legalized institution.

'Unquestionably the stress which most writers have laid upon the beauty of nature's plans for perpetuating the plant and animal species, and the effort to have the child carry over into human life some sense of that beauty has come from a most commendable instinct to protect the child from the natural shock of the revelation of so much that is unesthetic and revolting in human sex life. The nearness of the sex organs to the excretory organs, the pain and messiness of childbirth are elements which certainly need some compensating antidote to prevent their making too disagreeable and disproportionate an impress on the child's mind.

'The results are doubtless good as far as they go, but they do not go nearly far enough. What else is there to call upon to help out? Why, the one thing which has been persistently neglected by practically all the sex writers—the emotional side of sex experience. Parents and teachers have been afraid of it and distrustful of it. In not a single one of all the books for young people that I have thus far read has there been the frank unashamed declaration that the climax of sex emotion is an unsurpassed joy, something which rightly belongs to every normal human being, a joy to be proudly and serenely experienced. Instead there has been all too evident an inference that sex emotion is a thing to be ashamed of, that yielding to it is indulgence which must be curbed as much as possible, that all thought and understanding of it must be rigorously postponed, at any rate till after marriage.

'We give to young folks, in their general education, as much as they can grasp of science and ethics and art, and yet in their sex education, which rightly has to do with all of these, we have said, 'Give them only the bare physiological facts, lest they be prematurely stimulated.' Others of us, realizing that the bare physiological facts are shocking to many a sensitive child, and must somehow be softened with something pleasant, have said, 'Give them the facts, yes, but see to it that they are so related to the wonders of evolution and the beauties of the natural world that the shock is minimized.' But none of us has yet dared to say, 'Yes, give them the facts, given them the nature study, too, but also give them some conception of sex life as a vivifying joy, as a vital art, as a thing to be studied and developed with reverence for its big meaning, with understanding of its far-reaching reactions, psychologically and spiritually, with temperant restraint, good taste and the highest idealism.' We have contented ourselves by assuming that marriage makes sex relations respectable. We have not yet said that it is only beautiful sex relations that can make marriage lovely....

'Only such an understanding can be counted on to give them the self control that is born of knowledge, not fear, the reverence that will prevent premature or trivial connections, the good taste and finesse that will make their sex life when they reach maturity a vitalizing success.'

After the foregoing introduction comes the part devoted to sex instruction entitled, 'An Explanation for Young People.' It proceeds to explain sex life in detail both physiologically and emotionally. It describes the sex organs and their operation and the way children are begotten and born. It negatives the idea that the sex impulse is in itself a base passion, and treats it as normal and its satisfaction as a great and justifiable joy when accompanied by love between two human beings. It warns against perversion, venereal disease, and prostitution, and argues for continence and healthy mindedness and against promiscuous sex relations.

The pamphlet in discussing the emotional side of the human sex relation,

'It means that a man and a woman feel that they belong to each other in a way that they belong to no one else; it makes them wonderfully happy to be together; they find they want to live together, work together, play together, and to have children together, that is, to marry each other, and their dream is to be happy together all their lives. The idea of sex relations between people who do not love each other, who do not feel any sense of belonging to each other, will always be revolting to highly developed sensitive people.'

... 'Sex relations belong to love, and love is never a business. Love is the nicest thing in the world, but it can't be bought. And the sex side of it is the biggest and most important side of it, so it is the one side of us that we must be absolutely sure to keep in good order and perfect health, if we are going to be happy ourselves or make any one else happy.'

The government proved that the pamphlet was mailed to Mrs. C. A. Miles, Grottoes, Va.

Upon the foregoing record, of which we have given a summary, the trial judge charged the jury that the motive of the defendant in mailing the pamphlet was immaterial, that it was for them to determine whether it was obscene, lewd, or lascivious within the meaning of the statute, and that the test was 'whether its language has a tendency to deprave and corrupt the morals of those whose minds are open to such things and into whose hands it may fall; arousing and implanting in such minds lewd and obscene thought or desires.'

The court also charged that, 'even if the matter sought to be shown in the pamphlet complained of were true, that fact would be immaterial, if the statements of such facts were calculated to deprave the morals of the readers by inciting sexual desires and libidinous thoughts.'

The jury returned a verdict of guilty upon which the defendant was sentenced to pay a fine of $300, and from the judgment of conviction she has taken this appeal.

Before SWAN, AUGUSTUS N. HAND, and CHASE, Circuit Judges.

AUGUSTUS N. HAND, Circuit Judge (after stating the facts as above).

… It was perhaps proper to exclude the evidence offered by the defendant as to the persons to whom the pamphlet was sold, for the reason that such evidence, if relevant at all, was part of the government's proof. In other words, a publication might be distributed among doctors or nurses or adults in cases where the distribution among small children could not be justified. The fact that the latter might obtain it accidently or surreptitiously, as they might see some medical books which would not be desirable for them to read, would hardly be sufficient to bar a publication otherwise proper. Here the pamphlet appears to have been mailed to a married woman. The tract may fairly be said to be calculated to aid parents in the instruction of their children in sex matters. As the record stands, it is a reasonable inference that the pamphlet was to be given to children at the discretion of adults and to be distributed through agencies that had the real welfare of the adolescent in view. There is no reason to suppose that it was to be broadcast among children who would have no capacity to understand its general significance….

But the important consideration in this case is not the correctness of the rulings of the trial judge as to the admissibility of evidence, but the meaning and scope of those words of the statute which prohibit the mailing of an 'obscene, lewd or lascivious pamphlet.' It was for the trial court to determine whether the pamphlet could reasonably be thought to be of such a character before submitting any question of the violation of the statute to the jury…. And the test most frequently laid down seems to have been whether it would tend to deprave the morals of those into whose hands the publication might fall by suggesting lewd thoughts and exciting sensual desires….

It may be assumed that any article dealing with the sex side of life and explaining the functions of the sex organs is capable in some circumstances of arousing lust. The sex impulses are present in every one, and without doubt cause much of the weal and woe of human kind. But it can hardly be said that, because of the risk of arousing sex impulses, there should be no instruction of the young in sex matters, and that the risk of imparting instruction outweighs the disadvantages of leaving them to grope about in mystery and morbid curiosity and of requiring them to secure such information, as they may be able to obtain, from ill-informed and often foul-minded companions, rather than from intelligent and high-minded sources. It may be argued that suggestion plays a large part in such matters, and that on the whole the less sex questions are dwelt upon the better. But it by no means follows that such a desideratum is attained by leaving adolescents in a state of inevitable curiosity, satisfied only by the casual gossip of ignorant playmates.

The old theory that information about sex matters should be left to chance has greatly changed, and, while there is still a difference of opinion as to just the kind of instruction which ought to be given, it is commonly thought in these days that much was lacking in the old mystery and reticence. This is evident from the current literature on the subject, particularly such pamphlets as 'Sex Education,' issued by the Treasury Department United States Public Health Service in 1927.

The statute we have to construe was never thought to bar from the mails everything which might stimulate sex impulses. If so, much chaste poetry and fiction, as well as many useful medical works would be under the ban. Like everything else, this law must be construed reasonably with a view to the general objects aimed at. While there can be no doubt about its constitutionality, it must not be assumed to have been designed to interfere with serious instruction regarding sex matters unless the terms in which the information is conveyed are clearly indecent....

The defendant's discussion of the phenomena of sex is written with sincerity of feeling and with an idealization of the marriage relation and sex emotions. We think it tends to rationalized and dignify such emotions rather than to arouse lust. While it may be thought by some that portions of the tract go into unnecessary details that would better have been omitted, it may be fairly answered that the curiosity of many adolescents would not be satisfied without full explanation, and that no more than that is really given. It also may reasonably be thought that accurate information, rather than mystery and curiosity, is better in the long run and is less likely to occasion lascivious thoughts than ignorance and anxiety. Perhaps instruction other than that which the defendant suggests would be better. That is a matter as to which there is bound to be a wide difference of opinion, but, irrespective of this, we hold that an accurate exposition of the relevant facts of the sex side of life in decent language and in manifestly serious and disinterested spirit cannot ordinarily be regarded as obscene. Any incidental tendency to arouse sex impulses which such a pamphlet may perhaps have is apart from and subordinate to its main effect. The tendency can only exist in so far as it is inherent in any sex instruction, and it would seem to be outweighed by the elimination of ignorance, curiosity, and morbid fear. The direct aim and the net result is to promote understanding and self-control.

No case was made for submission to the jury, and the judgment must therefore be reversed.

United States v. Dennett, 39 F.2d 564 (C.C.A.2 N.Y. 1930).

7   The Age of Consent and the Protection of Females

1. *The Woman's Christian Temperance Union was instrumental in states' reforms of statutory rape laws at the end of the nineteenth century; most states raised the age of consent from 10 or 12 to 16 or 18. In states in which women could not yet vote, petitions like the one below served to get the attention of lawmakers. Space was left under the text of the petition for the names and addresses of those wishing to sign it. The "ruin" to which it refers is the losing of one's virginity outside of marriage, making one "fallen" and therefore less marriageable.*

Petition of the Woman's Christian Temperance Union for the Protection of Women

To the Senate and House of Representatives:

The increasing and alarming frequency of assaults upon women, and the frightful indignities to which even little girls are subject, have become the shame of our boasted civilization.

A study of the Statutes has revealed their utter failure to meet the demands of that newly-awakened public sentiment which requires better legal protection for womanhood and girlhood.

Therefore we, women of _____, State of _____, do most earnestly appeal to you to enact such statutes as shall provide for the adequate punishment of crimes against women and girls. We also urge that the age at which a girl can legally consent to her own ruin be raised to at least eighteen years; and we call attention to the disgraceful fact that protection of the person is not placed by our laws upon so high a plane as protection of the purse.

Woman's Christian Temperance Union (WCTU). 1888. "Petition of the Woman's Christian Temperance Union for the Protection of Women." Washington, D.C.: National Archives and Records Administration.

*2. Emily Blackwell was a leader in the campaign to reform statutory rape laws by rais-
ing the age of consent from 10–12 to 16–18. Below she reflects the popular narrative that there was a "traffic in girls" when she notes that poorer and working-class
girls were most vulnerable to being taken advantage of, even being made unwilling
prostitutes, when on their own in cities to work. She also draws attention to the
"double standard" of morality by which women who had sex before marriage were
viewed much more harshly than men who had engaged in the same activities.*

By fixing the age of legal majority the State declares that under this
age young people have not the experience nor the maturity of judgment
which would qualify them for independent action in matters of importance
affecting their own interests. They are in consequence made incapable of
such action. Their consent cannot relieve a guardian from responsibility in
the management of their property. Except in a few exceptional cases they
cannot make a contract which will be binding when they come of age. A
minor cannot legally marry without the consent of the guardian. Surrepti-
tious marriage with a minor is an offense punishable by law, and such a
marriage can be annulled upon the application of the guardian. Thus their
power of action is, in their own interest, so limited that their consent is not
sufficient to make valid even perfectly legitimate transactions, nor does it
avail to protect adults who assume it as sufficient authority.

Even in crime youth is allowed as an extenuating circumstance, from the
general feeling that the young are less able to resist external influences,
and are less responsible for their actions than the adult. The establishment
of reformatories for juvenile offenders testifies to the belief that their characters are still unformed for good or for evil.

In the case of girls, the State has not only extended exceptional protection to them as minors in reference to their legitimate social relations, it
has also established a sort of legal majority in reference to those that are
illegitimate. It has fixed an age below which girls are held to be incom-
petent of assent to such illegitimate relations. "Consent," as it is termed,
varied in all the different States, until recently, from the age of seven
to twelve years, and in many of them it is still only ten or twelve. This
arrangement amounted virtually to the protection of children only for the
years during which their physical abuse is so brutal an offense as to excite
indignation even among the majority of persons of vicious life. The protection accorded in other respects to minors was distinctly and emphatically
withdrawn from girls during the first few years of early womanhood, when
it is most needed.

Such legislation is directly in the interests of vice. The line is drawn just
where those who are interested in vice would have it. It is certainly as illogi-
cal as cruel that an age when a girl's consent is not held sufficient for legal
marriage, it should be held sufficient to justify her destruction. A man may
not legally marry the minor daughter of another without his consent, but
he is legally free to seduce her if he can.

It would seem that our present legislation was influenced more by respect for property, than by consideration for personal protection. Virtually it is effective only in regard to the well-to-do class in which property consider- ations enter largely into the question of marriage. In this class the daugh- ters live at home, under the protection of parents and family connections, to mature age. The only danger to which they are actually exposed is to that of an imprudent marriage, and against that the law fully protects them.

The case is entirely different with the majority of girls where poverty obliges them to go to work as soon as they are capable of earning. Ignorant, inexperienced, impulsive, they enter the great world of work, usually into wearisome and ill-paid labor, under the control and direction of men. For except in domestic service, girls do not come much in contact with the great body of respectable elder women who should be their natural guides. These are withdrawn from their world of industry, and are occupied in domestic life, and those whom the girls do meet in work are usually not in positions of influence or authority. It is with men largely that the girls deal, and upon them they depend for direction and occupation. Even in domestic service girls are removed from home life, and thrown among associates of the most varied character, and for whom the mistress usually feels little responsibil- ity. There is no class in society so helpless, so surrounded by temptation, as young working girls just growing up. They are surrounded by a network of snares and pitfalls. For this is the class which is coveted as a prey by the licentious and by those who live by pandering to licentiousness.

Though unacknowledged and working under cover, there exists virtually an organized system of temptation, controlled by old experienced agents of vice, aiming to sweep as much of this fresh material as possible into their nets. How constant and insidious this work is, what craft and what indirect means are employed to entice young girls into some of the many devious paths that lead downward, can only be realized by those whose attention and thought have been especially called to the subject. The testimony given ... in the reference to the international traffic in girls, is full of terrible testimony to the extent of youthful prostitution in great cities, to the endless ways in which the victims are tempted or entrapped, and the difficulty of escape when once they fall into bad hands ... all tell the same story with endless variations, of the dangers which encompass these years of early womanhood on its entrance into work of all kinds outside of the home.

Society unconsciously works into the hands of the tempters. As cruelly severe toward women as it is criminally indulgent toward men in these respects, it is enough for a girl to be compromised, or even suspected, to make it difficult for her to obtain employment and keep in the ranks of the honest. The whole situation grows out of the different standard of virtue for men and women, that while chastity is the one absolute prerequisite to social consideration and even to decent life among women, it is regarded as an absolutely impossible virtue in men. Consequently seduction is a minor offense in a man—though it means destruction to the woman. Virtually a man who seduces a young woman commits a greater crime than if he killed her, as moral death is a greater misfortune than physical death. Would not most parents consider the death of a daughter less of a misfortune than that she should take the first step toward a life of vice?

So long as the State acknowledges any special obligation toward minors in protection of property and person, it is certainly bound by duty and interest to extend it to those who most need it. To assume that a girl of fourteen or fifteen is not to be trusted in making a legal marriage, but that a girl of eleven or twelve is competent to understand and accept the consequences of an illegitimate connection, is a glaring absurdity, only to be accounted for by the different motives on which such action is based. No reason can be given for the low age of consent that would not tell equally upon every restriction on the freedom of minors. It is surely to the interest of the State that its girls should grow up virtuous women. It cannot be its interest to facilitate the work of those who would compass its destruction, in order to increase the temptations to vice, already too powerful, which surround young men.

Wherever the age of protection has been raised the result has been for good only. It acts as a deterrent upon those who would mislead youth. It strengthens the hands of the individuals and societies who work for the protection and help of friendless youth. It would seem sufficient to state the case fairly to accomplish our end, but the great long-continued effort that has been needed to partially accomplish this end testifies to the contrary. And constant vigilance is needed to keep even what is gained. Vice is always watching its opportunity. Two years ago a bill to lower the age of consent to its old standard came very near passing the New York Legislature, and was only defeated by the timely effort of a single member. It is said to be good policy to do what your enemy opposes, and there is no doubt that all the vicious element of our cities is opposed to our efforts. They recognize that our present legislation is just what is to their advantage.

It is often objected to the advocates of woman suffrage, that women can have all the legal rights they can justly claim without it, that men are always ready to remove any proved injustice to them. Yet the fact remains that the first States to raise the age of consent to that of majority were those in which women had a direct voice in politics—Wyoming and Kansas. There can be no doubt that had women a share in legislation, the present agitation would be unnecessary, for these disgraceful enactments would long ago have been erased from our statute books. Indeed they would never have been placed there in the first instance.

So long as the State assumes any obligation on the matter, the only just and logical ground to take is that the age of consent should be raised to that for independent legal majority.

Blackwell, Emily. 1895. "Age of Consent Legislation." *Philanthropist* 9: 2–3.

3. *Also known as the Mann Act, the White-Slave Traffic Act was passed in response to the United States having signed an international treaty to curb the "social evil" of prostitution. More broadly, it was also passed in response to a moral panic not only over young, working-class girls who were supposedly being forced into prostitution in U.S. cities, but also due to concern over a growing sexual independence among those same urban girls. As such, the Act was also used to punish consensual relationships between unmarried people. Since its passage in 1910, it has been amended—but never entirely repealed.*

CHAP. 395—An Act to further regulate interstate commerce and foreign commerce by prohibiting the transportation therein for immoral purposes of women and girls, and for other purposes.

Be it enacted by the Senate and House of Representatives of the United States of America in Congress assembled, That the term "interstate commerce," as used in this Act, shall include transportation from any State or Territory or the District of Columbia, and the term "foreign commerce," as used in this Act, shall include transportation from any State or Territory or the District of Columbia to any foreign country and from any foreign country to any State or Territory or the District of Columbia.

SEC. 2. That any person who shall knowingly transport or cause to be transported, or aid or assist in obtaining transportation for, or in transporting, in interstate or foreign commerce, or in any Territory or in the District of Columbia, any woman or girl for the purpose of prostitution or debauchery, or for any other immoral purpose, or with the intent and purpose to induce, entice, or compel such woman or girl to become a prostitute or to give herself up to debauchery, or to engage in any other immoral practice; or who shall knowingly procure or obtain, or cause to be procured or obtained, or aid or assist in procuring or obtaining, any ticket or tickets, or any form of transportation or evidence of the right thereto, to be used by any woman or girl in interstate or foreign commerce, or in any Territory or the District of Columbia, in going to any place for the purpose of prostitution or debauchery, or for any other immoral purpose, or with the intent or purpose on the part of such person to induce, entice, or compel her to give herself up to the practice of prostitution, or to give herself up to the practice of debauchery, or any other immoral practice, whereby any such woman or girl shall be transported in interstate or foreign commerce, or in any Territory or the District of Columbia, shall be deemed guilty of a felony, and upon conviction thereof shall be punished by a fine not exceeding five thousand dollars, or by imprisonment of not more than five years, or by both such fine and imprisonment, in the discretion of the court.

SEC. 3. That any person who shall knowingly persuade, induce, entice, or coerce, or cause to be persuaded, induced, enticed, or coerced, or aid or assist in persuading, inducing, enticing or coercing any woman or girl to go from one place to another in interstate or foreign commerce, or in any Territory or the District of Columbia, for the purpose of prostitution

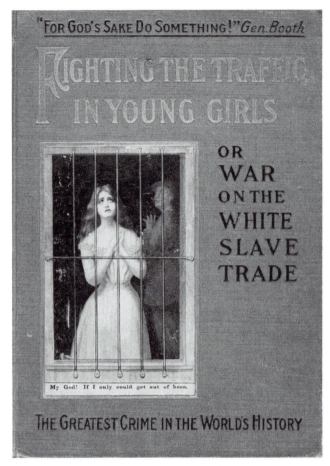

The above is the cover of Ernest A. Bell's (1910) *Fighting the Traffic in Young Girls: or, War on the White Slave Trade* (Chicago: n.p.). Tracts like it were part of a moral panic over the sexuality of young, working-class females at the turn of the century. Reformers fashioned a narrative of passive, white females being kidnapped and forced into prostitution; this fit their beliefs that females would not willingly have sex outside of marriage. While it is unlikely that such kidnappings were occurring, it was true that white, unmarried females were exploring their sexuality, which many reformers saw as akin to prostitution. It was due to this panic that the White-Slave Traffic Act (or Mann Act) was passed.

or debauchery, or for any other immoral purpose, or with the intent and purpose on the part of such person that such woman or girl shall engage in the practice of prostitution or debauchery, or any other immoral practice, whether with or without her consent, and who shall thereby knowingly cause or aid or assist in causing such woman or girl to go and be carried or transported as a passenger upon the line or route of any common carrier or carriers in interstate or foreign commerce, or any Territory or the District of Columbia, shall be deemed guilty of a felony and on conviction thereof shall be punished by a fine of not more than five thousand dollars, or by imprisonment for a term not exceeding five years, or by both fine and imprisonment, in the discretion of the court.

SEC. 4. That any person who shall knowingly persuade, induce, entice or coerce any woman or girl under the age of eighteen years from any State or Territory or the District of Columbia to any other State or Territory or the District of Columbia, with the purpose and intent to induce or coerce her, or that she shall be induced or coerced to engage in prostitution or debauchery, or any other immoral practice, and shall in furtherance of such purpose knowingly induce or cause her to go and to be carried or transported as a passenger in interstate commerce upon the line or route of any common carrier or carriers, shall be deemed guilty of a felony, and in conviction there of shall be punished by a fine of not more than ten thousand dollars, or by imprisonment for a term not exceeding ten years, or by both such fine and imprisonment, in the discretion of the court.

SEC. 5. That any violation of any of the above sections two, three, and four shall be prosecuted in any court having jurisdiction of crimes within the district in which said violation was committed, or from, through, or into which any such woman or girl may have been carried or transported as a passenger in interstate or foreign commerce, or in any Territory or the District of Columbia, contrary to the provisions of any of said sections.

SEC. 6. That for the purpose of regulating and preventing the transportation in foreign commerce of alien women and girls for purposes of prostitution and debauchery, and in pursuance of and for the purpose of carrying out the terms of the agreement of project of arrangement for the suppression of the white-slave traffic, adopted July twenty-fifth, nineteen hundred and two, for submission to their respective governments by the delegates of various powers represented at the Paris conference and confirmed by a formal agreement signed at Paris on May eighteenth, nineteen hundred and four, and adhered to by the United States on June sixth, nineteen hundred and eight, as shown by the proclamation of the President of the United States, dated June fifteenth, nineteen hundred and eight, the Commissioner-General of Immigration is hereby designated as the authority of the United States to receive and centralize information concerning the procuration of alien women and girls with a view to their debauchery, and to exercise supervision over such alien women and girls, receive their declarations, establish their identity, and ascertain from them who induced them to leave their native countries, respectively;

and it shall be the duty of said Commissioner-General of Immigration to receive and keep on file in his office the statements and declarations which may be made by such alien women and girls, and those which are hereinafter required pertaining to such alien women and girls engaged in prostitution and debauchery in this country, and to furnish receipts for such statements and declarations provided for in this act to the persons, respectively, making and filing them.

Every person who shall keep, maintain, control, support or harbor in any house or place for the purpose of prostitution, or for any other immoral purpose, any alien woman or girl within three years after she shall have entered the United States from any country, party to the said arrangement for the suppression of the white-slave traffic, shall file with the Commissioner-General of Immigration a statement in writing setting forth the name of such alien woman or girl, the place at which she is kept, and all facts as to the date of her entry into the United States, the port through which she entered, her age, nationality, and parentage, and concerning her procuration to come to this country within the knowledge of such person, and any person who shall fail within thirty days after such person shall commence to keep, maintain, control, support, or harbor in any house or place for the purpose of prostitution, or for any other immoral purpose, any alien woman or girl within three years after she shall have entered the United States from any of the countries, party to the said arrangement for the suppression of the white-slave traffic, to file such statement concerning such alien woman or girl with the Commissioner-General of Immigration, or who shall knowingly and willfully state falsely or fail to disclose in such statement any fact within his knowledge or belief with reference, to the age, nationality, or parentage of any such alien woman or girl, or concerning her procuration to come to this country, shall be deemed guilty of a misdemeanor, and on conviction shall be punished by a fine of not more than two thousand dollars, or by imprisonment for a term not exceeding two years, or by both such fine and imprisonment, in the discretion of the court.

In any prosecution brought under this section, if it appear that any such statement required is not on file in the office of the Commissioner-General of Immigration, the person whose duty it shall be to file such statement shall be presumed to have failed to file said statement, as herein required, unless such person or persons shall prove otherwise. No person shall be excused from furnishing the statement, as required by this section, on the ground or for the reason that the statement so required by him, or the information therein contained, might tend to criminate him or subject him to a penalty or forfeiture, but no person shall be prosecuted or subjected to any penalty or forfeiture under any law of the United States for or on account of any transaction, matter, or thing, concerning which he may truthfully report in such statement, as required by the provisions of this section.

SEC. 7. That the term "Territory," as used in this Act, shall include the district of Alaska, the insular possessions of the United States, and the Canal Zone. The word "person," as used in this Act, shall be construed to import both the plural and the singular, as the case demands, and shall include corporations, companies, societies, and associations. When construing and enforcing the provisions of this Act, the act, omission, or failure of any officer, agent, or other person, acting for or employed by any other person or by any corporation, company, society, or association, within the scope of his employment or office, shall in every case be also deemed to be the act, omission, or failure of such other person, or of such company, society, or association as well of that of the person himself.

SEC. 8. That this Act shall be known and referred to as the "White-slave traffic Act."

White-Slave Traffic Act of 1910, 61st Cong., 3rd sess., *Congressional Record* 85 (25 June 1910).

4. *Statutory rape laws in the United States initially set the age of consent at 10 or 12. At the end of the nineteenth century, most states raised it to 16 or 18 due to strong lobbying efforts by the Woman's Christian Temperance Union and others. Today, such laws are not uniform across the states—the states set different ages of consent, from 15 to 18; most require that the perpetrator be a certain number of years older than the victim (the number of years varies across the states), but some prosecute same-age perpetrators. Below are some examples: New York's law in 1881, 1916 (as amended in 1895), and 2005 (as amended in 1965 and 2001); one can see the change in the perception of the crime in the changing age of consent, requiring the perpetrator to be older, and the use of gender-neutral language. In Vermont, there is no requirement for the perpetrator to be older than the victim. In California the perpetrator must be older to be prosecuted at the felony level but can be prosecuted at the misdemeanor level at any age. Note also that California links the prosecution of statutory rape to the prevention of teen pregnancy.*

REVISED STATUTES OF NEW YORK 1881, BANKS AND BROTHERS SEVENTH EDITION

Part 4, Ch. 1 (Of Crimes and Punishments), Title 2 [Offences Against One Person]

Every person who shall be convicted of rape, either,

1. By carnally and unlawfully knowing any female child under the age of ten years: or,
2. By forcibly ravishing any woman of the age of ten years or upwards:

Shall be punished by imprisonment in a state prison, not less than ten years.

MCKINNEY'S CONSOLIDATED LAWS OF NEW YORK, 1916. WEST PUBLISHING CO.

§ 2010. Rape defined:

... A person who perpetrates an act of sexual intercourse with a female, not his wife, under the age of eighteen years, under circumstances not amounting to rape in the first degree [forcible rape], is guilty of rape in the second degree, and punishable with imprisonment for not more than ten years.

NEW YORK STATE CONSOLIDATED LAWS [CURRENT THROUGH 2005]

Chapter 40, New York Penal Law, Part 3—Specific Offenses, Title H—Offenses Against the Person Involving Physical Injury, Sexual Conduct, Restraint, and Intimidation

Article 130—Sex Offenses

§ 130.25 Rape in the third degree.

A person is guilty of rape in the third degree when:

1. He or she engages in sexual intercourse with another person who is incapable of consent by reason of some factor other than being less than seventeen years old;
2. Being twenty-one years old or more, he or she engages in sexual intercourse with another person less than seventeen years old; or
3. He or she engages in sexual intercourse with another person without such person's consent where such lack of consent is by reason of some factor other than incapacity to consent.

Rape in the third degree is a class E felony.

§ 130.30 Rape in the second degree.

A person is guilty of rape in the second degree when:

1. being eighteen years old or more, he or she engages in sexual intercourse with another person less than fifteen years old; or
2. he or she engages in sexual intercourse with another person who is incapable of consent by reason of being mentally disabled or mentally incapacitated.

It shall be an affirmative defense to the crime of rape in the second degree as defined in subdivision one of this section that the defendant was less than four years older than the victim at the time of the act.

Rape in the second degree is a class D felony.

§ 130.35 Rape in the first degree.

A person is guilty of rape in the first degree when he or she engages in sexual intercourse with another person:

1. By forcible compulsion; or
2. Who is incapable of consent by reason of being physically helpless; or

3. Who is less than eleven years old; or

4. Who is less than thirteen years old and the actor is eighteen years old or more.

Rape in the first degree is a class B felony.

VERMONT STATUTES TITLE 13: CRIMES AND CRIMINAL PROCEDURE [CURRENT THROUGH 2005]

Chapter 72: Sexual Assault

§ 3252. Sexual assault

(a) A person who engages in a sexual act with another person and
    (1) Compels the other person to participate in a sexual act:
        (A) Without the consent of the other person; or
        (B) By threatening or coercing the other person; or
        (C) By placing the other person in fear that any person will suffer imminent bodily injury; or
    (2) Has impaired substantially the ability of the other person to appraise or control conduct by administering or employing drugs or intoxicants without the knowledge or against the will of the other person; or
    (3) The other person is under the age of 16, except where the persons are married to each other and the sexual act is consensual; or
    (4) The other person is under the age of 18 and is entrusted to the actor's care by authority of law or is the actor's child, grandchild, foster child, adopted child or step-child; shall be imprisoned for not more than 20 years, or fined not more than $10,000.00, or both.
(b) A person who engages in a sexual act with another person under the age of 16 and
    (1) the victim is entrusted to the actor's care by authority of law or is the actor's child, grandchild, foster child, adopted child or step-child; or
    (2) the actor is at least 18 years of age, resides in the victim's household and serves in a parental role with respect to the victim; shall be imprisoned for not more than 35 years, or fined not more than $25,000.00, or both.

CALIFORNIA CODES, CALIFORNIA PENAL CODE [CURRENT THROUGH 2005]

Part 1 Of Crimes and Punishments, Title 9 Of Crimes Against the Person Involving Sexual Assault, and Crimes Against Public Decency and Good Morals, Chapter 1. Rape, Abduction, Carnal Abuse of Children, and Seduction.

§ 261.5. (a) Unlawful sexual intercourse is an act of sexual intercourse accomplished with a person who is not the spouse of the perpetrator, if the person is a minor. For the purposes of this section, a "minor" is a person under the age of 18 years and an "adult" is a person who is at least 18 years of age.

(b) Any person who engages in an act of unlawful sexual intercourse with a minor who is not more than three years older or three years younger than the perpetrator, is guilty of a misdemeanor.

(c) Any person who engages in an act of unlawful sexual intercourse with a minor who is more than three years younger than the perpetrator is guilty of either a misdemeanor or a felony, and shall be punished by imprisonment in a county jail not exceeding one year, or by imprisonment in the state prison.

(d) Any person 21 years of age or older who engages in an act of unlawful sexual intercourse with a minor who is under 16 years of age is guilty of either a misdemeanor or a felony, and shall be punished by imprisonment in a county jail not exceeding one year, or by imprisonment in the state prison for two, three, or four years.

(e) (1) Notwithstanding any other provision of this section, an adult who engages in an act of sexual intercourse with a minor in violation of this section may be liable for civil penalties in the following amounts:

   (A) An adult who engages in an act of unlawful sexual intercourse with a minor less than two years younger than the adult is liable for a civil penalty not to exceed two thousand dollars ($2,000).

   (B) An adult who engages in an act of unlawful sexual intercourse with a minor at least two years younger than the adult is liable for a civil penalty not to exceed five thousand dollars ($5,000).

   (C) An adult who engages in an act of unlawful sexual intercourse with a minor at least three years younger than the adult is liable for a civil penalty not to exceed ten thousand dollars ($10,000).

   (D) An adult over the age of 21 years who engages in an act of unlawful sexual intercourse with a minor under 16 years of age is liable for a civil penalty not to exceed twenty-five thousand dollars ($25,000).

   (2) The district attorney may bring actions to recover civil penalties pursuant to this subdivision. From the amounts collected for each case, an amount equal to the costs of pursuing the action shall be deposited with the treasurer of the county in which the judgment was entered, and the remainder shall be deposited in the Underage Pregnancy Prevention Fund, which is hereby created in the State Treasury. Amounts deposited in the Underage Pregnancy Prevention Fund may be used only for the purpose of preventing underage pregnancy upon appropriation by the Legislature.

   (3) In addition to any punishment imposed under this section, the judge may assess a fine not to exceed seventy dollars ($70) against any person who violates this section with the proceeds of this fine to be used in accordance with Section 1463.23. The court shall, however, take into consideration the defendant's ability to pay, and no defendant shall be denied probation because of his or her inability to pay the fine permitted under this subdivision.

Examples of Statutory Rape Laws: New York in 1881, 1916, and 2005; Vermont 2005; California 2005.

8 Teen Pregnancies and Responses to Them

1. The first Florence Crittenden Mission opened in New York City in 1883 to redeem "fallen" young women; by the end of the nineteenth century, this focused almost entirely on young, unwed mothers. The following statement from one Crittenden Home in West Virginia, explaining its mission and its work, was printed on the first anniversary of its founding.

The Florence Crittenden Rescue Home will be one year old to-day, and its work so far has been carried on very successfully by the Women's Christian Temperance Union. The following statement of what has been accomplished at the home, and an expression of thanks from the secretary will prove interesting at this time.

The Florence Crittenden Rescue Home which was opened April 1, 1895, is situated on Seventeenth Street, No. 71. The object of this rescue home is to aid fallen and betrayed girls to lead pure lives. No board on price is asked or taken from an inmate. Neither is there any compulsion used to keep one. No one can remain in the home unless she declares her purpose to lead a good life and obey the matron and the rules of the house. Our first desire is to reinstate a girl in the hearts of her kindred, and in that way a number who were supposed to be dead by their parents or friends, or worse than dead, have been invited to return to the home of their childhood. During the year we have sheltered (some for months) twenty-six girls. As I write, the faces and sad histories of many pass before me. I could write until the public would grow weary, and then the half would not have been told. Most of our girls plead guilty—but few blame their parents. It is usually the story of late hours at night, and drink, and how bitterly they grieve over their own destruction. When inmates of the jail, or of "houses of shame" are told that there are women that pity them and are reaching out their hands to help them, they think it a delusion and snare to entrap them, and the quiet little house on Seventeenth Street they fear is a prison.

The girls of the rescue home do the work of the house and dew, and usually in a few weeks desire places to earn their living. The board of managers do all they can to help all who are able to get places, and encourage them to be faithful in all things. If one falls sick or finds she cannot give satisfaction, we will take her in until she secures another home. The public has been very kind to us, giving us money and kind words—trusting us one year ago when we had nothing to show them or tell them. Now we can tell you that we used the money you gave us, in the fear of God, for the uplifting of the forsaken and say to you for them: "Blessed are the merciful, for they shall obtain mercy."

The women of the Woman's Christian Temperance Union expect to continue this work as long as a girl says, "I am so tired, I wish I was dead."

Our home can be seen during every day, but the Sabbath, by visitors. The matron will kindly give any information required.

We of the board of managers thank the public again for the great confidence shown us, and can say that after a year's contact with the sorrowing, we have more faith in the All Father and humanity than we ever had.

We thank all the newspapers of the city. Also the chief of police and staff for their kindness to us.

We thank all who have aided us and ask that they continue their gifts; although they may seem small to the donor, yet to us they are great. While we need help for the coming year, we are glad to say our "Rescue Home is free from debt and we are very hopeful for the future."

He, the Maker, knows what is best,

Hope is strength, and trust is rest.

The Board of Managers of the Florence Crittenden Rescue Home. 1896. "The Rescue Home. To-day is the First Anniversary of Its Organization. An Official Statement." *Wheeling Daily Intelligencer,* 1 April.

2. *Decided in 1981,* Michael M. v. Superior Court of Sonoma County *is the only case heard by the United States Supreme Court dealing with statutory rape. Here the Court held that gender-specific statutory rape laws (prosecuting only males and protecting only females) were constitutional. The Court stated that such a law would serve as a means to deter teenage pregnancies; the justices reasoned that females should feel deterred from (heterosexual) sex by fear of getting pregnant, and a law punishing only males would "'equalize' the deterrents on the sexes." The dissenters wrote that pregnancy prevention was never the purpose behind such laws; rather, they were intended to preserve female chastity before marriage.*

JUSTICE REHNQUIST ANNOUNCED THE JUDGMENT OF THE COURT AND DELIVERED AN OPINION, IN WHICH THE CHIEF JUSTICE, JUSTICE STEWART, AND JUSTICE POWELL JOINED

The question presented in this case is whether California's "statutory rape" law ... violates the Equal Protection Clause of the Fourteenth Amendment. Section 261.5 defines unlawful sexual intercourse as "an act of sexual intercourse accomplished with a female not the wife of the perpetrator, where the female is under the age of 18 years." The statute thus makes men alone criminally liable for the act of sexual intercourse.

In July, 1978, a complaint was filed in the Municipal Court of Sonoma County, Cal., alleging that petitioner, then a 17 1/2-year-old male, had had unlawful sexual intercourse with a female under the age of 18, in violation of § 261.5. The evidence adduced at a preliminary hearing showed that, at approximately midnight on June 3, 1978, petitioner and two friends approached Sharon, a 16 1/2-year-old female, and her sister as they waited at a bus stop. Petitioner and Sharon, who had already been drinking, moved away from the others and began to kiss. After being struck in the face for rebuffing petitioner's initial advances, Sharon submitted to sexual intercourse with petitioner. Prior to trial, petitioner sought to set aside the information on both state and federal constitutional grounds, asserting that § 261.5 unlawfully discriminated on the basis of gender. The trial court and the California Court of Appeal denied petitioner's request for relief, and petitioner sought review in the Supreme Court of California....

Canvassing "the tragic human costs of illegitimate teenage pregnancies," including the large number of teenage abortions, the increased medical risk associated with teenage pregnancies, and the social consequences of teenage childbearing, the court concluded that the State has a compelling interest in preventing such pregnancies. Because males alone can "physiologically cause the result which the law properly seeks to avoid," the court further held that the gender classification was readily justified as a means of identifying offender and victim. For the reasons stated below, we affirm the judgment of the California Supreme Court.

... In *Reed v. Reed*, for example, the Court stated that a gender-based classification will be upheld if it bears a "fair and substantial relationship" to legitimate state ends, while in *Craig v. Boren*, the Court restated the test to require the classification to bear a "substantial relationship" to "important governmental objectives."

... But because the Equal Protection Clause does not "demand that a statute necessarily apply equally to all persons" or require "'things which are different in fact ... to be treated in law as though they were the same,'" ... this Court has consistently upheld statutes where the gender classification is not invidious, but rather realistically reflects the fact that the sexes are not similarly situated in certain circumstances....

We are satisfied not only that the prevention of illegitimate pregnancy is at least one of the "purposes" of the statute, but also that the State has a strong interest in preventing such pregnancy. At the risk of stating the obvious, teenage pregnancies, which have increased dramatically over the last two decades, have significant social, medical, and economic consequences for both the mother and her child, and the State. Of particular concern to the State is that approximately half of all teenage pregnancies end in abortion. And of those children who are born, their illegitimacy makes them likely candidates to become wards of the State.

We need not be medical doctors to discern that young men and young women are not similarly situated with respect to the problems and the risks of sexual intercourse. Only women may become pregnant, and they suffer disproportionately the profound physical, emotional, and psychological consequences of sexual activity. The statute at issue here protects women from sexual intercourse at an age when those consequences are particularly severe.

The question thus boils down to whether a State may attack the problem of sexual intercourse and teenage pregnancy directly by prohibiting a male from having sexual intercourse with a minor female. We hold that such a statute is sufficiently related to the State's objectives to pass constitutional muster.

Because virtually all of the significant harmful and inescapably identifiable consequences of teenage pregnancy fall on the young female, a legislature acts well within its authority when it elects to punish only the participant who, by nature, suffers few of the consequences of his conduct. It is hardly unreasonable for a legislature acting to protect minor females to exclude them from punishment. Moreover, the risk of pregnancy itself constitutes a substantial deterrence to young females. No similar natural sanctions deter males. A criminal sanction imposed solely on males thus serves to roughly "equalize" the deterrents on the sexes.

We are unable to accept petitioner's contention that the statute is impermissibly underinclusive and must, in order to pass judicial scrutiny, be *broadened* so as to hold the female as criminally liable as the male. It is argued that this statute is not *necessary* to deter teenage pregnancy because a gender-neutral statute, where both male and female would be subject to prosecution, would serve that goal equally well. The relevant inquiry, however, is not whether the statute is drawn as precisely as it might have been, but whether the line chosen by the California Legislature is within constitutional limitations. ...

In any event, we cannot say that a gender-neutral statute would be as effective as the statute California has chosen to enact. The State persuasively contends that a gender-neutral statute would frustrate its interest in effective enforcement. Its view is that a female is surely less likely to report violations of the statute if she herself would be subject to criminal prosecution. In an area already fraught with prosecutorial difficulties, we decline to hold that the Equal Protection Clause requires a legislature to enact a statute so broad that it may well be incapable of enforcement.

We similarly reject petitioner's argument that § 261.5 is impermissibly overbroad because it makes unlawful sexual intercourse with prepubescent females, who are, by definition, incapable of becoming pregnant. Quite apart from the fact that the statute could well be justified on the grounds that very young females are particularly susceptible to physical injury from sexual intercourse ... it is ludicrous to suggest that the Constitution requires the California Legislature to limit the scope of its rape statute to older teenagers and exclude young girls.

There remains only petitioner's contention that the statute is unconstitutional as it is applied to him because he, like Sharon, was under 18 at the time of sexual intercourse. Petitioner argues that the statute is flawed because it presumes that, as between two persons under 18, the male is the culpable aggressor. We find petitioner's contentions unpersuasive. Contrary to his assertions, the statute does not rest on the assumption that males are generally the aggressors. It is, instead, an attempt by a legislature to prevent illegitimate teenage pregnancy by providing an additional deterrent for men. The age of the man is irrelevant, since young men are as capable as older men of inflicting the harm sought to be prevented.

In upholding the California statute, we also recognize that this is not a case where a statute is being challenged on the grounds that it "invidiously discriminates" against females. To the contrary, the statute places a burden on males which is not shared by females. But we find nothing to suggest that men, because of past discrimination or peculiar disadvantages, are in need of the special solicitude of the courts.... [T]he statute instead reasonably reflects the fact that the consequences of sexual intercourse and pregnancy fall more heavily on the female than on the male.

Accordingly the judgment of the California Supreme Court is *Affirmed.*

JUSTICE BLACKMUN, CONCURRING IN THE JUDGMENT

It is gratifying that the plurality recognizes that, "[a]t the risk of stating the obvious, teenage pregnancies ... have increased dramatically over the last two decades," and "have significant social, medical, and economic consequences for both the mother and her child, and the State."

... I am persuaded that, although a minor has substantial privacy rights in intimate affairs connected with procreation, California's efforts to prevent teenage pregnancy are to be viewed differently from Utah's efforts [through a statute criminalizing performing an abortion on a minor unless her parents were notified] to inhibit a woman from dealing with pregnancy once it has become an inevitability.

... I think too that it is only fair, with respect to this particular petitioner, to point out that his partner, Sharon, appears not to have been an unwilling participant in at least the initial stages of the intimacies that took place the night of June 3, 1978. Petitioner's and Sharon's nonacquaintance with each other before the incident; their drinking; their withdrawal from the others of the group; their foreplay, in which she willingly participated and seems to have encouraged; and the closeness of their ages (a difference of only one year and 18 days) are factors that should make this case an unattractive one to prosecute at all, and especially to prosecute as a felony, rather than as a misdemeanor chargeable under § 261.5. But the State has chosen to prosecute in that manner, and the facts, I reluctantly conclude, may fit the crime.

JUSTICE BRENNAN, WITH WHOM JUSTICES WHITE AND MARSHALL JOIN, DISSENTING

... I fear that the plurality opinion and JUSTICES STEWART and BLACKMUN reach the opposite result by placing too much emphasis on the desirability of achieving the State's asserted statutory goal—prevention of teenage pregnancy—and not enough emphasis on the fundamental question of whether the sex-based discrimination in the California statute is substantially related to the achievement of that goal....

The State of California vigorously asserts that the "important governmental objective" to be served by § 261.5 is the prevention of teenage pregnancy. It claims that its statute furthers this goal by deterring sexual activity by males—the class of persons it considers more responsible for causing those pregnancies. But even assuming that prevention of teenage pregnancy is an important governmental objective and that it is, in fact, an objective of § 261.5 ... California still has the burden of proving that there are fewer teenage pregnancies under its gender-based statutory rape law than there would be if the law were gender-neutral. To meet this burden, the State must show that, because its statutory rape law punishes only males, and not females, it more effectively deters minor females from having sexual intercourse....

The State has not produced such evidence in this case. Moreover, there are at least two serious flaws in the State's assertion that law enforcement problems created by a gender-neutral statutory rape law would make such a statute less effective than a gender-based statute in deterring sexual activity....

There are now at least 37 States that have enacted gender-neutral statutory rape laws. Although most of these laws protect young persons (of either sex) from the sexual exploitation of older individuals, the laws of Arizona, Florida, and Illinois permit prosecution of both minor females and minor males for engaging in mutual sexual conduct....

In addition, the California Legislature in recent years has revised other sections of the Penal Code to make them gender-neutral....

Until very recently, no California court or commentator had suggested that the purpose of California's statutory rape law was to protect young women from the risk of pregnancy. Indeed, the historical development of § 261.5 demonstrates that the law was initially enacted on the premise that young women, in contrast to young men, were to be deemed legally incapable of consenting to an act of sexual intercourse. Because their chastity was considered particularly precious, those young women were felt to be uniquely in need of the State's protection. In contrast, young men were assumed to be capable of making such decisions for themselves; the law therefore did not offer them any special protection.

It is perhaps because the gender classification in California's statutory rape law was initially designed to further these outmoded sexual stereotypes, rather than to reduce the incidence of teenage pregnancies, that the State has been unable to demonstrate a substantial relationship between the classification and its newly asserted goal....

I would hold that § 261.5 violates the Equal Protection Clause of the Fourteenth Amendment, and I would reverse the judgment of the California Supreme Court.

JUSTICE STEVENS, DISSENTING

Local custom and belief—rather than statutory laws of venerable but doubtful ancestry—will determine the volume of sexual activity among unmarried teenagers....

In my opinion, the only acceptable justification for a general rule requiring disparate treatment of the two participants in a joint act must be a legislative judgment that one is more guilty than the other.... The fact that the California Legislature has decided to apply its prohibition only to the male may reflect a legislative judgment that, in the typical case the male is actually the more guilty party. Any such judgment must, in turn, assume that the decision to engage in the risk-creating conduct is always—or at least typically—a male decision. If that assumption is valid, the statutory classification should also be valid. But what is the support for the assumption? It is not contained in the record of this case or in any legislative history or scholarly study that has been called to our attention. I think it is supported to some extent by traditional attitudes toward male-female relationships. But the possibility that such a habitual attitude may reflect nothing more than an irrational prejudice makes it an insufficient justification for discriminatory treatment that is otherwise blatantly unfair. For, as I read this statute, it requires that one, and only one, of two equally guilty wrongdoers be stigmatized by a criminal conviction....

I respectfully dissent.

Michael M. v. Superior Court of Sonoma County, 450 U.S. 464 (1981). http://www.law.cornell.edu/supct/html/historics/USSC_CR_0450_0464_ZO.html

3. Also known as the Welfare Reform Act, the Personal Responsibility and Work Opportunity Reconciliation Act (PRWORA) replaced the federal guarantee of cash assistance formerly provided by Aid to Families with Dependent Children. It stressed replacing welfare with work, collecting child support, and reducing dependency. But the PRWORA had social objectives as well, most of which emphasized the need to change the sexual and reproductive behavior of the poor, young, and unmarried. With its first words, "marriage is the foundation of a successful society," it goes on to link teen pregnancy to welfare dependency, low educational attainment, and juvenile delinquency. To combat these problems, the PRWORA funds programs that decrease teen births and abortions, prosecute statutory rape, and promote teens' abstinence from sexual activity.

An Act to provide for reconciliation pursuant to section 201(a)(1) of the concurrent resolution on the budget for fiscal year 1997.

Be it enacted by the Senate and House of Representatives of the United States of America in Congress assembled,

SECTION 1. SHORT TITLE

This Act may be cited as the 'Personal Responsibility and Work Opportunity Reconciliation Act of 1996'....

TITLE I—BLOCK GRANTS FOR TEMPORARY ASSISTANCE FOR NEEDY FAMILIES

SEC. 101. FINDINGS

The Congress makes the following findings:

(1) Marriage is the foundation of a successful society.

(2) Marriage is an essential institution of a successful society which promotes the interests of children.

(3) Promotion of responsible fatherhood and motherhood is integral to successful child rearing and the well-being of children.

(4) In 1992, only 54 percent of single-parent families with children had a child support order established and, of that 54 percent, only about one-half received the full amount due. Of the cases enforced through the public child support enforcement system, only 18 percent of the caseload has a collection.

(5) The number of individuals receiving aid to families with dependent children (in this section referred to as 'AFDC') has more than tripled since 1965. More than two-thirds of these recipients are children. Eighty-nine percent of children receiving AFDC benefits now live in homes in which no father is present.

    (A)(i) The average monthly number of children receiving AFDC benefits—

(I) was 3,300,000 in 1965;

(II) was 6,200,000 in 1970;

(III) was 7,400,000 in 1980; and

(IV) was 9,300,000 in 1992.

(ii) While the number of children receiving AFDC benefits increased nearly threefold between 1965 and 1992, the total number of children in the United States aged 0 to 18 has declined by 5.5 percent.

(B) The Department of Health and Human Services has estimated that 12,000,000 children will receive AFDC benefits within 10 years.

(C) The increase in the number of children receiving public assistance is closely related to the increase in births to unmarried women. Between 1970 and 1991, the percentage of live births to unmarried women increased nearly threefold, from 10.7 percent to 29.5 percent.

(6) The increase of out-of-wedlock pregnancies and births is well documented as follows:

(A) It is estimated that the rate of nonmarital teen pregnancy rose 23 percent from 54 pregnancies per 1,000 unmarried teenagers in 1976 to 66.7 pregnancies in 1991. The overall rate of nonmarital pregnancy rose 14 percent from 90.8 pregnancies per 1,000 unmarried women in 1980 to 103 in both 1991 and 1992. In contrast, the overall pregnancy rate for married couples decreased 7.3 percent between 1980 and 1991, from 126.9 pregnancies per 1,000 married women in 1980 to 117.6 pregnancies in 1991.

(B) The total of all out-of-wedlock births between 1970 and 1991 has risen from 10.7 percent to 29.5 percent and if the current trend continues, 50 percent of all births by the year 2015 will be out-of-wedlock.

(7) An effective strategy to combat teenage pregnancy must address the issue of male responsibility, including statutory rape culpability and prevention. The increase of teenage pregnancies among the youngest girls is particularly severe and is linked to predatory sexual practices by men who are significantly older.

(A) It is estimated that in the late 1980's, the rate for girls age 14 and under giving birth increased 26 percent.

(B) Data indicates that at least half of the children born to teenage mothers are fathered by adult men. Available data suggests that almost 70 percent of births to teenage girls are fathered by men over age 20.

(C) Surveys of teen mothers have revealed that a majority of such mothers have histories of sexual and physical abuse, primarily with older adult men.

(8) The negative consequences of an out-of-wedlock birth on the mother, the child, the family, and society are well documented as follows:

(A) Young women 17 and under who give birth outside of marriage are more likely to go on public assistance and to spend more years on welfare once enrolled. These combined effects of 'younger and longer' increase total AFDC costs per household by 25 percent to 30 percent for 17-year-olds.

(B) Children born out-of-wedlock have a substantially higher risk of being born at a very low or moderately low birth weight.

(C) Children born out-of-wedlock are more likely to experience low ver-
bal cognitive attainment, as well as more child abuse, and neglect.

(D) Children born out-of-wedlock are more likely to have lower cognitive scores, lower educational aspirations, and a greater likelihood of
becoming teenage parents themselves.

(E) Being born out-of-wedlock significantly reduces the chances of the
child growing up to have an intact marriage.

(F) Children born out-of-wedlock are 3 times more likely to be on welfare
when they grow up.

(9) Currently 35 percent of children in single-parent homes were born out-
of-wedlock, nearly the same percentage as that of children in single-parent
homes whose parents are divorced (37 percent). While many parents
find themselves, through divorce or tragic circumstances beyond their
control, facing the difficult task of raising children alone, nevertheless,
the negative consequences of raising children in single-parent homes are
well documented as follows:

(A) Only 9 percent of married-couple families with children under 18
years of age have income below the national poverty level. In contrast,
46 percent of female-headed households with children under 18
years of age are below the national poverty level.

(B) Among single-parent families, nearly 1/2 of the mothers who never
married received AFDC while only 1/5 of divorced mothers received
AFDC.

(C) Children born into families receiving welfare assistance are 3 times
more likely to be on welfare when they reach adulthood than children not born into families receiving welfare.

(D) Mothers under 20 years of age are at the greatest risk of bearing low
birth weight babies.

(E) The younger the single-parent mother, the less likely she is to finish
high school.

(F) Young women who have children before finishing high school are
more likely to receive welfare assistance for a longer period of time.

(G) Between 1985 and 1990, the public cost of births to teenage mothers
under the aid to families with dependent children program, the food
stamp program, and the medicaid program has been estimated at
$120,000,000,000.

(H) The absence of a father in the life of a child has a negative effect on
school performance and peer adjustment.

(I) Children of teenage single parents have lower cognitive scores, lower
educational aspirations, and a greater likelihood of becoming teenage parents themselves.

(J) Children of single-parent homes are 3 times more likely to fail and
repeat a year in grade school than are children from intact 2-parent
families.

(K) Children from single-parent homes are almost 4 times more likely to
be expelled or suspended from school.

(L) Neighborhoods with larger percentages of youth aged 12 through 20
and areas with higher percentages of single-parent households have
higher rates of violent crime.

(M) Of those youth held for criminal offenses within the State juvenile justice system, only 29.8 percent lived primarily in a home with both parents. In contrast to these incarcerated youth, 73.9 percent of the 62,800,000 children in the Nation's resident population were living with both parents.

(10) Therefore, in light of this demonstration of the crisis in our Nation, it is the sense of the Congress that prevention of out-of-wedlock pregnancy and reduction in out-of-wedlock birth are very important Government interests and the policy contained in part A of title IV of the Social Security Act (as amended by section 103(a) of this Act) is intended to address the crisis....

PART A—BLOCK GRANTS TO STATES FOR TEMPORARY ASSISTANCE FOR NEEDY FAMILIES

SEC. 401. PURPOSE

(a) IN GENERAL- The purpose of this part is to increase the flexibility of States in operating a program designed to—
   (1) provide assistance to needy families so that children may be cared for in their own homes or in the homes of relatives;
   (2) end the dependence of needy parents on government benefits by promoting job preparation, work, and marriage;
   (3) prevent and reduce the incidence of out-of-wedlock pregnancies and establish annual numerical goals for preventing and reducing the incidence of these pregnancies; and
   (4) encourage the formation and maintenance of two-parent families.
(b) NO INDIVIDUAL ENTITLEMENT- This part shall not be interpreted to entitle any individual or family to assistance under any State program funded under this part....

SEC. 402. ELIGIBLE STATES; STATE PLAN

(a) IN GENERAL- As used in this part, the term 'eligible State' means, with respect to a fiscal year, a State that, during the 2-year period immediately preceding the fiscal year, has submitted to the Secretary a plan that the Secretary has found includes the following:
   (1) OUTLINE OF FAMILY ASSISTANCE PROGRAM
      (A) GENERAL PROVISIONS- A written document that outlines how the State intends to do the following:
         (i) Conduct a program, designed to serve all political subdivisions in the State (not necessarily in a uniform manner), that provides assistance to needy families with (or expecting) children and provides parents with job preparation, work, and support services to enable them to leave the program and become self-sufficient.
         (ii) Require a parent or caretaker receiving assistance under the program to engage in work (as defined by the State) once the State determines the parent or caretaker is ready to engage in work, or once the parent or caretaker has received assistance under the

program for 24 months (whether or not consecutive), whichever is earlier.

(iii) Ensure that parents and caretakers receiving assistance under the program engage in work activities in accordance with section 407.

(iv) Take such reasonable steps as the State deems necessary to restrict the use and disclosure of information about individuals and families receiving assistance under the program attributable to funds provided by the Federal Government.

(v) Establish goals and take action to prevent and reduce the incidence of out-of-wedlock pregnancies, with special emphasis on teenage pregnancies, and establish numerical goals for reducing the illegitimacy ratio of the State (as defined in section 403(a)(2)(B)) for calendar years 1996 through 2005.

(vi) Conduct a program, designed to reach State and local law enforcement officials, the education system, and relevant counseling services, that provides education and training on the problem of statutory rape so that teenage pregnancy prevention programs may be expanded in scope to include men....

SEC. 905. ESTABLISHING NATIONAL GOALS TO PREVENT TEENAGE PREGNANCIES

(a) IN GENERAL- Not later than January 1, 1997, the Secretary of Health and Human Services shall establish and implement a strategy for—
   (1) preventing out-of-wedlock teenage pregnancies, and
   (2) assuring that at least 25 percent of the communities in the United States have teenage pregnancy prevention programs in place.

(b) REPORT- Not later than June 30, 1998, and annually thereafter, the Secretary shall report to the Congress with respect to the progress that has been made in meeting the goals described in paragraphs (1) and (2) of subsection (a).

SEC. 906. SENSE OF THE SENATE REGARDING ENFORCEMENT OF STATUTORY RAPE LAWS

(a) SENSE OF THE SENATE- It is the sense of the Senate that States and local jurisdictions should aggressively enforce statutory rape laws.

(b) JUSTICE DEPARTMENT PROGRAM ON STATUTORY RAPE- Not later than January 1, 1997, the Attorney General shall establish and implement a program that—
   (1) studies the linkage between statutory rape and teenage pregnancy, particularly by predatory older men committing repeat offenses; and
   (2) educates State and local criminal law enforcement officials on the prevention and prosecution of statutory rape, focusing in particular on the commission of statutory rape by predatory older men committing repeat offenses, and any links to teenage pregnancy.

(c) VIOLENCE AGAINST WOMEN INITIATIVE- The Attorney General shall ensure that the Department of Justice's Violence Against Women initiative addresses the issue of statutory rape, particularly the commission of statutory rape by predatory older men committing repeat offenses....

SEC. 912. ABSTINENCE EDUCATION

Title V of the Social Security Act (42 U.S.C. 701 et seq.) is amended by adding at the end the following section:

SEPARATE PROGRAM FOR ABSTINENCE EDUCATION

SEC. 510. (a) For the purpose described in subsection (b), the Secretary shall, for fiscal year 1998 and each subsequent fiscal year, allot to each State which has transmitted an application for the fiscal year under section 505(a) an amount equal to the product of—
  (1) the amount appropriated in subsection (d) for the fiscal year; and
  (2) the percentage determined for the State under section 502(c)(1)(B)(ii).
(b)(1) The purpose of an allotment under subsection (a) to a State is to enable the State to provide abstinence education, and at the option of the State, where appropriate, mentoring, counseling, and adult supervision to promote abstinence from sexual activity, with a focus on those groups which are most likely to bear children out-of-wedlock.
  (2) For purposes of this section, the term 'abstinence education' means an educational or motivational program which—
    (A) has as its exclusive purpose, teaching the social, psychological, and health gains to be realized by abstaining from sexual activity;
    (B) teaches abstinence from sexual activity outside marriage as the expected standard for all school age children;
    (C) teaches that abstinence from sexual activity is the only certain way to avoid out-of-wedlock pregnancy, sexually transmitted diseases, and other associated health problems;
    (D) teaches that a mutually faithful monogamous relationship in context of marriage is the expected standard of human sexual activity;
    (E) teaches that sexual activity outside of the context of marriage is likely to have harmful psychological and physical effects;
    (F) teaches that bearing children out-of-wedlock is likely to have harmful consequences for the child, the child's parents, and society;
    (G) teaches young people how to reject sexual advances and how alcohol and drug use increases vulnerability to sexual advances; and
    (H) teaches the importance of attaining self-sufficiency before engaging in sexual activity.
(c)(1) Sections 503, 507, and 508 apply to allotments under subsection (a) to the same extent and in the same manner as such sections apply to allotments under section 502(c).
  (2) Sections 505 and 506 apply to allotments under subsection (a) to the extent determined by the Secretary to be appropriate.

(d) For the purpose of allotments under subsection (a), there is appropriated, out of any money in the Treasury not otherwise appropriated, an additional $50,000,000 for each of the fiscal years 1998 through 2002. The appropriation under the preceding sentence for a fiscal year is made on October 1 of the fiscal year....

Personal Responsibility and Work Opportunity Reconciliation Act [PRWORA] of 1996, PL 104–193, 110 Stat 2105 (August 22, 1996).

9 Images of Adolescent Sexuality

The first 14 images in this chapter are from the Social Welfare History Archives, University of Minnesota Libraries. They are part of a 96-poster series, 48 for boys and 48 for girls. The boys' series, begun in 1918 by the U.S. Public Health Service and the Young Men's Christian Association, was called "Keeping Fit"; the girls' series was adapted from it in 1922 by the American Social Hygiene Association and was called "Youth and Life." The posters were widely seen; one early report claimed that by the 1920s, they had been viewed by 750,000 people. This sex education program begins with positive images of being "fit": taking care of one's hygiene and diet, exercising, and reading. It then continues on to emphasize the negatives of sexual thoughts and sexual activity before marriage. While some images or texts were used in both series, those that differed from one another showed the ways in which males and females were assumed to be quite different in temperament, values, and goals.

The remaining images depict scenes from contemporary film: *Blue Denim* (1959), *The Last Picture Show* (1971), and *Kids* (1995). They have been reproduced, respectively, courtesy of Twentieth Century Fox, Columbia Pictures, and Miramax Film Corp.

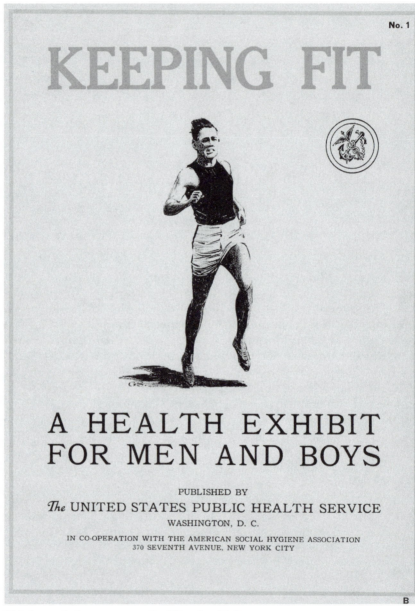

This image is the cover page for "Keeping Fit."

Outdoor Life

1. Athletics
2. Abundant outdoor life
3. Wholesome companions
4. Lots of good fun
5. Constant employment
6. Will power

will help a boy break the habit called "self-abuse" (in case he has acquired the habit) and recover from any harm it may have done. This habit does not produce the terrible effects some ignorant people say it does. Most boys who have abused themselves stop before any great harm is done. Self-abuse may, however, seriously hinder a boy's progress toward vigorous manhood. It is a selfish, childish, stupid habit. The strong boy will "cut it out"

B

"Outdoor Life" was the fourteenth image of "Keeping Fit"; it was preceded by images of boys engaged in sports such as running, baseball, and football. The accompanying text emphasized proper exercise, diet, cleanliness, and sleeping habits. This image appears at first to follow along those lines, but note the fine print: if a boy engages in all of these exercises and he works, it will help a boy stop engaging in "self abuse" (masturbation), a "selfish, childish, and stupid habit."

How the Mind Affects the Body

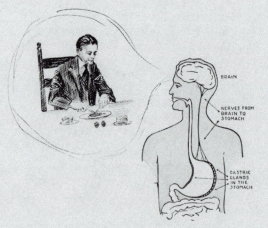

The thought of food when one is hungry causes a secretion to flow from the gastric glands of the stomach

Merely thinking how a lemon tastes will increase the flow of saliva

Sex thoughts cause the blood to flow to the sex organs and so produce excitement. Continued thinking about sex matters is harmful

B

After two images telling boys that nocturnal seminal emissions are normal and to be expected, "How the Mind Affects the Body" warns that "continued thinking about sex matters is harmful."

By Courtesy of St. Nicholas

This girl may become an invalid for life if she marries a man who has had gonorrhea not entirely cured

Gonorrhea Causes

1. Many surgical operations upon women
2. Much invalidism among innocent wives
3. Many childless marriages

B

After a number of images advising boys to use their minds constructively with reading good books, and using their bodies constructively by exercising, the text warns boys that they must exercise self-control—they must not "indulge in sexual intercourse with immoral girls," because they might catch a venereal disease. "Girl Shouldn't Marry Man with Gonorrhea," shows in soft focus the wholesome girl who is out there waiting for the boy to marry her, and the following image warns that just as boys expect their future wives to be pure when they go to the altar, the boys should be pure as well.

Do Not Believe Him

if some "wise guy" tells you that sexual intercourse is not dangerous

---

The facts are

A girl who would yield to one man has probably had relations with another. Very likely she is diseased

Most prostitutes (private or public) have either syphilis or gonorrhea or both

Furthermore, there are no antiseptics, prophylactic treatments or other preventives which assure absolute safety

B

"Do Not Believe Him" warns boys not to have sex with girls who are willing to have sex with them. She is either immoral or a prostitute. If a girl is willing to have sex, she has probably had sex before and might be carrying a disease, for which there is no quick cure.

Reproduction in the Plant

Pollen carried from another flower by a bee to the top of pistil

Pollen containing a "sperm" or male cell

Pistil Stamen

Sperm cell from pollen traveling through pistil to an ovum

"Ovum" or female cell

B

The parts of the flower are
the sex organs of the plant

"Reproduction in the Plant" begins a series of five images about reproduction. Following "Reproduction in the Plant" are pictures of reproduction in salmon, chicks, and rabbits. Relating human reproduction to plants and animals was common in sex education tracts.

Human Reproduction

The human baby also develops within the body of the mother. The ovum, or egg cell, within the mother is fertilized by the male cell, or sperm, which comes from the father

The fertilized egg cell develops within the body of the mother for about nine months, and then the child is born

Without the reproductive, or sex organs, the boy could not become a father

B

"Human Reproduction," unlike the pictures and drawings of chicks and rabbits carrying developing young inside them, displays a painting of a lovely white mother and her equally lovely child. While the text is accurate, it may not have taught boys and girls much about how to reproduce. The images following this one extol the virtues of family and purity, and the last few display famous men who have achieved greatness though keeping fit in body and mind.

YOUTH AND LIFE

AN EXHIBIT FOR GIRLS AND YOUNG WOMEN

APPROVED BY

THE UNITED STATES PUBLIC HEALTH SERVICE

PUBLISHED BY

THE AMERICAN SOCIAL HYGIENE ASSOCIATION
370 SEVENTH AVENUE, NEW YORK CITY

© Campbell Art Co.

Youth and Life Exhibit. Part No. 1. (Forty-eight Parts.) Copyright 1922, by The American Social Hygiene Association

"Youth and Life" was the girls' series, four years after the boys' series. Unlike the cover page of "Keeping Fit," showing the boy exercising, this cover shows a girl properly dressed and apparently contemplating all that life has to offer her if she is fit.

By courtesy of St. Nicholas

The secretion of the ovaries makes the girl grow into a woman

The secretion in the testes makes the boy grow into a man

The ovaries and testes also make possible fatherhood and motherhood—reproduction

Youth and Life Exhibit. Part No. 17. (Forty-eight Parts.) Copyright 1922, by The American Social Hygiene Association

Like "Keeping Fit," this series begins with talking about health and fitness. There are some differences for girls, however. The first few images mention motherhood and its importance, and subsequent images talk about beauty being on the inside and stemming from health and how much fun walking can be if one is wearing the proper shoes (i.e., not high heels). It then segues into a series about glands and what function they perform in the body. This wholesome image is accompanied by text more direct than that for boys, in its use of the words ovaries and testes.

The Baby

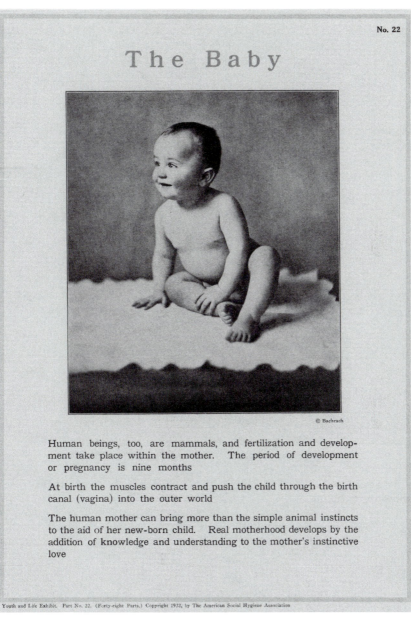

© Bachrach

Human beings, too, are mammals, and fertilization and development take place within the mother. The period of development
or pregnancy is nine months

At birth the muscles contract and push the child through the birth
canal (vagina) into the outer world

The human mother can bring more than the simple animal instincts
to the aid of her new-born child. Real motherhood develops by the
addition of knowledge and understanding to the mother's instinctive
love

Youth and Life Exhibit. Part No. 22. (Forty-eight Parts.) Copyright 1922, by The American Social Hygiene Association

Following an almost identical series from "Keeping Fit," showing reproduction
in the plant, chick, and rabbit, "The Baby" is different from the boys' equivalent
("Human Reproduction," showing a painting of a mother and child). The text is
different as well: rather than talking about a fertilized egg developing in the mother,
this one tells girls exactly how the baby enters the world.

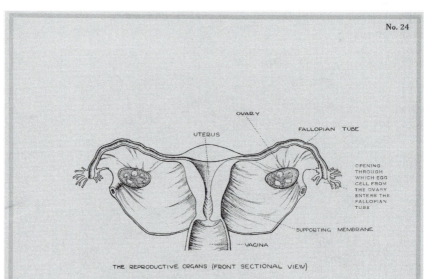

OVARY

UTERUS

FALLOPIAN TUBE

OPENING
THROUGH
WHICH EGG
CELL FROM
THE OVARY
ENTERS THE
FALLOPIAN
TUBE

SUPPORTING MEMBRANE

VAGINA

THE REPRODUCTIVE ORGANS (FRONT SECTIONAL VIEW)

The female reproductive system consists of

1. Two ovaries—glands in which develop the ova or egg cells

2. Two fallopian tubes—through which the egg cells reach the uterus

3. Uterus (womb)—a chamber with muscular walls in which the fertilized egg grows into a baby. The uterus enlarges as the baby grows

4. Vagina—a tube connecting the uterus with the outside

Almost immediately following "The Baby" is a drawing of the female reproductive system; there is no equivalent in the boys' series.

Danger In Familiarities

The Correct Dancing Position

Conventions are the fences society has built to protect you and the race

Familiarities arouse dangerous desires. They waste your power for the finest human companionship and love

Physical attraction alone will never wholly satisfy

Complete and lasting love is of the mind as well as of the body

Youth and Life Exhibit. Part No. 33. (Forty-eight Parts.) Copyright 1922, by The American Social Hygiene Association

Following the female reproductive system are images of healthy boys and girls, with accompanying text about what great things the properly controlled sex impulse can bring to the boy (strength, vigor), the girl (beauty, warmth), and "the race" (the culture of civilization). However, danger lurks in not controlling this instinct. "Danger in Familiarities" warns that dancing too closely and acting on physical attraction is not only dangerous in and of itself, but flouts "the fences society has built to protect you and the race."

Beware of Chance Acquaintances

"Pick-up" acquaintances often take girls autoriding, to cafès, and to theatres with the intention of leading them into sex relations. Disease or child-birth may follow

Avoid the man who tries to take liberties with you He is selfishly thoughtless and inconsiderate of you

Believe no one who says it is necessary to indulge sex desire

Know the men you associate with

h and Life Exhibit. Part No. 34. (Forty-eight Parts.) Copyright 1922, by The American Social Hygiene Association

Along the same lines as "Danger in Familiarities," is "Beware of Chance Acquaintances," telling girls not to get "picked up." Men who would seduce unmarried women into sexual intercourse are to be avoided at all costs. The image following this one shows a girl bringing a boy home to meet her mother—that is the proper way for girls and boys to get to know one another. If one does not do so, warn the several images following, one may get a venereal disease that would harm the baby that the girl will have someday.

For A Happy Married Life

By courtesy of Edison Lamp Works

Love is essential, and mutual respect, common interests, and unselfish consideration are the foundations of love

Sexual abstinence before marriage for both man and woman is the only reliable safeguard for the welfare of the family

To be sure that both man and woman are physically fit, each should have a medical examination before marriage. The laws of several states now require such an examination

Youth and Life Exhibit. Part No. 41. (Forty-eight Parts.) Copyright 1922, by The American Social Hygiene Association

"For a Happy Married Life" follows on the heels of the series about gonorrhea and syphilis, and portrays a suited man carving a turkey—this is the goal of sexual abstinence, a loving marriage. The images following show pictures of laughing, red-cheeked white children, and extol the virtues of "home-making," which is both a "talent" and a "science." The series ends with the notion that "Women are largely the makers of the home and the conservers of its spirit," and then lists numerous famous women who had achieved goals outside the home.

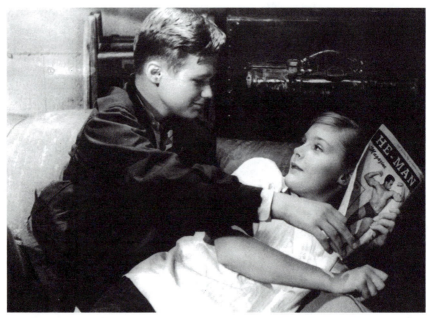

Blue Denim (1959) illustrates how moviemakers in the 1950s may have felt pressured by standards of the time period. When Janet becomes pregnant by Arthur, the film ends not with the abortion which Arthur tries to arrange, but with their parents providing them with a toaster and a car with which to begin their life as married parents. *Blue Denim*.

The Last Picture Show (1971) broke new ground with its representation of adolescent sex. Sonny engages in an affair with the older wife (Ruth) of his football coach, but stops seeing her when his best friend Duane and his girlfriend Jacy break up. He then pursues Jacy instead, but the movie closes with his talking to Ruth. *The Last Picture Show.* © 1971, renewed 1999 Columbia Pictures Industries, Inc. All Rights Reserved. Courtesy of Columbia Pictures.

Kids (1995), unlike some portrayals of adolescent sexuality in the 1990s that emphasized teen sensitivity or cool detachment, shows teens engaging in casual sexual encounters with little regard for consequences. Telly, the main character, thinks he is "safe" by having sex only with virgins, but the movie centers on one of his past conquests—who has had sex only once with him—discovering she is HIV-positive and trying to find him in order to tell him before he infects someone else. Photography from *Kids* used under license from Miramax Film Corp. All Rights Reserved.

10 Recent Statistics on Adolescent Sexuality

The first four illustrations in this chapter are based on interview data collected during the 2002 National Survey of Family Growth (NSFG). The 12,571 respondents were men and women, aged 15-44, residing in the United States. The interviews were administered in the homes of the respondents by female interviewers trained by the University of Michigan's Institute for Social Research, under the supervision of the National Center for Health Statistics. Those respondents aged 15–17 were required to have signed consent from a parent or guardian to participate. The over-all response rate for the survey was about 79 percent. For teenagers the response rate was 81 percent.

The final illustration is a map depicting birthrates in the United States (1999) for teenagers aged 15–19. It was originally published in 2001 under the auspices of the U.S. Department of Health and Human Services, Centers for Disease Control and Prevention.

Figure 10.1

Percent of never married females and males 15–17 years of age who have ever had sexual intercourse: United States 1988–2002

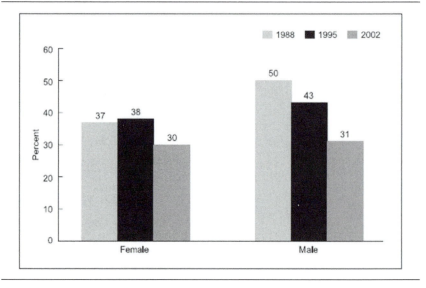

The 2002 National Survey of Family Growth (NSFG) was based on 12,571 interviews with men and women aged 15-44 in the United States. The interviews were administered in the selected person's homes in 2002-03 by female interviewers trained by the University of Michigan's Institute for Social Research, under the supervision of the National Center for Health Statistics. Those aged 15-17 were required to have signed consent from a parent or guardian to participate. The response rate for the survey was about 79 percent. For teenagers, the response rate was 81 percent.

For the above chart, interviewees were asked the following: [Male] "Have you ever had sexual intercourse with a female (sometimes this is called making love, having sex, or going all the way)?" [Female] "At any time in your life, have you ever had sexual intercourse with a man, that is, made love, had sex, or gone all the way?"

Source: Abma, J. C., Martinez, G. M., Mosher, W. D., Dawson, B. S. 2004. "Teenagers in the United States: Sexual Activity, Contraceptive Use, and Childbearing, 2002." National Center for Health Statistics. *Vital Health Statistics* 23 (24). p. 5.

Figure 10.2
Percent of never married females and males 18–19 years of age who have ever had sexual intercourse: United States 1988–2002

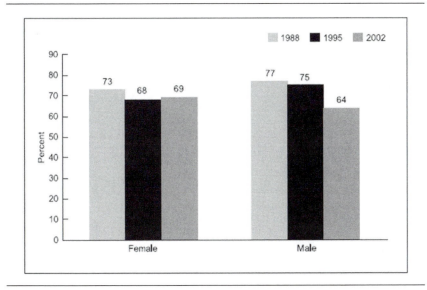

As in the previous chart, interviewees were asked the following: [Male] "Have you ever had sexual intercourse with a female (sometimes this is called making love, having sex, or going all the way)?" [Female] "At any time in your life, have you ever had sexual intercourse with a man, that is, made love, had sex, or gone all the way?"

Source: Abma, J. C., Martinez, G. M., Mosher, W. D., Dawson, B. S. 2004. "Teenagers in the United States: Sexual Activity, Contraceptive Use, and Childbearing, 2002." National Center for Health Statistics. *Vital Health Statistics* 23 (24). p. 6.

Figure 10.3

Percent of females and males 18–24 years of age at interview who had their first intercourse before age 20, by how much they wanted their first intercourse to happen when it did: United States 2002

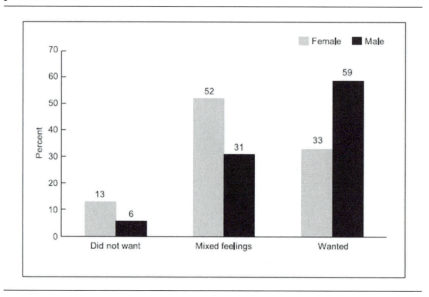

For this chart, interviewees were asked the following: "Think back to the very first time you had vaginal intercourse with a (person of the opposite sex). Which would you say comes closest to describing how much you wanted that first vaginal intercourse to happen?"

- I really didn't want it to happen at the time...
- I had mixed feelings—part of me wanted it to happen at the time and part of me didn't...
- I really wanted it to happen at the time...

Note that in another part of the questionnaire, respondents were asked if their first sexual experience was "voluntary" or "not voluntary." Of the females above who said they had not wanted the encounter to occur, 47.2 percent described it as voluntary and 52.8 percent as not voluntary; of those who said they had mixed feelings about the encounter, 96.2 percent described it as voluntary and 3.8 percent as not voluntary; of those who said they had wanted the encounter to occur, 98.4 percent described it as voluntary and 1.6 percent as not voluntary.

Source: Abma, J. C., Martinez, G. M., Mosher, W. D., Dawson, B. S. 2004. "Teenagers in the United States: Sexual Activity, Contraceptive Use, and Childbearing, 2002." National Center for Health Statistics. *Vital Health Statistics* 23 (24). pp. 6, 23, 48.

Figure 10.4

Percent of females 15–19 years of age who have ever had sexual intercourse, who have used the pill, the 3-month injectable (Depo-Provera), and the male condom, by race and Hispanic origin: United States 2002

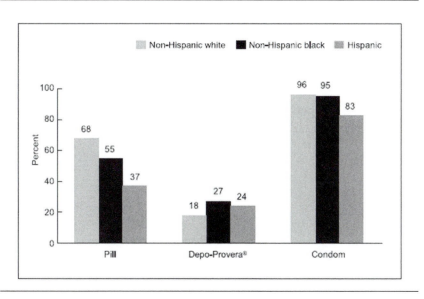

For this chart, interviewees were asked the following: "[Here are some] methods that some people use to prevent pregnancy or to prevent sexually transmitted disease. As I read each one, please tell me if you have ever used it for any reason. Please answer yes even if you have only used the method once."

- Have you ever used birth control pills?
- Have you ever used condoms or rubbers with a partner?
- Have you ever used Depo-Provera or injectables (or shots)?

In all, the interviewer listed 19 methods. Although it is not charted here, "withdrawal" was very common, used at some point by 60.7 percent of Non-Hispanic whites, 41.1 percent of Non-Hispanic blacks, and 52.1 percent of Hispanics—less common than the pill for the first two groups, and more common for the last.

Source: Abma, J. C., Martinez, G. M., Mosher, W. D., Dawson, B. S. 2004. "Teenagers in the United States: Sexual Activity, Contraceptive Use, and Childbearing, 2002." National Center for Health Statistics. *Vital Health Statistics* 23 (24). pp 6, 30.

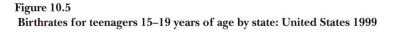

Figure 10.5
Birthrates for teenagers 15–19 years of age by state: United States 1999

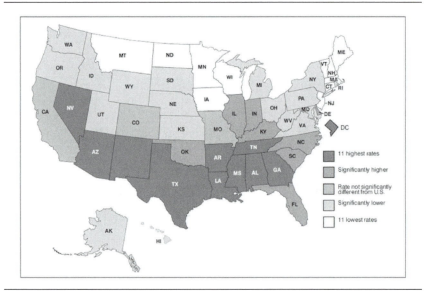

This map is from a 2001 publication under the auspices of the U.S. Department of Health and Human Services, Centers for Disease Control and Prevention. It found generally that births to teens aged 15-19 have declined in the U.S. from the 1950s to the present, except for the late 1980s. The declines were different in each state, as the map above shows.

Source: Ventura, S. J., Mathews, T. J., Hamilton, B. E. 2001. "Births to Teenagers in the United States, 1940-2000." *National Vital Statistics Report* 49, (10). Hyattsville, MD: National Center for Health Statistics. p 7.

III Bibliography

11 Age of Consent and Statutory Rape

Alexander, Ruth. 1995. *The "Girl Problem": Female Sexual Delinquency in New York, 1900–1930*. Ithaca, NY: Cornell University Press.

Amelio, Anthony M. 1995. "Florida's Statutory Rape Law: A Shield or a Weapon?—A Minor's Right of Privacy under Florida Statute §794.05." *Stetson Law Review* 26: 407–436.

Andre-Clark, Alice Susan. 1992. "Note: Whither Statutory Rape Laws: Of Michael M., the Fourteenth Amendment, and Protecting Women from Sexual Aggression." *Southern California Law Review* 65: 1933–1992.

Bienen, Leigh. 1976. "Rape I." *Women's Rights Law Reporter* 3 (Winter): 45–57.

Bienen, Leigh. 1977. "Rape II." *Women's Rights Law Reporter* 3 (Spring/Summer): 90–137.

Bienen, Leigh. 1980. "Rape III: National Developments in Rape Reform Legislation." *Women's Rights Law Reporter* 6 (Spring/Summer): 170–213.

Bienen, Leigh. 1980. "Rape IV." *Women's Rights Law Reporter* 6 (Spring/Summer): Supplement. Rutgers Law School.

Bienen, Leigh. 1998. "Defining Incest. [Symposium: Throwing Away the Key: Social and Legal Responses to Child Molesters.] Part II: Social, Cultural, and Legal Context." *Northwestern University Law Review* 92 (Summer): 1501–80.

Bossing, Lewis. 1998. "Now Sixteen Could Get You Life: Statutory Rape, Meaningful Consent, and the Implications for Federal Sentencing Enhancement." *New York University Law Review* 73 (October): 1205–50.

Califia, Pat. 1981. "Man/Boy Love and the Lesbian/Gay Movement." In *The Age Taboo: Gay Male Sexuality, Power, and Consent*, ed. D. Tsang, 133–146. Boston: Alyson Publications.

Califia, Pat. 1994. *Public Sex: The Culture of Radical Sex*. San Francisco: Cleis Press.

Campbell, Colin. 1997. "Mistake or Lack of Information as to Victim's Age as Defense to Statutory Rape." *American Law Reports* 46: n.p.

Cavallaro, Rosanna. 1996. "Criminal Law: A Big Mistake: Eroding the Defense of Mistake Fact about Consent in Rape." *Journal of Criminal Law and Criminology* 86: 815–60.

Chamallas, Martha. 1988. "Consent, Equality, and the Legal Control of Sexual Conduct." *Southern California Law Review* 61: 777–861.

Clarke, S. C. 1995. "Advance Report of Final Marriage Statistics, 1989 and 1990." *Monthly Vital Statistics Report* 43 (12): Supplement. Hyattsville, MD: National Center for Health Statistics.

Cocca, Carolyn. 2002. "From 'Welfare Queen' to 'Exploited Teen': Welfare Dependency, Statutory Rape, and Moral Panic." *National Women's Studies Association Journal* 14 (2): 56–79.

Cocca, Carolyn. 2002. "The Politics of Statutory Rape Laws: Adoption and Reinvention of Morality Policy in the States, 1971–1999." *Polity* (Fall): 51–72.

Cocca, Carolyn. 2002. "Prosecuting Mrs. Robinson? Gender, Sexuality, and Statutory Rape Laws." *Michigan Feminist Studies* 16 (Summer): 61–84.

Cocca, Carolyn. 2004. *Jailbait: The Politics of Statutory Rape Laws in the United States.* Albany, NY: State University of New York Press.

Connerton, Kelly C. 1997. "The Resurgence of the Marital Rape Exemption: The Victimization of Teens by Their Statutory Rapists." *Albany Law Review* 61: 237–343.

Dangerous Bedfellows Collective, eds. 1996. *Policing Public Sex: Queer Politics and the Future of AIDS Activism.* Boston: South End Press.

DeLaMothe, Cassandra. 1996. "Liberta Revisited: A Call to Repeal the Marital Exemption for All Sex Offenses in New York's Penal Law." *Fordham Urban Journal* 23: 857–92.

D'Emilio, John, and Estelle B. Freedman. 1997. *Intimate Matters: A History of Sexuality in America.* 2nd ed. Chicago: University of Chicago Press.

Donnino, William. 1997. "Practice Commentary: McKinney's Consolidated Laws of New York Annotated, Penal Law, Chapter 40 of the Consolidated Laws, Part 3 Specific Offenses, Title H Offenses against the Person Involving Physical Injury, Sexual Conduct, Restraint and Intimidation, Article 130 Sex Offenses." New York: West Group.

Donovan, Patricia. 1997. "Can Statutory Rape Laws Be Effective in Preventing Adolescent Pregnancy?" *Family Planning Perspectives* 29 (1): 30–34.

DuBois, Ellen, and Linda Gordon. 1984. "Seeking Ecstasy on the Battlefield: Danger and Pleasure in Nineteenth Century Feminist Sexual Thought." In *Pleasure and Danger: Exploring Female Sexuality*, ed. C. Vance, 31–49. 2nd edition, 1992. New York: Pandora.

Duggan, Lisa, Nan D. Hunter, and Carole Vance. 1995. "False Promises." In *Sex Wars: Sexual Dissent and Political Culture*, ed. L. Duggan and N. D. Hunter, 43–67. New York: Routledge.

Eidson, Rita. 1980. "The Constitutionality of Statutory Rape Laws." *UCLA Law Review* 27: 757–815.

Elstein, Sharon G., and Noy Davis. 1997. *Sexual Relationships between Adult Males and Young Teen Girls: Exploring the Legal and Social Responses.* Chicago: American Bar Association, Center on Children and the Law.

Fisch, Joseph. 1998. "Sentencing in Crimes against Children." *New York Law Journal* 219 (14): n.p. (January 22).

Freedman, Estelle B. 1987. "'Uncontrolled Desires': The Response to the Sexual Psychopath, 1920–1960." *Journal of American History* 74: 83–106.

Fuentes, Luisa. 1994. "Note: The Fourteenth Amendment and Sexual Consent: Statutory Rape and Judicial Progeny." *Women's Rights Law Reporter* 16: 139–52.

Galvin, Harriett. 1986. "Shielding Rape Victims in the State and Federal Courts: A Proposal for the Second Decade." *Minnesota Law Review* 70: 763–916.

Garfinkle, Elizabeth. 2003. "Coming of Age in America: The Misapplication of Sex-Offender Registration and Community Notification Laws to Juveniles." *California Law Review* 91: 163–208.

Geraci, Joseph, ed. 1997. *Dares to Speak: Historical and Contemporary Perspectives on Boy-Love.* Norfolk, UK: Gay Men's Press.

Greenfield, Lawrence. 1997. *Sex Offenses and Offenders.* Washington, DC: U.S. Department of Justice.

Guerrina, Britton. 1998. "Mitigating Punishment for Statutory Rape." *University of Chicago Law Review* 65 (Fall): 1251–77.

Higgins, Tracy. 1995. "'By Reason of Their Sex': Feminist Theory, Postmodernism, and Justice." *Cornell Law Review* 80: 1536–94.

Hsu, Gracie. 1996. "Statutory Rape: The Dirty Secret Behind Teen Sex Numbers." *Family Policy* 9 (3): 1–16.

Jenkins, Philip. 1998. *Moral Panic: Changing Concepts of the Child Molester in Modern America.* New Haven, CT: Yale University Press.

Kincaid, James R. 1992. *Child-Loving: The Erotic Child and Victorian Culture.* New York: Routledge.

Kincaid, James R. 1998. *Erotic Innocence: The Culture of Child Molesting.* Durham, NC: Duke University Press.

Kitrosser, Heidi. 1997. "Meaningful Consent: Toward a New Generation of Statutory Rape Laws." *Virginia Journal of Social Policy and the Law* 4: 287–338.

Kohn, Alan. 1992. "Underage Unwed Father Held Obligated to Support Child." *New York Law Journal* 208 (85):n.p.

Kunzel, Regina G. 1993. *Fallen Women, Problem Girls: Unmarried Mothers and the Professionalization of Social Work, 1890–1945.* New Haven, CT: Yale University Press.

Langum, David J. 1994. *Crossing over the Line: Legislating Morality and the Mann Act.* Chicago: University of Chicago Press.

Larson, Jane. 1997. "'Even a Worm Will Turn at Last': Rape Reform in Late Nineteenth Century America." *Yale Journal of Law and the Humanities* 9 (Winter): 1–71.

Lasch-Quinn, Elizabeth. 1997. "Progressives and the Pursuit of Agency." *Reviews in American History* 25 (2): 258–63.

Levesque, Roger. 1997. "Dating Violence, Adolescents, and the Law." *Virginia Journal of Social Policy and the Law* 4: 339–397.

Levine, Judith. 2002. *Harmful to Minors: The Perils of Protecting Children from Sex.* Minneapolis: University of Minnesota Press.

Levy, Michael. 1999. The Politics of Sex: The Age of Consent Debate in the Houses of Parliament. Paper presented at the annual meeting of the American Political Science Association, Atlanta, Georgia, 1–5 September.

Lynch, Michael. 1998. "Enforcing 'Statutory Rape'?" *The Public Interest* 132 (Summer): 3–16.

MacKinnon, Catharine. 1991. "Reflections on Sex Equality under Law." *Yale Law Journal* 10: 1281–328.

Marsh, Jeanne C., Alison Geist, and Nathan Caplan. 1982. *Rape and the Limits of Law Reform*. Boston: Auburn House.

McCollum, James. 1982. "Case Development: Constitutional Law—Statutory Rape—Gender-Based Classification Regarding Statutory Rape Law is Not Violative of the Equal Protection Clause of the Fourteenth Amendment: *Michael M. v. Superior Court*." *Howard Law Journal* 25: 341–65.

McNamara, Douglas. 1998. "Sexual Discrimination and Sexual Misconduct: Applying New York's Gender Specific Sexual Misconduct Law to Consenting Minors." *Touro Law Review* 14: 477–498.

Miller, Susannah. 1994. "Recent Developments: The Overturning of Michael M.: Statutory Rape Law Becomes Gender-Neutral in California." *UCLA Women's Law Journal* 5: 289–98.

Nathanson, Constance A. 1991. *Dangerous Passage: The Social Control of Sexuality in Women's Adolescence*. Philadelphia: Temple University Press.

National Law Journal Staff. 1995. "Sex Impersonation Charged." *National Law Journal*. January 9 (A10).

North American Man/Boy Love Association. 1981. "The Case for Abolishing Age of Consent Laws." In *The Age Taboo: Gay Male Sexuality, Power, and Consent*, ed. D. Tsang, 92–106. Boston: Alyson Publications.

Nowack, Sandy. 2000. "A Community Prosecution Approach to Statutory Rape: Wisconsin Pilot Policy Project." *DePaul Law Review* 50: 865–95.

Oberman, Michelle. 1994. "Turning Girls into Women: Reevaluating Modern Statutory Rape Law." *Journal of Criminal Law and Criminology* 85: 15–78.

Oberman, Michelle. 2000. "Regulating Consensual Sex with Minors: Defining a Role for Statutory Rape." *Buffalo Law Review* 48: 703–84.

Oberman, Michelle. 2001. "Girls in the Master's House: Of Protection, Patriarchy, and the Potential for Using the Master's Tools to Reconfigure Statutory Rape Law." *DePaul Law Review* 50: 799–826.

Odem, Mary E. 1995. *Delinquent Daughters: Protecting and Policing Adolescent Female Sexuality in the United States, 1885–1920*. Chapel Hill: University of North Carolina Press.

Olsen, Frances. 1984. "Statutory Rape: A Feminist Critique of Rights Analysis." *Texas Law Review* 63: 387–432.

Peiss, Kathy Lee. 1986. *Cheap Amusements: Working Women and Leisure in Turn-of-the-Century New York*. Philadelphia: Temple University Press.

Pearce, Diana. 1990. "Welfare Is Not for Women: Why the War on Poverty Cannot Conquer the Feminization of Poverty." In *Women, the State, and Welfare*, ed. L. Gordon, 265–278. Madison: University of Wisconsin Press.

Posner, Richard A., and Katharine B. Silbaugh. 1996. *A Guide to America's Sex Laws*. Chicago: University of Chicago Press.

Regan, Milton C., Jr. 1995. "Spousal Privilege and the Meanings of Marriage." *Virginia Law Review* 81: 2045–134.

Rivera, Jenny. 1994. "Domestic Violence against Latinas by Latino Males: An Analysis of Race, National Origin and Gender Differentials." *Boston College Third World Law Journal* 14: 231–257.

Roberts, Dorothy E. 1994. "Symposium: Gender Issues and the Criminal Law: Foreword: The Meaning of Gender Equality in Criminal Law." *Journal of Criminal Law and Criminology* 85: 1–14.

Roberts, Dorothy E. 1997. *Killing the Black Body: Race, Reproduction, and the Meaning of Liberty.* New York: Pantheon.

Rodman, Hyman. 1984. *The Sexual Rights of Adolescents: Competence, Vulnerability, and Parental Control.* New York: Columbia University Press.

Rubin, Gayle. 1984. "Thinking Sex: Notes for a Radical Theory of the Politics of Sexuality." In *Pleasure and Danger: Exploring Female Sexuality,* ed. C. Vance, 267–319. 2nd edition, 1992. New York: Pandora.

Schlossman, Steven, and Stephanie Wallach. 1985. "The Crime of Precocious Sexuality." *Harvard Educational Review* 48 (1): 65–94.

Schuijer, Jan. 1997. "The Netherlands Changes Its Age of Consent Law." In *Dares to Speak: Historical and Contemporary Perspectives on Boy-Love,* ed. J. Geraci, 207–212. Norfolk, UK: Gay Men's Press.

Searles, Patricia, and Ronald Berger. 1987. "The Current Status of Rape Reform Legislation: An Examination of State Statutes." *Women's Rights Law Reporter* 10 (Spring): 25–43.

Sinesio, Ronald. 1998. "Prosecution of Female as Principal for Rape." *American Law Reports* 67: 1127.

Smith-Rosenberg, Carroll. 1985. *Disorderly Conduct: Visions of Gender in Victorian America.* New York: A. A. Knopf.

Snyder, Howard N. 2000. *Sexual Assault of Young Children as Reported to Law Enforcement: Victim, Incident, and Offender Characteristics.* Washington, DC: U.S. Department of Justice.

Spohn, Cassia, and Julie Horney. 1992. *Rape Law Reform: A Grassroots Revolution and Its Impact.* New York: Plenum Press.

Stephens, Sharon, ed. 1995. *Children and the Politics of Culture.* Princeton, NJ: Princeton University Press.

Tennen, Ken. 1997. "Wake Up Maggie: Gender Neutral Statutory Rape Laws, Third-Party Infant Blood Extraction, and the Conclusive Presumption of Legitimacy." *Journal of Juvenile Law* 18: 1–33.

Trenkner, Thomas. 1998. "Constitutionality of Rape Laws Limited to Protection of Females Only." *American Law Reports* 99: n.p.

Tsang, Daniel, ed. 1981. *The Age Taboo: Gay Male Sexuality, Power, and Consent.* Boston: Alyson Publications.

Tsang, Daniel. 1981. "Introduction." In *The Age Taboo: Gay Male Sexuality, Power, and Consent,* ed. D. Tsang, 7–12. Boston: Alyson Publications.

Urban Institute. 1997. "Tougher statutory rape laws expected to have limited impact on teen childbearing," news release, 15 April.

U.S. Department of Justice, Bureau of Justice Statistics. 1995. *Sourcebook of Criminal Justice Statistics,* ed. K. Maguire and A. Pastore. Washington, DC: Government Printing Office.

Volpp, Leti. 2000. "Blaming Culture for Bad Behavior." *Yale Journal of Law and the Humanities* 12: 89–116.

Waites, Matthew. 2005. *The Age of Consent: Young People, Sexuality, and Citizenship.* New York: Palgrave Macmillan.

Walkowitz, Judith R. 1980. *Prostitution and Victorian Society: Women, Class, and the State.* New York: Cambridge University Press.

Walkowitz, Judith R. 1992. *City of Dreadful Delight: Narratives of Sexual Danger in Late-Victorian London.* Chicago: University of Chicago Press.

12 Teens and Contraception, Pregnancy, Birth, and Abortion

Abma J. C., G. M. Martinez, W. D. Mosher, and B. S. Dawson. 2004. "Teenagers in the United States: Sexual Activity, Contraceptive Use, and Childbearing, 2002." *Vital Health Statistics* 23(24).

Adams, Gina, Karen Pittman, and Raymond O'Brien. 1993. "Adolescent and Young Adult Fathers: Problems and Solutions." In *The Politics of Pregnancy: Adolescent Sexuality and Public Policy,* ed. A. Lawson and D. Rhode, 216–237. New Haven, CT: Yale University Press.

Alan Guttmacher Institute. 1994. *Sex and America's Teenagers.* New York: Alan Guttmacher Institute.

Alan Guttmacher Institute. 1997. "Welfare Reform, Marriage and Sexual Behavior," http://www.guttmacher.org/pubs/ib_welfare_reform.html.

Alan Guttmacher Institute. 1998. "Teenage Pregnancy and the Welfare Reform Debate," http://www.guttmacher.org/pubs/ib5.html.

Alan Guttmacher Institute. 1999. "Teen Sex and Pregnancy," http://www.guttmacher.org/pubs/fb_teen_sex.html.

Alan Guttmacher Institute. 2004. "U.S. Teenage Pregnancy Statistics: Overall Trends, Trends by Race and Ethnicity and State-by-State Information," http://www.guttmacher.org/pubs/state_pregnancy_trends.pdf.

Alexander, Ruth. (1995). *The "Girl Problem": Female Sexual Delinquency in New York, 1900–1930.* Ithaca, NY: Cornell University Press.

Bailey, Beth. 1999. *Sex in the Heartland.* Cambridge, MA: Harvard University Press.

Boonstra, Heather. 2002. "Teen Pregnancy: Trends and Lessons Learned." *Guttmacher Report on Public Policy* 5 (February), http://www.guttmacher.org/pubs/tgr/05/1/gr050107.html.

Cocca, Carolyn. 2002. "From 'Welfare Queen' to 'Exploited Teen': Welfare Dependency, Statutory Rape, and Moral Panic." *National Women's Studies Association Journal* 14 (2): 56–79.

Cocca, Carolyn. 2004. *Jailbait: The Politics of Statutory Rape Laws in the United States.* Albany, NY: State University of New York Press.

Coontz, Stephanie. 1992. *The Way We Never Were: American Families and the Nostalgia Trap.* New York: Basic Books.

Crews, Allison. 2001. "And So I Chose." In *Listen Up: Voices from the Next Feminist Generation,* new expanded ed., ed. B. Findlen, 142–152. Seattle, WA: Seal Press.

Elders, M. Jocelyn, and Alexa Albert. 1998. "Adolescent Pregnancy and Sexual Abuse." *Journal of the American Medical Association* 280 (7): 648–49.

Gebhard, Paul H., Wardell B. Pomeroy, Clyde E. Martin, and Cornelia V. Chistenson. 1958. *Pregnancy, Birth and Abortion.* New York: Harper.

Geronimus, Arline. 1997. "Teenage Childbearing and Personal Responsibility: An Alternative View." *Political Science Quarterly* 112 (3): 405–430.

Gilbert, Laurie. 2001. "You're Not the Type." In *Listen Up: Voices from the Next Feminist Generation,* new expanded ed., ed. B. Findlen, 74–83. Seattle, WA: Seal Press.

Gordon, Linda. 1994. *Pitied but Not Entitled: Single Mothers and the History of Welfare, 1890–1935.* New York: Free Press.

Harari, Susan, and Maris Vinovskis. 1993. "Adolescent Sexuality, Pregnancy, and Childbearing in the Past." In *The Politics of Pregnancy: Adolescent Sexuality and Public Policy,* ed. A. Lawson and D. L. Rhode, 23–58. New Haven, CT: Yale University Press.

Irvine, Janice M. 2002. *Talk about Sex: The Battles over Sex Education in the United States.* Berkeley: University of California Press.

Joffe, Carole. 1993. "Sexual Politics and the Teenage Pregnancy Prevention Worker in the United States." In *The Politics of Pregnancy: Adolescent Sexuality and Public Policy,* ed. A. Lawson and D. L. Rhode, 284–300. New Haven, CT: Yale University Press.

Jorgensen, Stephen. 1993. "Adolescent Pregnancy and Parenting." In *Adolescent Sexuality,* ed. T. Gulotta, G. Adams, and R. Montemayor, 103–140. New York: Sage Publications.

Kline, Wendy. 2001. *Building a Better Race: Gender, Sexuality, and Eugenics from the Turn of the Century to the Baby Boom.* Berkeley: University of California Press.

Kunzel, Regina G. 1993. *Fallen Women, Problem Girls: Unmarried Mothers and the Professionalization of Social Work, 1890–1945.* New Haven, CT: Yale University Press.

Landry, D. J., and J. D. Forrest. 1995. "How Old Are U.S. Fathers?" *Family Planning Perspectives* 27: 159–165.

Lawson, Annette. 1993. "Multiple Fractures: The Cultural Construction of Teenage Sexuality and Pregnancy." In *The Politics of Pregnancy: Adolescent Sexuality and Public Policy,* ed. A. Lawson and D. L. Rhode, 101–125. New Haven, CT: Yale University Press.

Lawson, Annette, and Deborah L. Rhode, eds. 1993. *The Politics of Pregnancy: Adolescent Sexuality and Public Policy.* New Haven, CT: Yale University Press.

Levin-Epstein, Jodie. 1997. *State TANF Plans: Out-of-Wedlock and Statutory Rape Provisions.* Washington, DC: Center for Law and Social Policy.

Lindberg, Laura Duberstein, Freya Sonenstein, Leighton Ku, and Gladys Martinez. 1997. "Age Difference between Minors Who Give Birth and Their Adult Partners." *Family Planning Perspectives* 29 (2): 61–66.

Lindsey, Ben B., and Wainwright Evans (1925). *The Revolt of Modern Youth.* New York: Boni and Liveright.

Luker, Kristin. 1984. *Abortion and the Politics of Motherhood*. Berkeley: University of California Press.

Luker, Kristin. 1996. *Dubious Conceptions: The Politics of Female Pregnancy*. Cambridge, MA: Harvard University Press.

MacIntyre, Sally, and Sarah Cunningham-Burley. 1993. "Teenage Pregnancy as a Social Problem: A Perspective from the United Kingdom." In *The Politics of Pregnancy: Adolescent Sexuality and Public Policy*, ed. A. Lawson and D. L. Rhode, 59–73. New Haven, CT: Yale University Press.

Mohr, James C. 1978. *Abortion in America: The Origins and Evolution of National Policy, 1800–1900*. New York: Oxford University Press.

Moran, Jeffrey P. 2000. *Teaching Sex: The Shaping of Adolescence in the 20th Century*. Cambridge, MA: Harvard University Press.

Nagin, Daniel, Greg Pogarsky, and David Farrington. 1997. "Adolescent Mothers and the Criminal Behavior of Their Children." *Law and Society Review* 31 (1): 137–62.

Nathanson, Constance A. 1991. *Dangerous Passage: The Social Control of Sexuality in Women's Adolescence*. Philadelphia: Temple University Press.

Odem, Mary E. (1995). *Delinquent Daughters: Protecting and Policing Adolescent Female Sexuality in the United States, 1885–1920*. Chapel Hill: University of North Carolina Press.

Peiss, Kathy Lee. 1986. *Cheap Amusements: Working Women and Leisure in Turn-of-the-Century New York*. Philadelphia: Temple University Press.

Phoenix, Ann. 1993. "The Social Construction of Teenage Motherhood: A Black and White Issue?" In *The Politics of Pregnancy: Adolescent Sexuality and Public Policy*, ed. A. Lawson and D. L. Rhode, 74–100. New Haven, CT: Yale University Press.

Pearce, Diana. 1993. "'Children Having Children': Teenage Pregnancy and Public Policy from the Woman's Perspective." In *The Politics of Pregnancy: Adolescent Sexuality and Public Policy*, ed. A. Lawson and D. L. Rhode, 46–58. New Haven, CT: Yale University Press.

Rangel, Maria Cristina. 2001. "Knowledge is Power." In *Listen Up: Voices from the Next Feminist Generation*, new expanded ed., ed. B. Findlen, 188–196. Seattle, WA: Seal Press.

Reagan, Leslie J. 1997. *When Abortion Was a Crime: Women, Medicine, and Law in the United States, 1867–1973*. Berkeley: University of California Press.

Reed, James. 1978. *The Birth Control Movement and American Society: From Private Vice to Public Virtue*. Princeton, NJ: Princeton University Press.

Reiss, Ira L. 1960. *Premarital Sexual Standards in America*. Glencoe, IL: Free Press.

Rhode, Deborah L. 1993. "Adolescent Pregnancy and Public Policy." In *The Politics of Pregnancy: Adolescent Sexuality and Public Policy*, ed. A. Lawson and D. L. Rhode, 301–335. New Haven, CT: Yale University Press.

Schlossman, Steven, and Stephanie Wallach. 1978. "The Crime of Precocious Sexuality: Female Juvenile Delinquency in the Progressive Era." *Harvard Educational Review* 48 (February): 65–94.

Sedlak, Michael W. 1983. "Young Women and the City: Adolescent Deviance and the Transformation of Educational Policy, 1870–1960." *History of Education Quarterly* 23 (Spring): 1–28.

Solinger, Rickie. 1992. *Wake Up Little Susie: Single Pregnancy and Race Before Roe v. Wade*. New York: Routledge.

Thompson, Sharon. 1995. *Going All the Way: Teenage Girls' Tales of Sex, Romance, and Pregnancy*. New York: Hill and Wang.

Tone, Andrea. 2001. *Devices and Desires: A History of Contraceptives in America*. New York: Hill and Wang.

Ulllman, Sharon R. 1997. *Sex Seen: The Emergence of Modern Sexuality in America*. Berkeley: University of California Press.

U.S. Bureau of the Census. 1975. *Historical Statistics of the United States: Colonial Times to 1970*. 2 vols. Washington, DC: U.S. Department of Commerce.

Ventura, S. J., T. J. Matthews, and P. E. Hamilton. 2001. "Births to Teenagers in the United States, 1940–2000." *National Vital Statistics Report* 49 (10) Hyattsville, MD: National Center for Health Statistics.

Vinovskis, Maris. 1988. *An "Epidemic" of Adolescent Pregnancy?: Some Historical and Policy Considerations*. New York: Oxford University Press.

Waller, Willard. 1937. "The Rating and Dating Complex." *American Sociological Review* 2: 727–34.

Weeks, John R. 1976. *Teenage Marriages: A Demographic Analysis*. Westport, CT: Greenwood Press.

13   Sex Education and Writings about Sex for Teens

Bailey, Beth L. 1988. *From Front Porch to Back Seat: Courtship in Twentieth-Century America*. Baltimore, MD: Johns Hopkins University Press.

Bay-Cheng, Laina. 2003. "The Trouble of Teen Sex: The Construction of Adolescent Sexuality through School-Based Sexuality Education." *Sex Education* 3: 61–74.

Beck, Lester F. 1949. *Human Growth: The Story of How Life Begins and Goes On, Based on the Educational Film of the Same Title*. With the assistance of Margie Robinson. New York: Harcourt, Brace.

Bigelow, Maurice A. 1924. "The Established Points in Social Hygiene Education, 1905–1924," *Journal of Social Hygiene* 10 (January): 2–11.

Bigelow, Maurice A. 1933. *The Established Points in Social Hygiene Education*. Rev. ed. New York: American Social Hygiene Association.

Brown, Lorna, ed. 1981. *Sex Education in the Eighties: The Challenge of Healthy Sexual Evolution*. New York: Plenum Press.

Brumberg, Joan Jacobs. 1997. *The Body Project: An Intimate History of American Girls*. New York: Random House.

Campbell, Patricia J. 1979. *Sex Education Books for Young Adults, 1892–1979*. New York: R. R. Bowker.

Carter, Julian B. 2001. "Birds, Bees, and Venereal Disease: Toward an Intellectual History of Sex Education." *Journal of the History of Sexuality* 10: 213–49.

Chen, Constance M. 1996. *"The Sex Side of Life": Mary Ware Dennett's Pioneering Battle for Birth Control and Sex Education*. New York: New Press.

Committee on Government Reform. 2004. *The Content of Federally Funded Abstinence-Only Education Programs*. Prepared for Rep. Henry A. Waxman, United States House of Representatives, http://www.democrats.reform.house.gov/Documents/20041201102153-50247.pdf.

Cook, Paul W. 1972. "A Great Experiment in Sex Education—The Anaheim Story." *Journal of School Health* 42: 7–9.

De Schweinitz, Karl. 1947. *Growing Up: The Story of How We Become Alive, Are Born and Grow Up.* Rev. ed. New York: Macmillan.

Dickerson, Roy E. 1948. *So Youth May Know: Sex Education for Youth.* Rev. ed. New York: Association Press.

Drake, Gordon V. 1968. *Is the School House the Proper Place to Teach Raw Sex?* Tulsa, OK: Christian Crusade Publications.

Eberwein, Robert T. 1999. *Sex Ed: Film, Video, and the Framework of Desire.* New Brunswick, NJ: Rutgers University Press.

Edson, Newell W. 1922. *Status of Sex Education in High Schools.* Washington, DC: Government Printing Office.

Ellis, Grace F., and T. Dinsmore Upton. 1915. "Sex Instruction in a High School." *Social Hygiene* 1: 271–72.

Ensler, Eve. 2001. *The Vagina Monologues.* New York: Villard.

Fine, Michelle. 1988. "Sexuality, Schooling, and Adolescent Females: The Missing Discourse of Desire." *Harvard Educational Review* 58: 29–53.

Force, Elizabeth S., and Edgar M. Finck. 1949. *Family Relationships: Ten Topics toward Happier Homes, a Handbook for Administrators and Teachers Who Use the Accompanying Study Guide.* Elizabethtown, PA: Continental Press.

Freeman, Susan Kathleen. Forthcoming. *Up for Discussion: Adolescent Girls and Sex Education in Mid-Twentieth Century Schools.* Urbana: University of Illinois Press.

Gambrell, Alan E. 1993. *Unfinished Business: A SIECUS Assessment of State Sexuality Education Programs.* New York: Sexuality Information and Education Council of the United States.

Gebhard, Bruno. 1948. "More Information Please." *Hygeia* 26: 545–47, 574–76.

Gilmore, Bob. 1947. "Sex Goes to School in Oregon." *Better Homes and Gardens,* September, 41.

Gruenberg, Benjamin C. 1939. *High Schools and Sex Education.* With the assistance of J. L. Kaukonen. Washington, DC: Government Printing Office.

Gudridge, Beatrice M. 1969. *Sex Education in Schools: A Review of Current Policies and Programs for the Guidance of School Board Members, Administrators, Teachers, and Parents.* Washington, DC: National School Public Relations Association.

Haffner, Debra Wayne, and William L. Yarber. 1996. *Guidelines for Comprehensive Sex Education: Kindergarten through Twelfth Grade.* 2nd ed. New York: National Guidelines Task Force.

Human Growth. 1947. Portland, OR: E. C. Brown Trust and Eddie Albert Productions. Filmstrip.

Irvine, Janice M., ed. 1994. *Sexual Cultures and the Construction of Adolescent Identities.* Philadelphia: Temple University Press.

Irvine, Janice M. 1995. *Sexuality Education across Cultures: Working with Differences.* San Francisco: Jossey-Bass.

Irvine, Janice M. 2002. *Talk about Sex: The Battles over Sex Education in the United States.* Berkeley: University of California Press.

Keliher, Alice V. 1938. *Life and Growth.* New York: D. Appleton-Century.

Kirkendall, Lester A. 1944. "Sex Education in 9 Cooperating High Schools, Part I." *Clearing House* 18: 387–91.

Kirkendall, Lester A. 1950. *Sex Education as Human Relations: A Guidebook on Content and Methods for School Authorities and Teachers.* New York: Inor.

Landers, Ann. 1963. *Ann Landers Talks to Teenagers about Sex.* Englewood Cliffs, NJ: Prentice-Hall, 1963.

Lentz, Gloria. 1972. *Raping Our Children: The Sex Education Scandal*. New Rochelle, NY: Arlington House.

Levine, Judith. 2002. *Harmful to Minors: The Perils of Protecting Children from Sex*. Minneapolis: University of Minnesota Press.

Martin, Michelle H. 2004. "'No One Will Ever Know Your Secret!' Commercial Puberty Pamphlets for Girls from the 1940s to the 1990s." In *Sexual Pedagogies: England, Australia, and America, 1879–2000*, ed. C. Nelson and M. H. Martin, 135–54. New York: Palgrave Macmillan.

Mast, Coleen Kelly. 1990. *Sex Respect: The Option of True Sexual Freedom*. Rev. ed. Bradford, IL: Respect, Inc.

Masten, Fannie B. 1953. "Family Life Education at Central High School, Charlotte, North Carolina." *Marriage and Family Living* 15: 105–8.

Mayo, Cris. 2004. *Disputing the Subject of Sex: Sexuality and Public School Controversies*. Lanham, MD: Rowman and Littlefield.

Moran, Jeffrey P. 2000. *Teaching Sex: The Shaping of Adolescence in the 20th Century*. Cambridge, MA: Harvard University Press.

National Public Radio, Kaiser Family Foundation, and Kennedy School of Government. 2004. Sex Education in America, http://www.kff.org/kaiserpolls/pomr012904oth.cfm.

Nelson, Claudia, and Michelle H. Martin, eds. 2004. *Sexual Pedagogies: Sex Education in Britain, Australia, and America, 1879–2000*. New York: Palgrave Macmillan.

Sears, James T., ed. 1992. *Sexuality and the Curriculum: The Politics and Practices of Sexuality Education*. New York: Teachers College Press.

Smith, Ken. 1999. *Mental Hygiene: Classroom Films, 1945–1970*. New York: Blast Books.

Social Hygiene. 1916. "The Matter and Methods of Sex Education." 2: 573–81.

Story of Menstruation. 1946. Burbank, CA: Walt Disney Productions. Filmstrip.

Strain, Frances Bruce. 1939. *Love at the Threshold: A Book on Dating, Romance, and Marriage*. New York: D. Appleton-Century.

Strain, Frances Bruce. 1946. *Teen Days: A Book for Boys and Girls*. New York: D. Appleton-Century.

Trudell, Bonnie Nelson. 1993. *Doing Sex Education: Gender Politics and Schooling*. New York: Routledge.

Usilton, Lida J., and Newell W. Edson. 1928. *Status of Sex Education in the Senior High Schools of the United States in 1927*. Washington, DC: Government Printing Office.

Welshimer, Helen. 1949. *The Questions Girls Ask*. New York: E. P. Dutton.

Whatley, Mariamne. 1985. "Male and Female Hormones: Misinterpretations of Biology in School Health and Sex Education." In *Women, Biology, and Public Policy*, ed. V. Shapiro, 67–89. Beverly Hills, Calif.: Sage Publications.

Wheeler, Leigh Ann. 2000. "Rescuing Sex from Prudery and Prurience: American Women's Use of Sex Education as an Antidote to Obscenity, 1925–1932." *Journal of Women's History* 12: 173–95.

Wheeler, Leigh Ann. 2004. *Against Obscenity: Reform and the Politics of Womanhood in America, 1873–1935*. Baltimore, MD: Johns Hopkins University Press.

14 Adolescence and Adolescent Sexuality, General

Alan Guttmacher Institute. 1994. *Sex and America's Teenagers*. New York: Alan Guttmacher Institute.

Albert, Bill, Sarah Brown, and Christine Flanagan, eds. 2003. *14 and Younger: The Sexual Behavior of Young Adolescents*. Washington, DC: National Campaign to Prevent Teen Pregnancy.

Alexander, Ruth. 1995. *The "Girl Problem": Female Sexual Delinquency in New York, 1900–1930*. Ithaca, NY: Cornell University Press.

Archard, David. 1998. *Sexual Consent*. Boulder: Westview Press.

Aries, P. 1962. *Centuries of Childhood: A Social History of Family Life*, trans. R. Baldick. New York: Vintage Books.

Bailey, Beth. 1988. *From Front Porch to Back Seat: Courtship in Twentieth-Century America*. Baltimore, MD: Johns Hopkins University Press.

Beisel, Nicola Kay. 1997. *Imperiled Innocents: Anthony Comstock and Family Reproduction in Victorian America*. Princeton, NJ: Princeton University Press.

Blau, Gary, and Thomas Gulotta. 1993. "Promoting Sexual Responsibility in Adolescence." In *Adolescent Sexuality*, ed. T. Gulotta, G. Adams, and R. Montemayor, 181–203. New York: Sage Publications.

Borneman, E. 1994. *Childhood Phases of Maturity: Sexual Developmental Psychology*, trans. M. Lombardi-Nash. Amherst, NY: Prometheus Books.

Breines, Wini. 1992. *Young, White, and Miserable: Growing Up Female in the Fifties*. Boston: Beacon Press.

Brewster, K. L., J.O.G. Billy, and W R. Grady. 1993. "Social Context and Adolescent Behavior: The Impact of Community and the Transition to Sexual Activity." *Social Forces* 71: 713–40.

Brown, Jane D., Jeanne R. Steele, and Kim Walsh-Childres, eds. 2002. *Sexual Teens, Sexual Media: Investigating Media's Influence on Adolescent Sexuality*. Mahwah, NJ: L. Erlbaum.

Brown, Lyn Mikel. 1998. *Raising Their Voices: The Politics of Girls' Anger.* Cambridge, MA: Harvard University Press.

Brumberg, Joan Jacobs. 1997. *The Body Project: An Intimate History of American Girls.* New York: Random House.

Bullough, Vern L. 1996. *Science in the Bedroom: A History of Sex Research.* New York: Basic Books.

Cott, Nancy. 1978. "Passionlessness: An Interpretation of Victorian Sexual Ideology, 1790–1850." *Signs* 4 (Winter): 219–36.

D'Emilio, John, and Estelle B. Freedman. 1997. *Intimate Matters: A History of Sexuality in America.* 2nd ed. Chicago: University of Chicago Press.

Elwin, Verrier. 1968. *The Kingdom of the Young.* London: Oxford University Press.

Erickson, Erik H. 1964. *Childhood and Society.* 2nd rev. ed. New York: Norton.

Erickson, Erik H. 1968. *Identity, Youth, and Crisis.* New York: Norton.

Faderman, Lillian. 1991. *Odd Girls and Twilight Lovers: A History of Lesbian Life in Twentieth-Century America.* New York: Columbia University Press.

Fass, Paula S., and Mary Ann Mason, eds. 2000. *Childhood in America.* New York: New York University Press.

Florsheim, Paul, ed. 2003. *Adolescent Romantic Relations and Sexual Behavior: Theory, Research, and Practical Implications.* Mahwah, NJ: L. Erlbaum.

Freud, Sigmund. 1908. "On the Sexual Theories of Children." In J. Strachey and A. Freud, eds. *The Standard Edition of the Complete Psychological Works of Sigmund Freud,* Vol. 9. London: Hogarth Press, 1962.

Green, Richard. 1987. *The "Sissy Boy" Syndrome and the Development of Homosexuality.* New Haven, CT: Yale University Press.

Gulotta, Thomas, Gerald Adams, and Raymond Montemayor, eds. 1993. *Adolescent Sexuality.* New York: Sage Publications.

Gutiérrez, Ramón. 1991. *When Jesus Came, the Corn Mothers Went Away: Marriage, Sexuality, and Power in New Mexico, 1500–1846.* Stanford, CA: Stanford University Press.

Hall, Granville Stanley. 1904. *Adolescence.* New York: D. Appleton.

Halpern, C. T., et al. 1994. "Testosterone and Religiosity as Predictor of Sexual Attitudes and Activity among Adolescent Males: A Biosocial Model." *Journal of Biosocial Sciences* 26: 217–34.

Halpern, C. T., et al. 2000. "Smart Teens Don't Have Sex (or Kiss Much Either)." *Journal of Adolescent Health* 26: 213–25.

Harari, Susan, and Maris Vinovskis. 1993. "Adolescent Sexuality, Pregnancy, and Childbearing in the Past." In *The Politics of Pregnancy: Adolescent Sexuality and Public Policy,* ed. A. Lawson and D. L. Rhode, 23–58. New Haven, CT: Yale University Press.

Heins, Marjorie. 2001. *Not in Front of the Children: "Indecency," Censorship and the Innocence of Youth.* New York: Hill and Wang.

Hersch, Patricia. 1998. *A Tribe Apart: A Journey into the Heart of American Adolescence.* New York: Fawcett Columbine.

Hine, Thomas. 1999. *The Rise and Fall of the American Teenager.* New York: Bard.

Hyde, Janet Shelby, and Sara R. Jaffee. 2000. "Becoming a Heterosexual Adult: The Experience of Young Women." *Journal of Social Issues* 56: 283–96.

Jenkins, Henry, ed. 1998. *The Children's Culture Reader.* New York: New York University Press.

Kaiser Foundation. 2003. *National Survey of Adolescents and Young Adults: Sexual Health Knowledge, Attitudes, and Experiences.* Menlo Park, CA: Kaiser Foundation.

Kellogg, John Harvey. 1884. *Plain Facts for Old and Young.* Burlington, Iowa: I. F. Segner.

Kinsey, Alfred C., Wardell B. Pomeroy, and Clyde E. Martin. 1948. *Sexual Behavior in the Human Male.* Philadelphia: W. B. Saunders.

Kinsey, Alfred C., Wardell B. Pomeroy, Clyde E. Martin, and P. Gebhard. 1953. *Sexual Behavior in the Human Female.* Philadelphia: W. B. Saunders.

Kunzel, Regina G. 1993. *Fallen Women, Problem Girls: Unmarried Mothers and the Professionalization of Social Work, 1890–1945.* New Haven, CT: Yale University Press.

Lawson, Annette. 1993. "Multiple Fractures: The Cultural Construction of Teenage Sexuality and Pregnancy." In *The Politics of Pregnancy: Adolescent Sexuality and Public Policy,* ed. A. Lawson and D. L. Rhode, 101–125. New Haven, CT: Yale University Press.

Levine, Judith. 2002. *Harmful to Minors: The Perils of Protecting Children from Sex.* Minneapolis: University of Minnesota Press.

Martinson, Floyd. 1973. *Infant and Child Sexuality: A Sociological Perspective.* St. Peter, MN: Book Mark, Gustavus Adolphus College.

McClintock, Martha K., and Gilbert Herdt. 1996. "Rethinking Puberty: The Development of Sexual Attraction." *Current Directions in Psychological Science* 5: 178–83.

Nathanson, Constance. 1991. *Dangerous Passage: The Social Control of Sexuality in Women's Adolescence.* Philadelphia: Temple University Press.

Owens, Robert E. 1998. *Queer Kids: The Challenges and Promise for Lesbian, Gay, and Bisexual Youth.* New York: Haworth Press.

Palladino, Grace. 1996. *Teenagers: An American History.* New York: Basic Books.

Peiss, Kathy Lee. 1986. *Cheap Amusements: Working Women and Leisure in Turn-of-the-Century New York.* Philadelphia: Temple University Press.

Percy, William A. 1996. *Pederasty and Pedagogy in Archaic Greece.* Urbana: University of Illinois Press.

Pomeroy, Sarah B. 2000. *Spartan Women.* New York: Oxford University Press.

Raymond, Diane. 1994. "Homophobia, Identity, and the Meanings of Desire: Reflections on the Cultural Construction of Gay and Lesbian Adolescent Sexuality." In *Sexual Cultures and the Construction of Adolescent Identities,* ed. J. M. Irvine, 115–50. Philadelphia: Temple University Press.

Reed, Rita. 1997. *Growing Up Gay: The Sorrows and Joys of Gay and Lesbian Adolescence.* New York: Norton.

Rossi, Alice S., ed. 1985. *Gender and the Life Course.* New York: Aldine.

Schlegel, Alice, and Herbert Barry III. 1991. *Adolescence: An Anthropological Inquiry.* New York: Free Press.

Sorenson, Robert C. 1973. *Adolescent Sexuality in Contemporary America: Personal Values and Sexual Behavior, Ages Thirteen to Nineteen.* New York: World Publishing.

Spurlock, John C. 2002. "From Reassurance to Irrelevance: Adolescent Psychology and Homosexuality in America." *History of Psychology* 5: 38–51.

Symons, D. 1979. *The Evolution of Human Sexuality.* New York: Oxford University Press.

Tessina, Tina B. 1989. *Gay Relationships for Men and Women: How to Find Them, How to Improve Them, How to Make Them Last.* Los Angeles: J. P. Tarcher.

Thompson, Sharon. 1995. *Going All the Way: Teenage Girls' Tales of Sex, Romance, and Pregnancy.* New York: Hill and Wang.

Thornton, A. 1990. "The Courtship Process and Adolescent Sexuality." *Journal of Family Issues* 11: 239–73.

Tolman, Deborah L. 2002. *Dilemmas of Desire: Teenage Girls Talk about Sexuality.* Cambridge, MA: Harvard University Press.

Van Oss, M. B., et al. 2000. "Older Boyfriends and Girlfriends Increase Risk of Sexual Initiations in Young Adolescents." *Journal of Adolescent Health* 27: 409–18.

Vergari, Sandra. 2001. "Morality Politics and the Implementation of Abstinence-Only Sex Education: A Case of Policy Compromise." In *The Public Clash of Private Values: The Politics of Morality Policy,* ed. C. Z. Mooney, 201–210. New York: Chatham House.

von Krafft-Ebing, Richard. 1893. *Psychopathia Sexualis, with Especial Reference to Contrary Sexual Instinct: A Medico-Legal Study,* trans. C. G. Chaddock from the 7th German ed. Philadelphia: F. A. Davis.

Walker, Rebecca. 2001. "Lusting for Freedom." In *Listen Up: Voices from the Next Feminist Generation,* new rev. ed., ed. B. Findlen, 19–24. Seattle, WA: Seal Press.

INTERNET SOURCES, ADOLESCENT SEXUALITY, GENERAL

Alan Guttmacher Institute. http://www.guttmacher.org/

H-Net: Humanities and Social Sciences Interdisciplinary Organization of Professors, Teachers, and Students. http://www.h-net.org/

Legislation of Interpol Member States on Sexual Offenses against Children. http://www.interpol.int/Public/Children/SexualAbuse/NationalLaws/Default.asp

Marriage, Women, and the Law, 1815–1914 (RLG Digital Collections Project). http://www.rlg.org/scarlet/

National Sexuality Resource Center. http://nsrc.sfsu.edu/Index.cfm

SIECUS: Sexuality Information and Education Council of the United States. http://www.siecus.org/

Bibliography of the History of Western Sexuality. http://www.univie.ac.at/Wirtschaftsgeschichte/Sexbibl/

World Health Organization Resource Guide on Adolescent Sexual and Reproductive Health, from the International Women's Health Coalition. http://www.iwhc.org/resources/who_resource_guide/adolescents.cfm

15   Films about Teens and Sex

FOR SEXUAL EDUCATION

Human Growth. 1947. Portland, OR: E. C. Brown Trust and Eddie Albert Productions. Filmstrip.
Story of Menstruation. 1946. Burbank, CA: Walt Disney Productions. Filmstrip.

FROM HOLLYWOOD

All Fall Down. 1962. Directed by John Frankenheimer.
All Quiet on the Western Front. 1930. Directed by Lewis Milestone.
American Beauty. 1999. Directed by Sam Mendes.
Another Country. 1984. Directed by Marek Kamievska.
Are These Our Children. 1931. Directed by W. Ruggles.
Baby Doll. 1956. Directed by Elia Kazan.
Blue Denim. 1959. Directed by Philip Dunne.
Blue Lagoon. 1980. Directed by Randall Kleiser.
Bob and Carol and Ted and Alice. 1969. Directed by Paul Mazursky.
Boys Don't Cry. 1999. Directed by Kimberly Peirce.
Boys in the Band, The. 1970. Directed by W. Friedkin.
Carnal Knowledge. 1971. Directed by Mike Nichols.
A Clockwork Orange. 1971. Directed by Stanley Kubrick.
Cynthia. 1948. Directed by Robert Leonard.
A Date with Judy. 1949. Directed by Richard Thorpe.
Deep End. 1971. Directed by Jerzy Skolimowski.
East of Eden. 1954. Directed by Elia Kazan.
Easy Rider. 1969. Directed by Dennis Hopper.
Endless Love. 1981. Directed by Franco Zeffirelli.
Equus. 1977. Directed by Sidney Lumet.

Five Finger Exercise. 1962. Directed by Daniel Mann.

Foxes. 1980. Directed by Adrian Lyne.

Friends. 1972. Directed by Lewis Gilbert.

Get Real. 1999. Directed by Simon Shore.

Go Between, The. 1971. Directed by Joseph Losey.

Graduate, The. 1967. Directed by Mike Nichols.

Happy Birthday Gemini. 1980. Directed by Richard Benner.

Her First Beau. 1941. Directed by Theodore Reed.

High School. 1940. Directed by George Nichols Jr.

Janie. 1944. Directed by M. Curtiz.

Jeremy. 1973. Directed by Arthur Barron.

Junior Miss. 1945. Directed by George Seaton.

Kids. 1995. Directed by Larry Clark.

Klute. 1971. Directed by Alan J. Pakula.

Last American Virgin, The. 1982. Directed by Boaz Davidson.

Last Picture Show, The. 1971. Directed by Peter Bogdanovich.

Last Tango in Paris. 1973. Directed by Bernardo Bertolucci.

Little Girl Who Lives Down the Lane, The. 1976. Directed by Nicolas Gessner.

Lolita. 1962. Directed by Stanley Kubrick.

Manhattan. 1977. Directed by Woody Allen.

Maurice. 1987. Directed by James Ivory.

Midnight Cowboy. 1969. Directed by John Schlesinger.

Mildred Pierce. 1944. Directed by Michael Curtiz.

Miss Annie Rooney. 1942. Directed by Edwin Marin.

My Beautiful Laundrette. 1985. Directed by Stephen Frears.

My Own Private Idaho. 1999. Directed by Gus Van Sant.

Ode to Billy Joe. 1976. Directed by Max Baer.

Peyton Place. 1957. Directed by Mark Robson.

Pretty Baby. 1976. Directed by Louis Malle.

Rebel without a Cause. 1955. Directed by Nicholas Ray.

Rich Kids. 1979. Directed by Robert M. Young.

Risky Business. 1983. Directed by Paul Brickman.

Romeo and Juliet. 1968. Directed by Franco Zeffirelli.

Say Anything. 1989. Directed by Cameron Crowe.

Silkwood. 1983. Directed by Mike Nichols.

Splendor in the Grass. 1961. Directed by Elia Kazan.

Summer of '42. 1971. Directed by Robert Mulligan.

A Summer Place. 1958. Directed by Delmer Daves.

Taxi Driver. 1976. Directed by Martin Scorcese.

Tea and Sympathy. 1956. Directed by Vincente Minneli.

Thirteen. 2003. Directed by Catherine Hardwicke.

Where the Boys Are. 1960. Directed by Henry Levin.

Who's Afraid of Virginia Woolf? 1966. Directed by Mike Nichols.

You're a Big Boy Now. 1966. Directed by Francis Ford Coppola.

Index

About the Editor and Contributors

THE EDITOR

CAROLYN COCCA is associate professor of politics and Director of the Women's Center at the State University of New York, College at Old Westbury. She is the author of *Jailbait: The Politics of Statutory Rape Laws in the United States* (2004), and her current work is on teen marriage.

THE CONTRIBUTORS

VERN BULLOUGH, RN, PhD, was California State University Outstanding Professor Emeritus, State University of New York Distinguished Professor Emeritus, and former dean of the Faculty of Natural and Social Sciences at SUNY Buffalo; he taught within history, sociology, and nursing programs at numerous academic institutions. He worked with such organizations as the NAACP and the ACLU and was a founder of the Center for Sex Research at California State University-Northridge, as well as of gay caucuses in the American Historical Association and the American Sociological Association. Along with being the recipient of dozens of grants and awards, he was the author of hundreds of refereed and popular articles, and the author, co-author, or editor of over fifty books on sexuality and on nursing. He passed away in 2006, as this volume went to press.

DAVID M. CONSIDINE coordinates the Media Literacy graduate program at Appalachian State University. An Australian, he is the author of *The Cinema of Adolescence* (1985), *Visual Messages: Integrating Imagery Into Instruction* (1999) and numerous articles about youth, media and media literacy.

SUSAN K. FREEMAN is assistant professor of women's studies at Minnesota State University, Mankato. She is the author of *Up for Discussion: Girls and Sex Education in Mid-Twentieth-Century Schools* (Forthcoming).

JAMES W. REED is professor of history at Rutgers University. He is the author of *The Birth Control Movement and American Society: From Private Vice to Public Virtue* (1983), served as Dean of Rutgers College from 1984 to 1993, and is currently at work on a history of biomedical sex research.

JOHN C. SPURLOCK is professor of history and chair of the Division of the Humanities at Seton Hill University. He has written *Free Love: Marriage and Middle-Class Radicalism in America, 1825 to 1860* (1988) and (with Cynthia Magistro) *New and Improved: The Transformation of American Women's Emotional Culture* (1998). His current work is on adolescent sexuality in the twentieth century.